ROAMING

LIVING AND WORKING ABROAD
IN THE 21ST CENTURY

CM PATHA

EITHER OR PRESS

EITHER ◐R PRESS

First Published by Either/Or Press in 2016

ISBN 978-0-993-49550-2

For press information, to book an event, to discuss special discounts for bulk
purchases, or to obtain permission to reproduce part of this book, please contact
Either/Or Press at eitherorpress@gmail.com.

Infographics designed by Andres Prieto
Typesetting by Istvan Szabo, Ifj. (Sapphire Guardian International)

To all roamers
and
to Harry and Rich

CONTENTS

PART I:
INTRODUCING THE ROAMER

CHAPTER 1
THE WORLD IS YOUR OYSTER

Passport, wallet, phone. What else do you really need when taking a trip? A toothbrush and pajamas are handy, but you can always buy them at your final destination. The passport and the wallet have been with us for ages, but at what point did a phone become indispensable to the art of travel?

* * *

When I boarded a flight bound for London Heathrow in September 1999, I carried my passport and wallet, but no phone. At the time, cell phones were largely in the domain of important business people, and were just starting to percolate down to the rest of us. For most of us, the word "phone" still referred to a piece of equipment that was firmly rooted in a physical location: an office, a telephone booth, or if you were lucky, your bedroom. Any other handheld device had a special prefix: a "cell" phone, a "mobile" phone, or even a "car" phone. Though mobile phones were entering the mass market, few had reliable international roaming software, and roaming fees were eye-wateringly expensive. It would have been pointless for me to get a mobile phone in Canada before moving to the United Kingdom. At the time, neither Facebook nor Skype existed, the iPod was two years away, and smartphones were still in the realm of science fiction. For girls like me, home was where the heart was, but above all, it was where the phone was.

So when I left Toronto to study abroad in London for a year, I also left my phone. Instead of a phone, my handbag contained a farewell gift from a friend—a small turtle paperweight on whose belly was inscribed "Wherever I roam, the world is my home." It was a thoughtful souvenir, but I had no plans to roam the world. Like the first soldiers of World War I, I'd enlisted in my course expecting to be back home by Christmas, or by summer at the latest. Little did I know that I would soon be following my turtle down his path: mobile, roaming, and carrying my "home" with me.

When my British Airways flight delivered me into the buzzing center of Tony Blair's "Cool Britannia," I was surprised by London's distinct lack of, well, Britishness. Of the twelve students in my master's course at the London School of Economics (LSE), only one was British. The rest came from America, Argentina, Turkey, and a potpourri of European countries. Having spent my junior year abroad in France where the majority of my friends had been French, I was unprepared to find only a smattering of native Brits in my classes and living in my halls of residence. Most graduate students at the LSE were just like me—young and hungry foreign students ready for adventure. The world was our oyster. Little did we know that we were also a microcosm of a much larger trend that was quietly revolutionizing how we would live and work in a globalized world.

After graduation, my fellow international students fell into three camps. The first group headed back to their native countries to pursue their careers. The second started working in London, married locals, and settled down in the United Kingdom. But a third, much larger group was embarking on an entirely different, untrodden path.

The idea of settling down somewhere, anywhere, just didn't apply to this third group. They began moving from country to country, taking jobs in far-flung places around the globe. They lived a few years here, a few years there. At home in any number of global cities, they had friends from around the world. Those who stayed in one city for many years still didn't lay down roots. They preferred to stay flexible, occasionally buying property in one country but often living in another. Others rented for many years to avoid either deciding where to settle down or dealing with the burden of having done so. Some of these itinerants didn't want to start a long-distance relationship only to have it result in a complicated commute, while others sought their romantic fortunes abroad because they couldn't find them next door. "Maybe I'll go to New York or Zurich," said my Portuguese friend Sofia, a banker who hadn't met a suitable partner in London. "Things might be different there." On the one hand, Sofia's logic was entirely sound—if you can't find what you're looking for, look elsewhere. On the other hand, it seemed totally crazy—why look internationally for solutions to personal relationships? A generation ago, most people "sourced" their partners locally through friends and family or from high school and university. When had this global flux become normal?

Belying the trend, I stayed in London, but like all my fellow migratory

10

birds, I stopped short of making a permanent nest. Inevitably each Christmas my mother would ask, "Where do you want to settle down? Do you want to stay in London?" My response—that the world just didn't work that way anymore—befuddled her. Settling down in your own home, preferably with a nice garden, was the badge of success for my mom's generation. For my peers and me, challenging careers and international adventures were the new American dream. By the time my mother was my age, she knew where she would live. Even though I'd been in London for nine, ten, and then eleven years, I was uncertain where I would spend the rest of my days. Every financial disclaimer will tell you that "past performance is not an indication of future performance," but it still looked as though the United Kingdom would be home. Why, then, couldn't I just tell my mom that I was settling down in London?

Perhaps I'd seen too many people come and go. Stephanie and Amol had moved from New York to London three years ago, and now they were off to Hong Kong. Ilan had moved from Brazil to New York, and he just arrived in London. Friends from the LSE, Edward and Nina had moved to Holland and Germany, came back to London for two years, and were off again to Africa with two kids in tow. Maybe I couldn't put my mom's mind to rest because there was a little voice at the back of mine saying, "You never know."

In January 2012, I left London. I didn't know if I'd won the lottery or drawn the short lot. My new partner had been offered the job of a lifetime in Singapore, and I agreed to join him there. G.K. Chesterton once said, "The function of the imagination is not to make strange things settled, so much as to make settled things strange." After seeing so many people move in and out of London and finding myself back on the road after a dozen years, I began wondering what on earth was happening. Why was no one staying put in one place anymore? If I, personally, could name a hundred people who had come and gone through London in my one, small life, were there thousands, maybe even millions, living and working in this "third way"? Who were all these people? Why didn't they just finally settle down somewhere? Did they never stop?

Looking back and comparing my moves to London and to Singapore, I found one conspicuous difference. When the plane touched down in Changi Airport in January 2012, my handbag contained not two, but three

11

indispensable travel companions—a passport, a wallet, and, this time, a mobile phone. Even before clearing customs, I had updated my Facebook status, made a quick Skype call from my iPhone, and received a few farewell text messages from friends in London. In the dozen or so intervening years between my two big moves, the mobile phone had become an essential item in the traveler's toolkit.

The mobile phone has revolutionized the way we live, work, and communicate on every level imaginable. It's a supremely useful and addictive gadget, but it's much more than that. It has become a metaphor for how our lives are changing in a globalized world.

When I left Canada in 1999, I'd had a fixed phone line and a fixed idea of home—Toronto. By the time I left London in 2012, the mobile phone had supplanted the virtually obsolete landline and was taking the very notion of home with it. I now had a mobile phone and a mobile idea of home. Depending on the situation, Toronto, London, and my newly adopted Singapore were *all* home to me. Maybe I would move after a few years, or maybe Singapore would be home forever. Worrying about the uncertainty made no sense. I could use my mobile phone in London just as easily as I could in Singapore. Of course, roaming came with a cost, but the convenience was incalculable.

Like phones, humans are undergoing a revolution and are now designed to roam. Individuals have "country code prefixes" and "contracts" with their passport countries, but they swap these as easily as they swap SIM cards. An entire generation of highly skilled, highly mobile individuals is now engaged in a lifestyle that I call global roaming, or just plain *roaming*. *Roamers* are forging a new way of life built on a peripatetic existence, moving from one exotic location to another at a rate and a scale that was never before imaginable. Some roamers stay in one place for a long time, but they still resist putting down roots. Roamers are not deliberately emigrating from one country or immigrating to another. They're simply migrating.

The numbers are staggering. One in ten Canadian, British, and Swiss citizens live in a foreign country. One in five New Zealanders and one in twenty Australians live abroad. From 2003 to 2007, Holland experienced net emigration—more people were leaving than coming in. Once again, immigrants outnumber emigrants in Holland, but *both* immigration and emigration are increasing to such a degree that they break records year-on-year. The United States is the only country other than Eritrea to tax its citizens who live abroad, but still almost seven million civilian Americans live overseas.

Throughout the twentieth century, North America, Europe, and the Antipodes attracted enormous numbers of immigrants. They still do. Migrants come because they expect a higher standard of living, greater safety, and more liberty. So why are these lands of milk and honey exporting so many of their own citizens?

Perhaps the answer lies not in persecution, but in freedom. A staggering 400,000 French nationals live in London alone. Many of them are influential bankers, lawyers, entrepreneurs—and voters. In 2007 President Nicolas Sarkozy became the first French presidential candidate to campaign in London. He was casting for support in the upcoming election, but he had a second agenda. Recognizing the loss of these valuable citizens, he begged them to come back home. "You've brought so much intelligence, imagination, passion for work, and desire for success with you to London that you have helped give it the vitality that Paris needs so much." He may have won their votes, but he didn't have much success coaxing these prodigal sons and daughters back to Paris. They had already cast their ballot, and voted for a return Eurostar ticket back to London.

The European Union (E.U.) allows for free movement of labor between its member states, so perhaps it isn't surprising that so many French and other Europeans live "abroad" within Europe. But visas and global tax programs don't seem to stop the rest of the world from moving around. The United Nations estimates that over 232 million people were living outside their home country in 2013. That's more people than the entire population of Mexico, Colombia, and Argentina combined. If these migrants formed their own country, they'd be the fifth most populous nation on earth just after China, India, the United States, and Indonesia. In 2000, the number of international migrants was only 175 million. In thirteen short years, the growth rate of global migration was a staggering 33 percent. In comparison, world population grew only 18 percent over the same period. There are more migrants today not only because the world's population has increased, but also because more people are deciding to pack their bags and move abroad. If we lowball that just 10 percent of the world's 232 million migrants are roamers, we're looking at a roaming population of over twenty-three million people living in a way that was unheard of a few decades ago.

We have lots of terms for people living abroad: migrant workers, expats, and immigrants, to name a few. Does the world really need another brand of foreigner? Can't roamers just slot into one of these categories? Is roaming a sufficiently different phenomenon to merit both a new entry into our lexicon and an entire book?

After several years of research, an online survey answered by over 500 people worldwide, and a hundred personal interviews, I've reached the conclusion that this lifestyle *is* different from anything that has gone on before. Millions of people are living in a way that isn't explained by any existing narrative. I coined the term *roaming*, but I didn't invent the phenomenon. Roamers are the great "other" living around the planet today, and they are hiding in plain sight.

Roamers can be hard to spot because, from the outside, they might be mistaken for the more familiar assortment of foreigners. But they're neither the classic expat who will head home after a few years working abroad nor the immigrant who desperately wants to emigrate from his home country into yours. Take for instance Julia and Pieter, a Dutch couple who have worked in Hong Kong for almost six years. Julia is an international school teacher, Pieter works in advertising, and their children attend high school in Hong Kong. When I told Julia about a Facebook group called *Hong Kong Expats*, she was unenthusiastic. "I have an allergy to these groups," she said. When asked why, Julia replied, "I just don't see myself as an expat." She and Pieter are not on expat contracts, and they don't have the privileges that those contracts typically convey. They don't know when or if they'll ever go back to the Netherlands. They may stay in Hong Kong indefinitely. Plenty of foreigners do. But Julia loves England and thinks that she would like to move there one day. "Or Cambodia, where my teaching skills could make a real difference," she says. Julia and Pieter are part of a growing cadre of people around the planet who are living in a gap that can best be described as a big yawning hole between an expat and an immigrant. The purpose of *Roaming* is not to convince people that they're either this or that, but rather to offer an alternative narrative for those like Julia who think that their way of life is misunderstood or underrepresented.

But it's more than that. It's not just a matter of semantics. You can't treat a disease that hasn't yet been identified; you can't make a choice until you know what the options are. You can't legislate, budget, or plan for something that you haven't identified. We are undergoing a massive paradigm shift. No historical precedent quite fits what is going on in the world today, yet governments continue to hopelessly legislate outdated ideas of who migrates and why. This new brand of migrant might have no burning desire to become a citizen, but she isn't staying for just a couple of years either.

Most lawmakers still think that the ideal model of citizenship is reflected in John F. Kennedy's patriotic appeal: "Ask not what your country can do for you; ask what you can do for your country." They have no clue what to do with an entire generation of people who respond, "I love my country, but I wouldn't want to *live* there." Passports and citizenship are meant to imply certain loyalties, predispositions, and final abodes, but they may no longer indicate any of that at all. How will societies cope with this constant flux of people moving into and out of their country? How do you represent or govern people who just can't sit still?

Mass urbanization defined the twentieth century. It produced a vast social, cultural, and economic gulf between rural and urban populations. As farming became increasingly mechanized, countryside migrants began moving to cities. This trend is still on the rise. An estimated one million people across the planet flood into cities and urban areas *every week*. Most of this migration is happening in countries that remain largely agrarian, but by no means is this a poor country syndrome. Even though America's population is still growing at a steady pace, 60 percent of its rural populations shrank in 2013, up from 40 percent in 1990. Wherever you live, you can witness this shift: Young people are moving out of villages and the countryside into metropolitan areas, leaving older populations and ghost towns in their wake. Why are all these migrants leaving for the big city? They're moving because they think that they'll be better off, and they often are. In plenty of cases, though, these migrants end up in shantytowns, favelas, or run-down suburbs where they have no access to clean water or sanitation and still have to pay extortionate rents. Even then, despite our idealized notions of the countryside, many of these migrants still believe that they are better off because when compared with their poor village counterparts, they live closer to schools and hospitals and have a wider variety of opportunities.

This rural-urban split has been the central fault line in every country around the world for the last century. Rural and urban populations are nominally part of the same country, but they're worlds apart. They vote differently, they have different income levels, they voice different concerns, and they diverge on a slew of other issues both big and small. By no stretch of the imagination is this yesterday's news. This division will continue for a long time yet, but there's a new challenge on the horizon. By the end of the twenty-first century, the single greatest socio-economic divide will no longer be between city dwellers and country folk. It will be between those living as "nationals" and those living as "globals," or roamers. The growing trend of roaming, perhaps even *mass* roaming, is about to spark a great debate, the next "clash of civilizations" of our times.

Many cities are already feeling the effects. Local residents of Singapore, London, and Paris are left scratching their heads wondering why property prices in their home cities have been skyrocketing when their national economy is flat or even shrinking. For roamers—many of whom are also priced out of the property market—the answer is clear: These global cities are attracting international investors who have little or nothing to do with the local or national economy.

So why are roamers moving around the world? Like countryside migrants, they too think that they'll be better off. By and large, they are right. Like urbanites in the twentieth century, the ultra-rich have a head start. They're already global. They flit between their homes in Geneva, Hong Kong, and Miami. Their companies are domiciled in the Cayman Islands, Jersey, and Luxembourg. Their tax lawyers work out how many days they're allowed to be in which country before having to pay tax there.

The vast majority of roamers are not in this league. Broadly speaking, they are middle class and are not going abroad because they'll be better off financially. Their roaming comes at a personal cost, and like the new arrivals in the slums of Calcutta, many will not end up wealthier than their counterparts who stay at home. Even then, roamers will have a wider variety of career prospects, more chances to spot business opportunities, access to more markets, and more varied socio-cultural experiences than those who remain in their home country. For many roamers, these things are enough to make them feel better off. Mirroring urbanization patterns, an increasing number of nationals will turn to roaming in the coming decades.

Roaming offers many benefits, but it's not entirely benign. Thirty years ago, we moved somewhere and lived there. Today people increasingly say that they're "based" somewhere. Should national governments be worried about that? In 2015, there were almost twice as many active SIM cards as people. Likewise, with dual nationality increasingly common, citizens must surely outnumber actual humans on the planet. Are people beginning to feel as loyal to their passport nation as they are to their mobile phone contract provider? Is citizenship becoming more of a "service contract" or "user agreement" with one country, rather than a description of the place where one lives, votes, and "is from"? Is such a loose tie to one's citizenship country a danger to society, or is it equivalent to the minor health risks associated with mobile phone use? What happens to traditional family and social relationships when your ties to a long-term place called "home" unravel? Can networks really replace community? What happens to children who don't feel connected to any particular country? Where do your fundamental loyalties lie when you're a "global citizen"?

On the other hand, are these traits a *good* thing? Can these global citizens contribute to promoting international understanding? Can roamers help reduce irrational business and political practices by providing alternative views from around the world? Hasn't nationalism caused enough conflicts already? Could the complete liberalization of labor actually make everyone better off?

Whether you roam or live at home, you will need to think about these things because you'll be on one side or the other of this coming divide. Roaming is not just a short-lived fad. It will be the defining way of living in the twenty-first century. If you're not roaming now, chances are your kids will be. Having an insight into roaming is vital to understanding your future in a globalized world.

When researching this phenomenon, I began to realize how deeply roaming is already ingrained. The simple question "For how long have you lived abroad?" sounds easy enough. Many people would have no trouble responding. Someone like Adi, however, would have to think harder. He was born in Indonesia, moved to Germany with his parents when he was 3, and became a German citizen. At the age of 18, he left Germany to study at Cambridge in the United Kingdom, and his parents moved back to Indonesia. At the age of 26, Adi landed a job that took him from London to Silicon Valley. What on earth does "living abroad" mean to Adi? Did he move abroad when he was 3, 18, or 23? If "home" isn't a clean concept, then neither is "abroad."

The key challenge of our time will be to integrate all these roamers into societies that don't require you to stay in one place for your whole life—societies where roamers can contribute and can feel as if they belong. *Roaming* not only identifies a new way of living; it's also asking the thornier and more naïve question of what this lifestyle actually means for governments, societies, and roamers themselves.

The ease of communication and the abundance of inexpensive flights have allowed roamers to embark on this lifestyle without a long-term commitment to living overseas. Once abroad, however, roamers sometimes find themselves stuck on the global circuit with no exit sign in sight. They follow worldwide job opportunities, regularly marry outside of their culture (often roamers from other nationalities), and raise their children in a third place not considered home to either partner. Can you really be at home abroad? Can you, should you, settle down somewhere? What are the pleasures and the pitfalls of living as a roamer?

Britt Lintner might be a poster child for roaming. She was born and grew up in the United States, studied in Wisconsin, and had no grand ambitions to work abroad. After university, she spent three years in New York working for the investment bank Lehman Brothers, which then asked her to move to London to work in institutional equity sales trading covering American clients from Europe. Britt thought it was a temporary move, but seventeen years later, she is married to a Frenchman, raising two boys, and still working in finance in London. One morning, Britt rang me in tears. "We're orphans here! Orphans!" she howled into the phone. She was on her way back from Heathrow Airport where her parents had just boarded a flight back home to the United States. Britt isn't an overly sentimental or emotional person. She is one of the most socially integrated, financially successful, and resolved people you'll ever meet. But as her family grows and her path leads her farther from her American birthplace, she's becoming keenly aware of the drawbacks of having her sister, parents, and old friends 5,000 miles away.

Just as using your mobile phone overseas allows you to be flexible but can result in a surprisingly high phone bill upon returning home, roaming also has hidden costs. And the bill for this lifestyle comes later, often many years after you start roaming. But this is the life roamers are building. They're encountering puzzles to which there are no easy solutions because no one has gone there in the same way before. Trailblazing is as exciting as it is frightening.

Most civilizations are built on a founding myth, and at the heart of almost each one lies a tale of mass migration or a heroic journey. The Epic of Gilgamesh, the Bible, the Ramayana, the Odyssey, and even America's Mayflower all glorify two seemingly incompatible but insatiable human desires: the need to travel across vast distances, and the yearning to find rest (after vanquishing the requisite monster or two, of course).

No historical or mythological precedent approximates what is going on in the world today. Roamers don't yet have a founding myth. They're not trying to reach a promised land, they don't have any Trojans or demon kings to defeat, and they have no perilous seas to cross. Perhaps roamers are more akin to those who heeded the call "Go west, young man" during America's gold rush. Even that analogy, however, has its limits. Roamers don't have one "west." They're coming from everywhere and they're going everywhere. And roaming isn't a temporary phenomenon. It is going to be the defining way of living in the twenty-first century.

CHAPTER 2
HOW TO SPOT A ROAMER IN THE WILD

It's hard to define hard-core pornography, but as one American judge put it, "I know it when I see it." Such neat logic would come in handy for defining the equally contentious term *roamer*, but you can't *see* what makes a roamer a roamer because it's not a collection of visual or quantifiable traits like *number of years abroad* that determines who makes the cut and who doesn't. What ultimately draws the distinction is an internal, emotional response that roamers themselves make: They don't feel like expats, migrant workers, immigrants, or any other phrase in use today. They also don't feel like locals—neither abroad nor at home.

Take for instance Brenda Howard, an American headhunter in her mid-30s living in Germany. She and her husband, Bill, a fellow American, have been in Frankfurt for three years. After renting an apartment for two years, the Howards bought a place in Frankfurt's trendy Sachsenhausen district. "We think we might stay here awhile," says Brenda. Born in a family that she says was "as American as apple pie," Brenda admits that she loved to travel, but while she was growing up in the suburbs of Atlanta, she never once considered living abroad.

After Brenda graduated from university, her first employer offered her the chance to work in its London office for a couple of years. She jumped at it. "It sounded so glamorous!" says Brenda. Freshly married, Brenda and Bill decided that the offer was too good to refuse, although it meant that Bill would have to quit his own job. The couple thought that their move would be a short-term international adventure, but after a few months in London, Bill found a job in a pharmaceutical industry, and three years later he had a job offer in Australia. Brenda and Bill decided to take the plunge, and stayed in Sydney for another three years. A new job opportunity brought them back to Europe, this time to Frankfurt. The language of communication in Brenda's office is English. "It's a really international environment," says Brenda. "Most people in the office are German, but there are lots of people from other countries, and they've all spent time abroad, so their English is excellent. Actually, thinking about it, their English is probably better than mine!" Brenda laughs.

Outside the office, Brenda's closest friends are people from all around the world, including many Americans abroad. She still keeps in touch with friends back in the United States, but she senses a widening transatlantic gap. "Americans living in the U.S. are just *so* American!" she says. "When I tell people in Atlanta that I went trekking in Bhutan, they look at me like I'm an alien." Brenda still feels staunchly American, but feels just as firmly that America is not the right home for her. "Bill and I invested in property back in Atlanta, but we don't imagine actually living there ever again. My entire professional life has been abroad."

Brenda and Bill are part of a growing cadre of roamers living around the world defying age-old notions of home, citizenship, and where one ultimately belongs. Brenda says, "My husband and I are American, born and bred, but now that we've lived abroad, we can't ever imagine going back."

So what exactly makes Brenda and Bill roamers? If you've got your binoculars at hand and you want to try spotting a roamer in the wild, there are three traits you should look for. Before elaborating on these, we'll look at a few urban myths that would lead you down the garden path.

Myth #1: "Roamer" is just a fancy name for an expat

When I first arrived in Singapore, a Singaporean friend invited me to dinner and assured me that I wouldn't feel out of place because other expats would be there too. A few days later, *Expat Living* magazine landed on my doorstep, and soon after that, I was invited to join an expat Facebook group. I began wondering why I was suddenly deemed an expat when no one had ever applied the word to me in the United Kingdom. I wasn't living any differently from how I had lived in London. I didn't know how long I would stay in Singapore, perhaps forever. I wasn't on any special package to compensate me for my move. I had found a local job on a local contract. My partner, an academic, and I lived in an apartment complex that had a few foreign residents, but most were Singaporean. Our job benefits didn't include cars or memberships to country clubs. The cultural context was different, the weather was better, but what else had suddenly changed to make me an expat? What, precisely, *is* an expat?

I contacted The Expatriate Archive Centre (E.A.C.) in The Hague to find out. The E.A.C. documents the social history of expatriate life across the world. Donna Worrall, head of public relations at the time, told me that they themselves were struggling with the expat designation. "I recently met a German man living in the Netherlands, and he laughed when I called him an expat," said Donna. "He replied, 'I'm just a German. I'm not an expat!' He didn't see himself as sufficiently different from the Dutch to be considered an expat."

Others shied away from the word for different reasons. "We found that many people living abroad, in particular those from Asia and Africa, don't like the word applied to themselves because it is associated with Western foreign domination," said Donna. In much of Asia and Africa, the term "expat" has a colonial heritage. In the seventeenth century European monarchies set up corporations to claim lands and import raw materials back to the homeland. The Dutch East India Company alone sent almost a million Europeans to work in the Asian trade from 1602 to 1796. Over time, these Europeans living *ex patria* (Latin for "outside of the fatherland") came to be known as *expatriates*. According to the Oxford English Dictionary, the word didn't enter into English usage until the early 1800s, first making its way into print in 1818.

By the mid-twentieth century, multinational companies had replaced colonial merchants as the main producers of expatriates. Almost exclusively from Europe and North America, these companies sent their own countrymen to new or developing markets where locals lacked specialist knowledge, skills, or experience. Now better known by their shorthand name as *expats*, these foreign workers didn't have the same privileges as the colonists, but they still had significant advantages over locals. To ease the hardship of transferring away from home, multinationals offered their employees abroad "expat packages," which often included housing, country club memberships, international schooling for children, and sometimes cars, drivers, maids, and cooks. Many expats were paid in foreign, "hard" currencies, not in the local currency. Three-year expat postings became common to prevent employees from going native and losing allegiance to the mothership back home. Though dwindling in number, expats working abroad on expat packages certainly continue to exist.

In the meantime, the spectrum of expats has expanded to include other groups. Plenty of those on expat packages are no longer from Western countries, and some so-called expats, like American or European retirees living in Mexico, are on no expat package at all. These retirees have effectively (and often officially) emigrated from their home country, but they're not called *Silver Emigrants* or *Senior Immigrants*. Why not?

Two factors seem to inform the use of the word "expat." First of all, immigrants are considered poorer than the average local, while expats are deemed to be wealthier. Silver Emigrants don't have a corporate expat package, but they too have a clear economic incentive for living overseas. In many cases it's not just the good weather that's drawing them abroad. Exchange rate asymmetries mean that they can often stretch their retirement savings further than they could at home. Often they enjoy a more lavish lifestyle than the average local retiree.

Roamers, on the contrary, don't have any economic benefits over locals in the same industry or station in life. If roamers are making more money than the average local while living abroad, that's only because they'd also be making more money than the average local at home.

The second factor is pretty blatantly racial. One morning while in my Singapore office, I asked my ethnically Chinese Singaporean colleague Yi Ling if she considered me an expat. She did. I asked her if she considered our colleague Zou Bing, a Chinese national working in Singapore, to be one as well. Yi Ling shook her head. "No, of course not!" she replied. I tried to find out what was the difference between Bing and me. "Bing is Chinese and lives in a Chinese way," Yi Ling said. I still have no idea what that was meant to imply, given that none of us was living in China.

Bing was born near Qingdao, studied in Tianjin, and is certainly more Chinese than I am, but she's also more German than I am. Having studied and worked in Munich for ten years, she speaks excellent German, celebrates Oktoberfest in one of her two traditional Bavarian dirndl dresses, and loves Bratwurst. After Germany, Bing moved to Beijing for two years, but then she moved abroad again, this time to Singapore where she has spent the past four years working as a program coordinator. Like many roamers, Bing and I communicate in English. Her English is flawless. Like me, Bing completed her studies in her birth country and went abroad for graduate studies. She has a local contract in Singapore, and as far as I can tell, has a higher income than I do. She loves going to museums, eating dim sum with friends, and participating in outdoor activities in a way that is very similar to my own lifestyle. Her parents, like mine, are middle-class professionals. Neither of us has a job that comes with a country club membership, a car and driver, or free international schools for children. Yes, Bing has a mother tongue and Chinese traditions that are different from mine, but mine are different from other "expats" of French, Australian, and other Western descent. When I asked Bing if she had ever felt like an expat in Singapore or in Munich, she looked at me as if I'd just fallen out of the sky. "I don't have an expat salary or benefits, but of course I'm not a local. I'm something different, something in between," she said.

In March 2015, the British national newspaper *The Guardian* ran a commentary titled "Why are white people expats when the rest of us are immigrants?" When I posted the article on my Facebook page, it provoked a flurry of responses. White people didn't consider themselves expats, and non-white people didn't consider themselves immigrants. French citizen Gaetane Prinselaar in Singapore wrote: "I don't consider myself an expat. I just live far away." Other curious responses on the *Guardian* website include the following replies:

- *I've never heard the phrase "illegal expat," have you?*
- *I recently moved to Dubai, as an Irishman, having lived for fifteen years in London. In London, I very much considered myself an immigrant. Here, I'm immediately labeled an expat.*
- *I think [immigrant refers] more to people from countries that we consider to be poor or in some way inferior. Doesn't make it any better though, and doesn't mean there's not a racist aspect to it.*
- *My friend's mother always called herself an expat, emigrating from the U.K., and immigrating into South Africa. [When I told her that she was in fact an immigrant, I thought] that she would have a heart attack. The look on her face was priceless—anyone close would have thought I had called her black.*
- *An Australian friend once told me (a white Brazilian) when we were both living in London, "Mate, I hate immigrants." The mind boggles.*

Yes, it truly does. Perhaps it's time to give the word *expat* a rest? Or perhaps we should relegate it to where it belongs—the dwindling number of people working abroad on expat contracts and those definitely returning to their "fatherland" after a few years abroad.

When I interviewed Cécile Courbon, a French project manager living in Singapore, straight off the bat she told me, "We're definitely not expats." She explained:

The only time we ever even see expats is on Friday nights at the airport when we're heading away for a long weekend. We know who they are, but they have their own life and social circuit. My husband and I were not lured to Singapore by high salaries and subsidies to compensate for the drawbacks of living abroad. We actively sought international opportunities. I lost my job at a bank in Paris in 2008 and instead of getting depressed, Antoine convinced me to look for work abroad so we could see what it was like to live and work in another country. I found work before arriving in Singapore, but Antoine only found his job once we were here. Everyone asks when we intend to return home, but the correct question isn't "When are you going home?" but "Where next?" As for me, "home" is currently Singapore. We'll probably go back to France, but we don't know when. All we know is that we're happy here now.

Some start life abroad as classic expats, but morph into something different along the way. When HSBC asked Jonathan McCullagh to move from London to Hong Kong, the company offered him an expat contract and the promise of a return ticket. When his contract ran out, Jonathan opted to stay in Hong Kong and switched to a local contract. In his case, the local contract actually earns him a higher wage than he had earned on his expat contract, but it also means that HSBC will not automatically repatriate him back to London. He doesn't lose sleep over it. "I'll always be English, but that doesn't mean I have to live within the borders of England ever again," he said.

Unlike many roamers, Jonathan is able to identify a clear homeland, but he doesn't necessarily expect to return. Donna Worrall of the Expatriate Archive Centre says that this lack of romantic yearning for home separates roamers from the traditional expat:

I was speaking to an Irish expat who has been in the Netherlands for over twenty years. She said when she left Ireland, it was a big commitment and undertaking, but now the young Irish people are taking flights like she used to take the bus. You see so many people coming and going from everywhere to everywhere, it's hard to identify in which place they're making an emotional investment. With expats, traditionally there has been a stronger sense of, and longing for, home.

When I met Americans Erin Sandral and Brenna Tinari in Singapore, I didn't know if they longed for home, but they certainly looked as if they would qualify as traditional expats, but looks can be deceiving. "We really have nothing in common with the vast majority of Americans in Singapore's American Club," said Erin. Brenna explained, "They continue living their American lives, eating super-sized food, and watching American television. They're here for a set period of two or three years, they know they're going back, so they don't bother to live their lives in a local way. I've only been here for a year, but my boyfriend is South African, and I don't know where we'll end up." Brenna was living abroad for the first time, but Erin was a veteran, growing up in Amsterdam and Paris before ending up in London for eighteen years as an adult. She never explicitly sought out the company of her fellow Americans because they felt so culturally unfamiliar to her. "When I was growing up, I only met Americans who were on a brief stint abroad and were all going 'home' eventually, that's to say true expats," she says. Erin always made local friends and learned the local language because she didn't know when, if ever, she'd be going back to the United States. Now married to an Australian, Erin still carries an American passport, but her feet are firmly planted in the here and now. Brenna and Erin want, maybe even need, to delve into local life because it might be home for a few years, or it might be home forever.

Foreigners who shy away from identifying as expats sometimes default to a trendy neologism: *global nomad*. Apart from the many things that separate roamers from nomads, one defining feature prevents the use of this seductively trendy word—nomads move in a group while roamers move entirely alone. At most, roamers might move with a partner or children, but certainly not en masse. They must build up a new community after every move. Individual opportunities and choices drive roamers to decide where to live and work. Nomads, in contrast, effectively travel with their neighborhood. Community is the *only* constant factor between locations. It provides them not only with kinship, but also with safety. The rest of us rely on modern institutions to provide peace and protection. If you've been burgled, your first call is most likely to the police, not to your uncle or your neighbor. Of course technology allows roamers to stay in touch with their uncles and neighbors, but as one roamer in Tokyo put it, "I discuss banalities with my parents and friends back home because they lack the everyday connection to my life." It's this everyday connection that provides the social glue for real nomads.

The term *global nomad* is a nice romantic allusion, and the word *expat* is still applicable in some instances, but what is happening today is something different, something entirely new.

So why are these entirely new things happening *now?*

Pulitzer-Prize winning journalist Thomas Friedman offers a simple solution: We're living differently because the world is different. In fact, it's radically different. In his award-winning book *The World Is Flat*, Friedman argues that we're in the midst of the third great wave of globalization.

Globalization 1.0 came after Columbus discovered the Americas in 1492. Spain, Portugal, Great Britain, France, and other monarchies competed to lay claim to colonies, sparking a global race for empire. In this era, *countries* (or monarchies) were the main drivers of global integration. The world shrank from large to medium.

Globalization 2.0 began when merchants formed companies like the British East India Company to carry out trade in the colonies. These early trading companies paved the way for the great multinational corporations that we now know today—Shell, General Electric, and Toyota, to name a few. *Companies* were the key players in this round of globalization. The world shrank again, this time from medium to small.

By the year 2000, Friedman argues, a third phase of globalization was gearing up, and this is where we find ourselves today. Globalization 3.0 is entirely new because neither countries nor companies are leading the way—*individuals* are.

Individuals around the world are increasing Wikipedia's global knowledge base.

Individual investors are using crowd-funding platforms like Kickstarter to fund *individual* entrepreneurs around the world.

Individuals aren't waiting for their country or company to send them abroad. They're doing it on their own.

Friedman says that the world has again become smaller, but this time it has shrunk so much that it's actually flat.

Under Friedman's paradigm, the people who moved overseas in the first two waves of globalization did so as expats, immigrants, and migrant workers. Just as countries and companies continue to play a major role in global affairs, these migrants still feature heavily in today's world. But Globalization 3.0 has given birth to a new breed of migrant, and these Migrants 3.0 are roamers.

Myth #2: Call them what you want, most roamers come from the West

Liu Ying Mei is from the East—China to be precise. She currently lives in Singapore. After Ying Mei gave birth to her first baby, she joined a Singapore Facebook group for young mothers, most of whom are from abroad. When a fellow mom posted a message saying that she was moving back to Europe and so her maid was looking for new employers, Ying Mei quickly responded to ask for the maid's contact details. The European mother's reply to Ying Mei was: "Hi Liu, I know she is keen to continue working with Western families so [you] might not be the best fit. Sorry ☺."

Ying Mei was stoic. "I didn't reply. What can you say to people like that? What is a Westerner?" Ying Mei is an internationally respected art dealer. She was educated in China and Germany. She's fluent in Mandarin, English, and German. For many years she was the owner of a successful art gallery in Shanghai, traveling extensively around the world to promote her artists. She moved to Singapore because her Dutch husband had an irresistible job offer, and with a baby on the way, the family wanted to stay together. She gave up the gallery in Shanghai but continues to deal for respected Chinese and Western artists. Besides, Ying Mei doesn't specify her citizenship or hometown on Facebook, so her name might indicate she is from China, but she could equally be from the United States, Germany, or anywhere else. Ying Mei didn't take the Facebook slight personally: "Some people live abroad, but still have the mentality of villagers. The woman just hasn't realized that world has changed."

Throughout the twentieth century, the main exporters of skills and knowledge were indeed *Westerners*. Expats on expat contracts were predominantly Western Europeans, North Americans, and Antipodeans who brought their education and skills to less developed markets. Immigrants and migrant workers often came from the poor South and headed North. This is simply not the case anymore. Today's roamers are Nigerian professionals working in Brussels, Argentines in Tokyo, Australians in Belgrade, Mexicans in Istanbul, and Americans still in Paris.

To a degree, roaming is a privileged person's game (you have to afford the airfare, be educated, and, often, speak a second language), but the idea that it's "Us from the West" roaming rather than "Them from Developing Countries" is a false notion that I regularly encounter. People are getting used to the idea that neither color nor religion indicates where you are from, and that a man with a strange name like Barack Obama can be president of the United States, but now we need to update our mindset about who is living abroad and why.

For this book, I surveyed over 500 people from around the world. The majority of respondents are indeed citizens of the West, but only by a tiny margin of 5 percent. If I add what was once considered Eastern Europe to that mix, that demographic rises to 68 percent. That still means that 32 percent come from South and Central America, the Middle East, Africa, and Asia.

There is, however, one clear correlation. Wherever they originate, most roamers studied in the West. It's easier to travel with a "good" passport, but it's also easier to travel if you have a "good" education. An astonishing 67 percent of roamers hold a master's degree or a Ph.D., and over 80 percent of these were completed in the Western world. Over 50 percent were completed in one of the Big Three education powerhouses— the United Kingdom, the United States, and France.

But American and European universities are losing their first-mover advantage as emerging markets catch up. Increasingly, roamers are choosing to study in places that were off the radar twenty years ago. American Dana Schwartz opted to do her master's degree abroad after a chance encounter. In 2009, Dana boarded a flight from San Francisco to New York, and the man next to her struck up a conversation. He turned out to be a respected businessman who had once been the Chief Scientist at Xerox. In the course of the conversation, Dana's plans for graduate studies came up, and her neighbor suggested that she look at Singapore. Dana had spent a summer abroad as an undergraduate, but she hadn't considered looking at graduate schools outside the United States. After a bit of research, Dana applied and was accepted to a master's degree course in public policy at the National University of Singapore (NUS). Now an alumna, Dana thinks that she made the right decision. "I now have an amazing global network spreading from South America to Africa, Europe, and Asia," she says. "It allows me to step outside and see things through other people's eyes, and perhaps try new ways of doing things that are not typically American." Dana made her choice based not only on the potential for international experience, but also on the quality of that experience. NUS consistently makes the top forty in worldwide university rankings.

Younger universities from so-called developing nations are growing in quality and reputation. During my interviews for this book, I met an admissions officer from France's INSEAD school of business at its Singapore campus. When I asked about INSEAD's nearest local rival, the NUS Business School, the admissions officer smirked and said, "We consider ourselves in a different league."

She may be right. In its global 2012 MBA rankings, *The Financial Times* put INSEAD in sixth place and NUS in twenty-third. But two years earlier, INSEAD was in fifth place, and NUS was not even ranked. To come out of nowhere and reach twenty-third place in two short years is no small achievement. INSEAD's current standing might merit a cocky attitude, but the league is getting bigger, and the contenders are getting stronger.

Newer schools are thundering past the veterans. In 2012 *The Financial Times* put Hong Kong's UST Business School and Ahmedabad's Indian Institute of Management (IIM) in tenth and eleventh place, well ahead of traditional MBA stalwarts Cornell University and IMD in Switzerland. In the year 2000, Cornell and IMD sat in tenth and eleventh place. Hong Kong's UST was ranked seventieth, and India's IIM didn't make the cut at all.

Nitpickers from Chicago to Shanghai can debate the value of university rankings, but one thing is certain: Names such as Oxford, Harvard and the Sorbonne still carry cachet, but in terms of quality, things are changing quickly.

In one of the most watched TED talks of all times, Hans Rosling, professor of international health at Karolinska Institute in Sweden, shows that Western notions of the average world citizen are woefully outdated. The headlines are not wrong: There is an increasing polarization between the rich and the poor. This is true *within* countries all over the world and when looking at the world's poorest billion citizens. Rosling, however, shows that in terms of income, health, life expectancy, fertility rates, and education, most countries are meeting in the middle. Across the world, fertility rates are converging between 1.5 and 2.5 children per woman. Life expectancy and incomes are increasing across the board, making huge leaps in countries like China and India. Although China's average life expectancy as a whole still lags behind wealthier countries, Shanghai's is higher than Washington, D.C.'s. Washington has an infant mortality rate *three times* higher than Shanghai. The distinction between the "have" and the "have not" countries is shrinking. Rosling predicts that China and India, as a whole, will achieve the same income levels and the same life expectancy as the United Kingdom and America in 2048.

Emerging economies are not only catching up, but also surpassing the old guard. In *The Economist*'s 2013 Quality of Life Index, Singapore sits in sixth place, ranking higher than New Zealand, the Netherlands, and Canada; Hong Kong comes in tenth, above Finland, Ireland, and Austria; Taiwan places higher than Belgium, Germany, and the United States; South Korea, Kuwait, and Chile are all ahead of France and Britain. In 1988, just twenty-five years earlier, the countries who stood at the top of this index were the United States, France, and West Germany, all of whom have fallen out of the top ten. While many people continue to divide the world's countries into the rich and the poor, the mindset does not correspond to the dataset, as Hans Rosling puts it.

Take for example Dr. Monica Araya, a Costa Rican now living in Oslo. Monica left Costa Rica to study at Yale University for two years, but wound up staying in the United States for eight years. When she completed her Ph.D. in environmental management in 2006, she looked for work in Europe. "During the Bush administration, nothing much was happening on the environmental front in America, so I looked towards the E.U. because it was the leader in climate change," says Monica. When Monica received a full-time job offer in Madrid with Climate Change Capital, she thought she was moving there for good. The Spanish government, however, had other plans. Because Monica didn't fit the profile of immigrants from Latin America, Spain wouldn't give her a work permit. Monica's company did all it could to help, but nothing worked. In Spain, the immigration officials put Monica's application into the same pile as anyone looking for a visa from Latin America, which is the same category as low-skilled migrant workers. Since Monica wasn't looking for low-skilled work, her visa was rejected. Monica says, "My lawyer told me if I had exactly the same education, skills, and a passport from Australia, I would have had a work permit. As a Costa Rican, I had no chance." The Spanish authorities couldn't wrap their heads around the idea that someone from a former colony could have higher and more specialized skills than a local Spaniard. So Climate Change Capital offered Monica a job in London, where she stayed for five years.

Legislators everywhere are utterly stuck in 1960s stereotypes of what an immigrant looks like. Monica was able to change her mindset and plans, but Spain missed out on a highly motivated and skilled addition to its society. Ironically, *The Economist* published an article in October 2012 about well-educated Latin Americans returning from Europe to their birth countries where economic growth and job opportunities had been flourishing. A previous generation of expats and migrant workers established South-North and East-West geographic corridors, but roamers are going in every direction imaginable.

Myth #3: Roamers come from a privileged background

One Berlin-dweller impressed upon me that "mobility is a privilege." It's true that roaming isn't available to the planet's poorest one billion who are struggling with the basics of clean water, elementary education, and preventable diseases, but this lifestyle is increasingly accessible to (and even required of) the middle classes throughout the world.

The majority of people I surveyed did not receive a private or elite education; over 60 percent attended common, state-funded primary and secondary schools. Certainly most roamers are "privileged" in that they didn't have to pull themselves up from the slums of Calcutta or the trailer parks of America, but broadly speaking, roamers are from the conventional middle classes.

Over 30 percent of roamers take home a pretax salary of under $50,000 USD, and 29 percent make between $50,000 and $100,000. Only 6 percent of roamers rake in over $300,000.

For a metropolitan area, where costs of living are very high, these are not salaries associated with excessive incomes. Depending on where in the world you live and how many dependents you have, your savings will be wildly different according to local taxes and the general cost of living. Two cities that are ranked side-by-side in AT Kearney's Global Cities Index— Hong Kong and Los Angeles—have vastly different costs of living. In 2012, the average rent for an 85-square-meter (900-square-foot) furnished apartment in an expensive area in Hong Kong was $4,400. In Los Angeles, you would have paid $2,100 for a similar apartment in a comparable part of town. Without accounting for income or property taxes, Hong Kong is

29 percent more expensive than Los Angeles. When you add income and sales taxes, the margin shrinks, but it's still there. So *where* you make your money is just as important as *how much* you make.

So is mobility a privilege? The mobile phone analogy again comes in handy. Mobile phones were a luxury thirty years ago. Today we feel as though we're missing an arm if we've forgotten our phone at home. Mobile phones are a blessing when you need to make a quick call and a curse when family dinnertime is interrupted by a ring from your boss or a client. Likewise, sometimes mobility is not only *not* a privilege, but a downright pain in the bum. Dutch national Eduard Visser works in the energy sector. He was once called to an impromptu meeting in Holland, which is a twelve-hour flight from his home in Calgary. Eduard had spent much of the past six weeks traveling, so he put his foot down. "I firmly 'asked' if I couldn't call in to the meeting." The board conceded, and Eduard attended the meeting via Skype. Because flights are relatively inexpensive and long-distance travel is considered commonplace, the board's first choice was to put Eduard on a flight without considering his health, local work commitments, or his family. In this case, Eduard got his way, but that doesn't always work. Eduard says, "Barely a week goes by when I'm not on a plane." Where is the privilege?

Myth #4: Most roamers are from Generation Y

In *The Rise of the Global Nomad*, Jim Matthewman squarely identifies a new breed of business professionals with no particular home base as a Generation Y way of life. It is true that roaming and the Gen Y generation contemporaneously came of age in the early twenty-first century, but that does not make roaming a uniquely Gen Y phenomenon.

If we use the standard definition of Gen Y as those born between the early 1980s and early 2000s, only 28 percent of those I surveyed fall into that category. Half (50 percent) are between the ages of 30 and 40, and a significant chunk (22 percent) is over 40, which is the generation one might associate with those returning home to raise a family. I met numerous couples in 40s who only recently started roaming, *after* having children.

Of course, there are differences across generations. Those now in their 40s or 50s who went abroad well before the digital age have a different approach to moving, making friends, and staying in touch. "I don't do

Facebook or Skype," says Tom Hodges in São Paulo. "I like to meet people in person." Members of Generation Y, on the other hand, grew up during the communications revolution, so they're used to staying in touch online. Many remain in contact with childhood friends via Facebook, Weibo, and other online tools. Generation Yers also grew up traveling to distant parts of the world at a more regular pace than previous generations. (George W. Bush will likely be the last person without a valid passport to be inaugurated president of the United States. In fact, every presidential candidate since then has campaigned abroad.)

Compared with previous generations, a higher percentage of Generation Yers will certainly find themselves roaming because it's becoming more and more common during their lifetime. Apparently they're already preparing themselves for it. A MOVE Guides poll reports that 93 percent of Generation Y students and young professionals expect to work abroad at some point in their career. My spidey sense tells me that they're right.

Myth #5: Roamers are just DINKYs having a good time before they settle down

Around the planet, there's a universal trend to delay marriage and childbearing. DINKYs (Double Income, No Kids Yet) are a growing segment in societies everywhere. DINKYs have greater spending power and freedom than those with families, so it's easier to work and travel the world without an expat package, childcare, or help from the extended family. Several people I interviewed speculated that most roamers are likely DINKYs. It makes sense that early in their careers, professionals may want to spend a few years gaining international experience before going home to start a family. Surprisingly, a high number of roamers have children—27 percent, which is a deceptively low percentage. Among university-educated and urban women, the average age for first-time mothers is rising well into the late 30s, and over half of my sample group (55 percent) is under the age of 35. When I discount roamers under the age of 40, 58 percent of my sample group has children.

Only 10 percent of my sample group receives an expat contract while abroad. As expat packages dwindle, you'd expect that those with families would be first in line to receive them. Surprisingly, that is not the case. Most people on expat packages, 63 percent, have no kids in tow.

Those who live abroad with children are, by and large, doing so out of their own pocket. The vast majority of roaming parents, 72 percent, are either employed under a local contract or running their own business. Some young roamers are DINKYs, but many are parents, and that doesn't stop them from roaming.

Myth #6: Roamers Are Just Third Culture Kids

In the late 1950s, American sociologist Ruth Hill Useem witnessed the upsurge of Americans working abroad and the subsequent explosion of international schools. She began questioning how these children were relating to their nationality while living in a culture that was different from, and often in conflict with, American values. They seemed to be building relationships to many cultures without having full ownership of any. Recognizing that these children were fusing together two (or more) cultures and creating their own unique "third culture," she christened them Third Culture Kids (TCKs). Regardless of nationality, Useem noticed that TCKs have more in common with each other than they do with people from their passport countries. As one of my interviewees, Joseph Pandey in New York, says, "Those of us with mixed backgrounds, we don't belong anywhere in particular. We always have a sense of belonging somewhere else." When someone asks Joseph where he's from, he simply says "Canada" to cut the conversation short. It's true that he's a Canadian citizen, but he's also of Indian origin, was born in Africa, grew up in Mauritius, and arrived in Canada with a thick French accent at the age of 16. Today, Joseph sounds like any other Canadian, but beneath the façade (and the passport) he's a citizen of TCK. Or as he puts it, "I'm a love child of globalization!"

It's hard to be an expatriate without knowing if you'll ever *re*patriate, especially if you have no clear idea of where the *patria* is. Those with mixed backgrounds, who grew up between cultures or in many different cultures, have a tangled relationship to the very notion of a home country. After reading *Third Culture Kids: Growing Up Among Worlds*, American Erin Sandral wrote me and said:

I cried when I read the book. It was the first time I realized that I wasn't alone...that there were others out there just like me who had no home and no roots. It was revelatory for me, because until then, I had only met others who were on a brief stint abroad and were all going "home" eventually (i.e., true expats). Many of the stories in the book were very similar to those I had experienced, for example, perfecting a local accent in order to fit in. Growing up in Amsterdam, I had a strange accent, something akin to a Dutch person speaking English. When I moved the States, I adopted a perfect American accent within three months. Though I stayed in the U.S. for only two years, I still haven't been able to get rid of the accent.

When I conducted my survey, I expected to find a high percentage of TCKs among roamers. It makes sense that those with early international exposure are more drawn to the roaming lifestyle. Indeed 25 percent of roamers self-identify as TCKs. This, however, means that the vast majority of roamers had a sedentary upbringing. In fact, 75 percent of roamers never lived outside of their birth country before the age of eighteen. They're not diplomatic, military, or expat brats. Even more astonishing is that 69 percent of roamers grew up in the same country where *both* of their parents had grown up. In other words, they're not of mixed heritage or children of immigrants. It turns out that most of today's roamers are not Neapolitan ice cream—they're plain vanilla. As easy as it would be to blame parents for today's rootless, mobile existence, the vast majority of roamers have found other inspirations for their international lifestyle.

O.K, enough with the urban myths. If roamers aren't expats, westerners, or DINKYS, if you can't identify them according to what school they attended or where their parents were born, what traits can you ascribe to roamers? It's not enough to say what they're not. What traits do roamers have in common, other than just living abroad and sharing a hazy feeling of being different?

Roamer Trait #1: Supranational

Alex Ljung co-founded the audio-sharing website SoundCloud in his home country of Sweden. But with a population of just ten million, Sweden has a small market, and Ljung was thinking big. Shortly after setting up in Stockholm, Ljung and his partner transplanted the company to Berlin where they had better access to world-class developers and a larger market. They soon landed financing from American investors and moved part of SoundCloud to the United States. Ljung now divides his time between the United States and Germany. So is Ljung's company American, German, or Swedish? I suspect Ljung's own answer would be "Who cares?" In an interview with *The New York Times*, Ljung said, "We're more like citizens of the Internet than citizens of a country."

Ljung might be a Swedish citizen, but his life stretches far beyond Sweden (and Germany or the United States). He no longer has a strong affinity to just one country because his interests demand that he look beyond national borders. His most enduring affiliation is now with the World Wide Web and other fellow netizens.

Ljung typifies the first trait that roamers share: **They see themselves in a global context that is *equal to or greater than* any single national context**. Although roamers typically describe themselves as *international*, more precisely they are **supranational**—their perspective doesn't range just between several countries, but it *transcends* national boundaries altogether. Unlike immigrants, expats, or migrant workers for whom a strong national link to the homeland is supplemented with a second strong national bond to their host country, roamers have a genuinely global outlook. As marketers might say, they have neither brand loyalty nor brand disloyalty.

Ilan Solot, a Brazilian banker living in London who spent several years working in New York, explains, "I don't feel part of any national community. I guess the community I feel closest to is the Latin dancing community, and that community is completely international." Married to a Serbian, Ilan says that his newborn son will be eligible for up to five passports. Nevertheless, when pressed, Ilan still admits a small penchant for those from his homeland. "The people I understand best or with whom I have the most in common are other Brazilians living abroad, followed closely by other international people living like I do."

Roamers like Ilan may find most in common with other co-nationals living as they do, but they do not necessarily seek each other out through their embassies, chambers of commerce, or national organizations. "My parents had friends who, almost exclusively, were other Korean immigrants," said American Susan Lee when I interviewed her in

Singapore in 2013. "I guess they were most comfortable around other Korean-language speakers, who had the same culture and a common immigrant history." Maybe Susan's parents were most at ease with other Koreans in the United States, but it's also possible that they didn't have much choice in the matter. It would take them months or even years to develop local knowledge and contacts. They were dependent on their welcoming committee, typically family members or other Korean immigrants. Today, roamers can access Facebook groups, networking events, and online communities like Meetup.com even before they go abroad. If you're Korean and love fly-fishing, it's probably more appealing to meet other fishing enthusiasts than it is to encounter other Koreans abroad who don't know their tigerfish from their trout. (Some roamers tell me that they go out of their way to *avoid* meeting people from their own country.)

Unlike her parents, Susan didn't go out of her way to seek out American friends. Instead, when Susan started a women's group, it was deliberately inclusive. Half of its members were local Singaporeans, and half were foreigners. "I seek to connect with people who share similar values—those who are open minded, big hearted, curious, generous people. So local or foreign, it's those shared traits that we bond over."

By bonding over shared values and pursuits, roamers are building a culture that spans cultures. "I find in the international community a sense of understanding that I cannot find in the country of my birth," says Kirsten Durward, a Scottish teacher living in Kuala Lumpur. "I try to be tolerant, but I get irritated with expatriates who talk about 'back home' and who complain that they can't find certain luxuries like cornflakes or marmite. On the other hand, in the long-term, I don't seek out a traditionally local experience because I find that limiting, too. I've met many marvelous men, but I've yet to have a fully committed relationship because everyone has wanted me to settle where they are, come live in their village, and I've just found that I can't do that."

Like Kirsten, roamers can feel alienated by a local mindset—be it that of their home country or their adopted country. While they may be proud of their home culture and well integrated into their local society, roamers tend to feel most at home in a globally minded community. Despite what may be a genuine desire to integrate into their adopted society, roamers too have a propensity to stick together, but because they're from all over the world, they're building a truly supranational global community. Incidentally, roamers who return home are still roamers. Back in their home, they'll often drift to those who share their worldview, typically other roamers—be they foreigners or locals who also have returned home.

These supranational attitudes are having unintended consequences. Australian John G. worked for a British student exchange organization in South America when it was almost entirely staffed by non-Brits. "I worked with an Egyptian, an Indian, a Nigerian, and locals. Only the director was British." Some local British nationals grumbled, but John challenged critics to view the situation in a positive light. "It shows how many anglophiles there are in the world!" he says. Unwittingly roamers are challenging the concept of a purely "national" institution.

Many people use the word *cosmopolitan* to describe what I call *supranational*, but I have carefully chosen the word because it is neutral. *Cosmopolitan* could be an appropriate description, but today it evokes everything from the namesake cocktail and the fashion magazine to the privileged demimonde who spend their time running around St. Tropez. Linking roaming to this sexy high life paints a false picture. Some roamers are members of this international jet set, but many more are not. While the single largest segment of roamers works in the borderless *beau monde* of banking and finance (18 percent), the second largest group works in the distinctly less lavish sector of education, academia, or research (12 percent). Those working in IT and telecommunications are just behind at 11 percent. Numerous industries are represented around the 5 percent mark, including heath care, government/U.N. agencies, advertising/marketing, energy/mining, and management consulting/business services. Roamers are academics, computer programmers, human rights workers, entrepreneurs, designers, and every other profession imaginable; they have families, they have pets, and they sometimes even go for quiet walks in the park. Roaming is not restricted to a particular industry, income level, age, or party scene. It is a trend that spans all of these divisions.

Stepping back from today's distortion of the word, *cosmopolitan* signifies more than a certain urban sophistication. It's often confused with *multicultural*, but plenty of places are home to many cultures without being cosmopolitan. A more appropriate description of a cosmopolitan person or place is one that faces out into the world instead of referring inwardly to itself. A cosmopolitan person is one who is able to become competent in other customs, views, and cultures without fearing the loss of his or her own identity. As cultural theorist Ulf Hannerz puts it, cosmopolitans become *aficionados* of cultures. Cosmopolitans develop an aesthetic appreciation for divergent cultural experiences in the same way you might appreciate art without becoming an artist yourself.

In this sense, roamers are indeed cosmopolitan, but they're also supranational. They're culturally fluent citizens of a given country, but above and beyond that, they genuinely see themselves as global citizens. Dagmar Baeuerle, a German-born American citizen in Hong Kong, says, "Our friends are from all over the world. Many are mixed couples from different countries, but we all share the same global values. We're all hardworking without being workaholics. We're all open and curious; we're interested in cultures and have a wide range of interests." As amorphous as that sounds, it's a good description of the supranational culture that roamers are building. Others offer a more concise and blunt description. As American Rafael Gutiérrez in Hong Kong puts it, "Everything outside this life feels provincial."

Roamer Trait #2: Outwardly mobile

"I'm driven by the content of what I do, not by location," says British citizen Iain Henderson. "Home and office are wherever in the world there's a WiFi connection—and ideally good coffee." When we met in Iain's "London office" (café Le Pain Quotidien in Notting Hill), Iain was just about to switch jobs. He was working with the World Wildlife Fund in China and would soon be moving to the United Nations Environment Programme in Geneva. "The more I travel, the more at home I feel everywhere. I'm not worried about where I am; what's important is what I'm doing," he says.

Upwardly mobile people pursue wealth, prestige, and connections in high society. Roamers like Iain are aspirational as well, but it's not financial enrichment that motivates them. Roamers are **outwardly mobile**. They pursue professional or personal goals unfettered by national borders. If the best career opportunity is on another continent, they won't hesitate to make the move. If they think it's important to speak Mandarin in the twenty-first century, they won't just take classes in the community college, they'll move to Beijing for a few years. If their home country's economy is tanking and they've just lost their job, they'll scope out prospects in parts of the world that are thriving. Given a crystal ball, *upwardly mobile* people would be crushed to learn that they'd never own a Porsche or the biggest house on the block. Au contraire, *outwardly mobile* roamers would be miserable to hear that they'll be spending the rest of their lives living on home soil, confined to whatever opportunities and experiences that offers. Even when living in their home country, roamers feel more content knowing that they can go abroad again should they wish.

We live in a capitalist world. *Financial capital* might be the leading currency, but by no means is it the only one. People with *social capital* might not have a shekel in their pocket, but they have durable networks of friends, colleagues, and other relationships that grant them special social status. People with high *cultural capital* have gained respect based on their intellect, influence, taste, or style.

Roamers have just added a new category to this list. *Mobility capital* is the ability to adapt to a new environment quickly and reliably without external support. Those with high *mobility capital* can land in a new country and start running without much hassle or complaint. They can set up a new office in a foreign country through their sheer determination. They'll have to learn some local customs and manners to get the job done, but they're used to adjusting to new cultures. The guy who asks his company to foot his taxi bills for six months because he can't figure out how use the local transportation system, for example, would have lower mobility capital than the one who downloaded the local transportation app (and dictionary) before arriving. The woman who can speak to her clients in their native tongue has higher mobility capital than the one who can't understand her client's accent. But it's not just about attitude and aptitude. Physical limitations can also curb a person's mobility capital—those who are physically unable to adapt to a new environment or regularly get ill because it is too hot, too cold, too humid, etc., will also fare lower on the mobility scale.

As with other forms of capital, *mobility capital* comes from a combination of nature and nurture. The Slumdog Millionaire managed to increase his financial capital through a combination of luck and skill, but as the old saying goes, "The easiest way to make a million is to start with a million." Likewise, people can set their minds to achieve mobility, but those who start early will have an advantage over those who come later into the game (i.e., it's easier to learn a new language when you already speak two).

Allan Ang, a Malaysian who spent eight years in the United Kingdom and recently moved to Sydney for work, says, "You need to stay flexible. If you're rigid in your ways, you'll never be able to adapt. You need to be dynamic." Allan originally went to the United Kingdom to study, and like many who go to university or abroad for the first time, Allan admits that he had to learn how to use a washing machine when he arrived. "I didn't have the slightest clue!" He laughs. Allan wasn't ready, but he was flexible enough to make himself ready when the challenge (in this case dirty socks) presented itself. Adopting this attitude a young age, Allan was globally ready when the next opportunity came up.

Like Allan, roamers don't make much fuss about moving overseas and are willing to learn on the road. Those who move abroad through a company might require certain basics, but roamers are dynamic. Some accept job offers without having ever set foot in the country that will be their new home, perhaps for many years to come. They simply are ready to dive headfirst into uncharted waters and do everything necessary to adapt to their new environment.

This all sounds great, but this global portability can have a grim underbelly. Some roamers are working so much that it doesn't really matter what the world outside of their window looks like. As Canadian Jackie Sung in Hong Kong says, "Same shit, different postcode." Samuel Kolehmainen has a more optimistic spin on his plug-and-play mode of living. "There's very few places in the world that have practices dedicated to my field of interest," he says. "When the opportunity to join the team came up, I jumped at it." A Finish lawyer previously living in Dublin, Samuel had never been to Singapore before moving there. He explains, "I'm more interested in the people I'm working with ten to twelve hours per day. They're the top people in my field, so our work environment stimulates me. Outside of work I spend much of my time with my wife. We're interested in learning about cultures and trying new things, so I'm not worried about our quality of life. I know we can find a way to be happy wherever we are."

These outwardly mobile roamers might expect a fair salary, but they're not primarily motivated by their paycheck. "I wanted a challenge on a professional, emotional, and linguistic level," says Tuck Meng Yee in

Shanghai. Tuck holds Malaysian and Australian citizenship. He had been working as private banking analyst in Singapore for six years before moving to Shanghai, where his girlfriend was already living. Instead of asking his girlfriend to move, Tuck took the challenge upon himself. "I wanted to see what I could achieve when living in a new environment," he says. Tuck got a job teaching finance at East China Normal University and Shanghai Jiaotong University. Tuck took a big paycut to go to Shanghai, but on a personal level, he feels that he took a significant step forward.

Tuck is not the only roamer who is tuning into the self-discovery channel. Almost one-third of roamers, 31 percent, say that their main impetus for going abroad was to seek adventure, to try something new, or for intellectual stimulation. A higher salary, on the other hand, motivated only 5 percent of roamers to move abroad. Overall, the single biggest magnet is a career opportunity, at 34 percent. There is, however, a gender gap. The number one reason for men to go abroad is a job opportunity, with 42 percent citing this as their main purpose, compared with only 28 percent of women. Women's top motive for going abroad is adventure, trying something new, and intellectual stimulation, with 37 percent saying these were the biggest draw.

Some roamers manage to be both upwardly and outwardly mobile, with 27 percent saying that they're earning significantly more money abroad than they could at home. Another 24 percent think that they have a moderately higher income. The other 49 percent, however, believe that they're gaining no monetary benefit from living abroad. In fact 23 percent think that they are saving less, including those who say, "I'm bleeding money, but it's worth it."

"It's not about money, it's about challenges," says dual Lebanese-Canadian citizen Antoine Massoud. After university, Antoine had hoped to work in a relative's property business in the United States, but he was unable to get a green card. Instead of counting his misfortunes or heading to safer shores back home, he picked himself up and headed to Guangzhou, China, to see what opportunities he might discover there. He and a friend started a catering business, which they later sold to a large food retailer. Now based in Hong Kong, Antoine says, "When you get to a certain point in your career, you want rewards that are not only monetary. You want to brave a few challenges." Like Antoine, 25 percent of roamers took the extraordinary risk of moving to a foreign country without having a job offer and only found employment or started a company once on the ground.

Daniel, an American hedge fund analyst in London, put it this way: "I'm probably not better off in London. I probably would have more disposable income in Chicago…or, well, I don't know. I'm not in it for the money. If I were, I'd be in Dubai. I once had a job offer in Dubai for stupid money. I thought, 'You're going to give me *that* much money? For what?!' I didn't take the job. I'm in London for the life experience."

For many roamers, part of the trick to staying outwardly mobile is having a Buddha-like detachment from worldly goods. Jennifer, a Ghanaian designer in London, told me, "I feel better waking up every morning knowing that I can leave, that I have no commitments." Flexibility, far above stability, is a central feature in the life of a roamer.

A king-size teak bed might seem like a good idea at the time and vintage copies of *Vogue* are priceless, but they all add up to commitments. Possessions can become a burden whether you're living at home or abroad, but it's one thing to pay for a U-Haul to move within a country, and an entirely different one to transport all your worldly goods by boat and shipping container halfway across the world, living out of a suitcase for weeks or months on end. Parents' homes, friends' attics, and storage units turn into receptacles for things desired, but not currently required. Sarah Ryan, an American in London, tells me that her wedding gifts are still in her parents' place in Chicago. She married fifteen years ago.

It's unsurprising that storage facilities are a booming trade, the fastest growing sector of the commercial real estate industry. Kenny Wong, an entrepreneur in Los Angeles, told me about friends who had left things in self-storage when they moved to a new country, uncertain how long they'd be gone. "They rented a storage unit for eight years!" he says. "Retrospectively, they couldn't afford it, and they really didn't know what to do with everything once they finally cleared it out." Zou Bing still pays for a storage locker in Munich—six years after moving back to Beijing and then on to Singapore. During a recent visit to Munich, Bing intended to clear out her locker, but failed miserably. "Every time I opened up a book I realized I couldn't throw anything out." So Bing took out a few items and quietly closed the locker door again.

Carlos Salcedo makes sure that doesn't happen to him. A half-Peruvian, half-British financial analyst who moved to New York after living in London, Carlos says, "I don't own anything. I have a laptop, some clothes, and a sound system. I travel light. I'm not accumulating anything, just my salary."

When you're roaming the world, staying financially liquid is a logical option. Despite low interest rates and unstable financial markets, over half of roamers (56 percent) have not invested in the most tangible commitment-entailing asset: property. This changes as roamers get older. (Carlos, for example, bought an apartment since our interview.) But even by the time they're 40, one-third of roamers still have not invested in property anywhere. Of those who do invest, half take the plunge to make a long-term commitment to their current country of residence by buying where they live. The other half bought property in their home country or in a third location.

Whether they live in their own property or rented accommodation, roamers build as much flexibility into their living arrangements as possible, which often requires proximity to an international airport. "London is perfect because it's easy to leave," says Mikhail, a Russian investment banker in London. "It's a great hub." The weather might be awful, but London is only a two-hour flight to the south of Spain or Turin.

I predict that in the next few years, headhunters the world over will start adding *mobility capital* to their list of job requirements. Roamers are lucky because they have a head start in this department. They might not know their Borges from their Beckett or score well on the financial capital scale, but they are adaptable, flexible, and reliable in a new environment. Their slogan might well be "You can parachute me into any place in the world, and I'll make it happen." It shouldn't be surprising that roamers score highly on the mobility scale. After all, they practically invented it.

Roamer Trait #3: Creative Class

The final trait common to roamers is that, by and large, they are *members of the Creative Class*. By Creative, I don't mean that roamers are artists and bohemians, but that their job is to "create meaningful new forms." This trait is not unique to roamers. Richard Florida popularized the phenomenon in his book *The Rise of the Creative Class*. This class is not defined by income (e.g., the middle class), but by how it generates economic value. The Creative Class produces economic value through the formation of ideas. Mark Zuckerberg and other flip-flop-wearing

45

entrepreneurs typify the Creative Class. It includes scientists inventing new vaccinations, writers scripting children's television programs, management consultants solving business problems, and programmers developing new source code. Creative workers are highly educated; they are expected to use their own judgment and tap into a vast body of knowledge to invent unique solutions to the task at hand. While the service sector edges toward an ever-greater standardization where workers are expected to use "Would you like a drink with your order?" and other preprogrammed phrases, Creatives are expected to work independently without much supervision. They're willing to take on personal responsibility in exchange for control—control over what they can wear to work, what hours they work, and what their workspace looks like. Creative Class workers attach so much importance to individuality, non-conformity, and flexibility that they might balk at the notion of a Creative Class. They don't believe in labels. They don't think outside the box because they don't see a box. Their motto might be: "The class is dead, long live the Creative Class!"

Dress-down Fridays and the "no-collar" workplace might make Creative workers look like slackers, but in fact they work hard—harder than anyone else. They spend longer hours at the office, lab, or studio than their service and working-class counterparts. They don't understand the concept of getting paid for working overtime. They work anytime, anywhere. But they are rewarded. On average, Creative workers make significantly more money than those employed in services or manufacturing. In the same way that the twentieth century saw the economic engine shift away from manufacturing and manual labor to services, the twenty-first century is witnessing a move away from the service sector to the creative sector.

While money is important, Creatives are not willing to work for manna alone. Florida says that in a survey of over 20,000 IT workers and managers, 67 percent say that "challenge" is what matters most to them in their jobs. Creatives want to get ahead not because they'll make more money, but because they're good at what they do and because the respect of their peers is what spurns them on. Unlike the corporate "lifer" of the 1950s, Creative workers don't expect to stay with their company for more than a few years. Creative employees ultimately work for *themselves*, not for a company. When their employers no longer provide them with the right incentives, Creative workers are ready to move to another company more in tune with their philosophy (or even start their own businesses).

Creatives believe in meritocracy. They want to do well in life because they're good at what they do. Plenty of roamers went abroad because they wanted to work with the best people around the world instead of being a big fish in a small pond. By moving abroad, roamers have little chance of resting on their laurels or the glory of a deal done a year ago in a distant country. They must prove themselves not once or twice, but over and over again, and in a new cultural environment. *The Economist* captured this sentiment well in this tongue-in-cheek advertorial for a charity: "Aim high. You've been an overachiever your whole life. Changing the world should be a piece of cake." (Incidentally, *The Economist* is the most read news source among roamers—37 percent are regular readers.)

All Creatives thrive on challenges and meritocracy, but roamers take the daring up a notch. They have done well in their home countries, but is that enough? Can they do it again in a place where the competition might be stiffer? Michelle Mouracade, a Lebanese working in banking in Hong Kong, says that she and her fellow roamers are go-getters. "About fifteen of my Lebanese friends lived in Paris around the same time, but only two have stayed. All the ambitious people left," she says. William Finn, a Kiwi corporate lawyer in Singapore, echoes her sentiments: "The hungry ones move abroad. They're the ones who live outside their comfort zone."

That was an expression I heard from roamers over and over again: "going out of your comfort zone." Or you might see it the other way around: Roamers *find* their comfort zone when doing something new, mentally challenging, or physically exhausting. Roamers by nature are adventurers. Mark Arasaratnam says, "I wasn't looking for a new job, but when I was in London for a wedding, a friend said, 'Why don't you drop in to meet the guys at my office?' I popped in, and suddenly within twenty-four hours I had a job offer." After working in Toronto for six years and reaching a plateau, frankly, Mark was getting a bit complacent. "I was ready for this new challenge. I wasn't looking for it, but when it came to me, I couldn't turn it down," he says. Adventure-seekers know that by trying something new in a different environment, the potential upside is big, but so is the downside. This didn't bother Mark, who says, "I think those of us living this life are more predisposed to taking risks."

Mark might have stayed in Toronto with his well-paid, safe job, but Creatives and roamers don't just want professional success. They set goals to reach new heights in their personal lives, too. By putting themselves in a foreign context, roamers confront their core values, cultural norms, and belief systems. Each and every person I interviewed had sophisticated views on the way they were living. Nyree Hu, a Canadian financial marketing professional in Hong Kong, put it this way: "You have to keep checking in with yourself. 'Why am I here? What are my motives? Am I here to further my career? What are my priorities? What about my personal life?' If you happen to be single and do not have the obligations of family as ballast, you have to ask yourself these questions every day. Nothing is given."

Here are a couple of quotes by roamers that could be straight out of a textbook on the Creative Class:

Kirsten Durward, Scottish teacher in Kuala Lumpur: *I decided to implement a career that would allow me to both contribute to the world and continue to explore it. For me this boiled down to either the foreign service or education. I decided on education as I preferred choosing my location, rather than being sent.*

Antoinette Roux, French project manager, Ho Chi Minh City: *Roamers expect a lot from life, but we ask a lot from ourselves, too. We want to make our lives, not just let them happen to us.*

In psychology there's a condition called "cognitive dissonance" that occurs when two beliefs (e.g., your personal values or ideas versus those of your company) conflict with each other, causing mental stress. By and large, Creative workers are not willing to accept cognitive dissonance for extended periods of time. They'd rather face the unknown than stay mired in a job that doesn't match their aspirations. That might mean finding a new job, starting a business, or going freelance.

Take for instance Hannah and Stefan. Hannah is Australian, and Stefan is Swiss. They met when Stefan was working in Australia for a Swiss multinational. After the couple married, Stefan's company relocated him to Hong Kong. "When we moved to Hong Kong," says Hannah, "we had business-class flights, health insurance, membership to two country clubs, a luxurious car, and a very good living allowance." But when the company wanted Stefan to move back to Switzerland, the couple faced a tough decision. "We just weren't ready to go," says Hannah. "They didn't give him a choice in the matter, so he quit and started his own business. We wanted to make our own destiny and not have someone dictate our lives to us."

Stefan and Hannah dove head first into their new adventure. Hannah quickly finished her Ph.D. and found a job in a language institute. Stefan started his company. Like many roamers, Hannah and Stefan were willing to trade their golden handcuffs for freedom, but it came at a price. "It was much harder than we thought," Hannah admits. "Suddenly we were on our own without any of the expat amenities, and it was a big change. We miss them, but we don't regret it. We value freedom and flexibility over a big compensation package that allows a company to dictate where we should live our lives."

Stefan and Hannah's decision baffled many friends and family members. Hannah's husband was leaving a great job at a great company. His company was, after all, just telling him to come home. What was the problem with that? Like other roamers, Stefan didn't conform to expectations based on his nationality, a decision that would flummox non-roamers. Like all Creative workers, Stefan ultimately works for himself first and for a company second. Like all roamers, he also sees himself as an individual first and as a citizen second.

Those of you still confused about how to spot roamers in the wild, at least you now know that you won't be able to identify them by the color of their feathers, their eating habits, or their mating calls. But if you're an expert tracker, you'll be able to identify a roamer by looking out for a supranational, outwardly mobile member of the Creative Class. Some of you who consider yourselves roamers are thinking, "That doesn't sound like me at all!" There will always be a few black swans to disprove the rule. You may just be a black swan. Or if you dig deeply into that dark cavernous backpack of the soul, it's possible that you're actually an immigrant, an expat, or part of a different species altogether (in which case, I'll leave it to you to write *that* book).

CHAPTER 3
IS THIS JUST A PHASE?

To get my mom on board with my lifestyle, I need to package it so that she can explain it to her friends.

—Michael Delfs, American urban designer in London

There's a particular pleasure in the "aha" moment when, in the blink of an eye, there's an answer, sometimes to a question we didn't know we had. It's why we read horoscopes; it's why we like to know if we're personality type A or ENTJ; it's why we watch experts on TED talks explain us to ourselves. These all supply eureka-like insights to help us create meaning now that religion, cultural practices, and social convention no longer provide a grand narrative for our lives. Today's narrative is "be whoever you want to be." That's liberating, but it can result in a great deal of soul searching and uncertainty. As neurologist and author Oliver Sacks wrote, "To live on a day-to-day basis is insufficient for human beings; we need to transcend, transport, escape; we need meaning, understanding, and explanation; we need to see over-all patterns in our lives." These patterns help us make sense of an increasingly complex world.

That's why marketing is such a powerful tool. Most of us simply don't have the bandwidth to sift through the vast array of options on offer, and marketing tries to convince us that from a huge selection of stuff, there's really only one option. This sense of certainty is reassuring, even if it may be false. That may be why several people urged me to package roamers into some basic personality types or "tribes." Boiling roamers down into prepackaged archetypes would make for neat sound bites and give traction to people who need to get their mom on board with this roaming lifestyle. After all, explaining to your mom that you roam because it's part of the zeitgeist just doesn't cut it.

Roamers, however, don't neatly slot into tidy little boxes because real life is made of messier stuff. Take for example Claudio, who left Argentina for graduate studies at the University of California in Los Angeles. He attended the university's job fairs and accepted a graduate trainee position at a management consultancy in Los Angeles. Part of his training included a stint in Shanghai, where he met his future wife, an Australian. Ten years later, Claudio finds himself in the middle of a divorce, but with no choice where to live because his two young children were born in Hong Kong, where the family currently resides. There's no "moving home" scenario available, neither for Claudio nor for his ex-wife. They've agreed on joint custody of the children, but staying in Hong Kong permanently is not what either of them had planned. For now, Hong Kong is their compromise.

Why does Claudio roam? You can't pin it down to a few particular traits. Claudio initially sought a world-class education, intellectual stimulation, and international adventure. His reasons for staying abroad have changed throughout the years. Claudio moved to Los Angeles, Shanghai, and Hong Kong to enhance his career prospects. He would now like to return to Los Angeles, but stays put in Hong Kong for the sake of his children. The longer you roam, the muddier the waters become.

So is roaming just a phase? Does it slot in somewhere just after university and before you "finally settle down," either going back home or becoming an immigrant somewhere else? The short answer is no. Some roamers will roam their entire lives, and others will stay put somewhere for a very long time without ever really settling down. The only clear trend is that a roamer's *impetus* for living abroad changes over the course of his or her lifetime. These motivations can be clustered into three main stages. Roamers might flit back and forth between these phases at any point in their lives, and they may skip some altogether. Most, however, begin their adventures as Active Explorers.

Phase 1: Active Explorers
Not All Those Who Wander Are Lost

"After university I took off traveling and loved living abroad so much that I decided to become an international school teacher," says Cate Dunham, an Australian teaching in Kenya. Her choice to live internationally for an extended period, or perhaps forever, is deliberate. Cate's mother is confounded by her life choices. Cate says, "My mum once told me I can't keep farting around the world." Cate laughs because that is precisely what she, more or less, set out to do. One person's trash is another person's treasure. Cate's mother doesn't understand or approve, but Cate has continued following this path for many years without regret. She has lived in fifteen countries so far. "I love living internationally, and I can't imagine anything else," she says.

Like Cate, many Active Explorers had a thirst for travel from a young age and hit the road as soon as they could. Others, however, began indulging their wanderlust much later in life. "We spent seven years deciding where to go," says Karin M. in Singapore. She and her husband were in their late 30s when they set off with three young children in tow. Despite having their parents, friends, great jobs, and a home in London, they felt the urge for some adventures abroad. One of their top choices was Singapore, and Karin's husband managed to transfer there with his employer. The family has been in Singapore for five years, but they haven't yet settled down. "We're just starting to get itchy feet again," admits Karin. The family's eyes are not trained back on London just yet. The next port of call could be anywhere from California to Dubai.

Karin expects that London will be her final cul-de-sac, but a full 25 percent of roamers left their home country with a "let's blow this pop stand" attitude knowing that they'd never return. They do not aim to immigrate permanently to one particular country, but they intentionally emigrated from their own. If they don't settle down abroad, they will remain *Active Explorers* for the rest of their lives. Most roamers, 75 percent, say that they intend to pack up and go home someday, but only 13 percent want home to be their next stop. A whopping 58 percent of roamers expect to move to a new destination next, and 12 percent intend to move back to city where they have already lived but not where they grew up.

There's no single motive that kick-starts roaming or keeps Active Explorers abroad. Some started studying abroad or got a job offer. Others went traveling and ended up staying abroad, and some actively sought international employment. Many continue to roam because the most challenging work and the most interesting social environments are not in their home country. Others simply enjoy moving around and discovering new ways of living. What connects all these Active Explorers is their lack of regret for not settling down. In their own way, they have settled into a peripatetic life of permanent temporariness, and they're perfectly happy with that.

Most roamers start out as Active Explorers purposefully embarking on an international experience. They remain Active Explorers as long as they continue to make an affirmative decision to stay abroad without any inclination to settle down. For some roamers, that means their entire lives. Others, however, shift into the second phase of roaming, also known as "oops."

Phase 2: Accidental Migrants
Definitely Maybe

"What the hell have I done?" is a question that roamers routinely ask themselves. After the initial rush of excitement and freedom wears off, many roamers hit a wall of doubt. They started out as Active Explorers, intentionally going abroad, but they forgot to implement an exit (or re-entry) strategy. They find themselves driving on a global highway with no exit labeled "Home."

"I didn't know what I was getting myself into," says Kiwi corporate lawyer William Finn in Hong Kong. In 2005, William was contentedly working in a law firm in Auckland with no particular ambition to move abroad. Unexpectedly, he received a call from a headhunter with a tempting proposition. "They were offering me a position at a top law firm in New York, with a good salary and support to pass the state bar exam." Unable to resist the temptation, William set off on a high-flying career that has taken him to New York, London, Hong Kong, and now Singapore. With his career moving from strength to strength, he believes that he made a smart career move. "By moving laterally—internationally—you get an advantage," he says. "You get the chance to move up the ladder more quickly than your colleagues who stayed at home."

At the same time, William shares some misgivings. "I don't like living so far from my family and old friends, but I don't know if I can ever go back now. I'm happy with my life and career, but I probably would have been as happy had I stayed in New Zealand, and my life would be less complicated," says William.

He has bought a house in New Zealand, but now with a long-term Singaporean girlfriend, William doesn't know if he'll ever move back. Once in a while he still has a few niggling doubts. "It's been a great adventure, but I'm not sure I made the right choice," he admits. But did William really have a choice? What curious, successful, and adventurous young man would say, "No thanks New York—I'll stay at home"?

American banker Dan S. in London also didn't have international aspirations, but an unexpected internal job offer lead him abroad. "I was 25 and wanted a new challenge," he says. Dan had never lived or studied abroad, but when his boss offered him the chance to start a team in London, he couldn't resist. It was an excellent career move, but it's had unexpected consequences. "When I left, I never dreamed that seventeen years on I'd still be living outside of the U.S. This has become my long semester abroad," he says.

William and Dan never intended to move out of their home countries permanently. They're neither immigrants where they currently live nor emigrants from their home countries. They're simply *Accidental Migrants*.

Roaming is like walking in a blizzard—your footprints are covered by new layers of snow as soon as you take the next step forward. With time, the footprints are erased. The longer and farther you walk, the harder it is to retrace your steps. Reluctant roamers can embark on a *new* adventure to make their way back home, but they can't simply *trace* their way back home.

Many roamers embark on international adventures at a young age without fully appreciating the significance of their choices. Plenty of roamers figure that fastest route between two points is not a straight line, but via a curve. They initially set out to get international experience to get a better job not abroad, but *at home*. They don't realize that their international experience may lead them away from home and for much longer than they ever expected, perhaps forever. Having spent ten years in Asia or Europe developing regional know-how, they have a hard time converting their international expertise into a job back home in São Paulo, Cape Town, or Chicago. Professionally, they have painted themselves into a corner.

"I was young and too naïve to understand the risks when I applied to INSEAD," says Nyree Hu, a Canadian in Hong Kong. After completing her undergraduate degree in Canada, Nyree opted to study at INSEAD business school in France because of its excellent reputation and its international student body. Intending to work in Canada or the United States after her studies, Nyree never imagined that by studying in France she was buying a one-way ticket from Canada. "All INSEAD recruiting is done in London, so virtually all of the jobs on offer were in Europe," she says. Nyree found a great job in London, where she spent six years, and then another excellent career opportunity brought her to Hong Kong.

Nyree's career has soared, but it's not leading her back any closer to Canada.

Most roamers aren't thinking about home when they first go abroad; they're thinking about expanding their horizons and learning something new. "Only when you go somewhere else do you realize how other people live and why they think differently. The more adaptive you become, the more tolerant you become," says Ayse Levent. Ayse is someone who knows about difference and tolerance. Ayse is a Turkish and French citizen who was born in Germany and lived in the United Kingdom for many years. She now works as a market researcher in New York. But knowledge comes at a price. Ayse says, "Sometimes I envy people who never left home and don't know about other ways of living. I wonder if it's easier than having many great international experiences, but then having to choose which path is right for you." That question dates back to the Garden of Eden, that great parable of blissful ignorance. To know or to not know: Therein lies the rub. As Ayse points out, "The more you know, the more choices you have."

What can be better than having choices? "Freedom of choice" is the ultimate mantra of democracy and capitalism. It implies that choice is inherently good. The more choices we have, the greater the chance to get exactly what we want and, consequently, the better off we are. Right?

"Wrong," says Barry Schwartz, an American psychologist. In his book *The Paradox of Choice—Why More Is Less*, Schwartz claims that too many choices cause anxiety rather than liberation in modern, affluent Western societies. With a surplus of choices, consumers typically face two negative consequences: paralysis and opportunity costs. If a consumer can overcome paralysis and make a selection, his or her enjoyment of the product or service is decreased by regret. Borrowing a concept from economics, Schwartz says that this regret is caused by "opportunity costs," or the notion that when you choose one thing, you're excluding all other options, which have other benefits. Because modern society offers so many alternatives, Schwartz says, "It's easy to imagine that you could have made another choice that would have been better."

As the choice of goods and services has expanded, so have consumer expectations. This is what Schwartz calls the "escalation of expectations." Schwartz illustrates his theory with a personal example:

There was a time when jeans came in one flavor, and you bought them, and they fit like crap, and they were incredibly uncomfortable, and if you wore them long enough and washed them enough times, they started to feel O.K. So I went to replace my jeans after years and years of wearing these old ones, and I say, "I want a pair of jeans. Here's my size." And the shopkeeper says, "Do you want slim fit, easy fit, relaxed fit? You want button fly or zipper fly? You want stonewashed or acid-washed? Do you want them distressed? You want boot cut, you want tapered, blah blah blah…" On and on he went. My jaw dropped, and after I recovered, I say, "I want the kind that used to be the only kind." He had no idea what that was, so I spent an hour trying on all these damn jeans, and I walked out of the store—truth!—with the best-fitting jeans I had ever had. I did better. All this choice made it possible for me to do better. But I felt worse. Why? I wrote a whole book to try to explain this to myself. The reason I felt worse is that, with all of these options available, my expectations about how good a pair of jeans should be went up. I had no particular expectations when they only came in one flavor. When they came in 100 flavors, damn it, one of them should've been perfect. And what I got was good, but it wasn't perfect. And so I compared what I got to what I expected, and what I got was disappointing in comparison to what I expected. Adding options to people's lives can't help but increase the expectations people have about how good those options will be. And what that's going to produce is less satisfaction with results, even when they're good results.

Roamers know all about a surplus of choice. When I interviewed Kate Menihan in New York, she and her fiancé were having trouble planning their wedding. "We can't decide where to get married," she said. Kate is Canadian, and her fiancé is British. Both live in New York. Canada, Britain, and New York all had competing advantages, financial ramifications, and interests for everyone involved. "I wish we could just have one of those big Indian weddings where your family organizes everything and essentially you just show up," she said, laughing. "This choice is paralyzing us. We've been engaged for more than five months, but we're no closer to planning the wedding." Kate and her fiancé were frozen by the thought of choosing the wrong location. The story, however, has a happy ending—eventually Kate and her fiancé managed to make a decision and have since married.

In an interview with the *Sunday Times Magazine*, Irish actor Colin Farrell said that he spent a year living in a hotel so he could deny that he was now living permanently in Los Angeles. "There's a whole lot of buyer's remorse that goes on when you take your life and invest it in a place that's not whence you came," he said. It's a nice way of putting it—buyer's remorse. Rather than buy and face the prospect of buyer's remorse, he lived in a hotel room to keep his options open. But as Schwartz points out, keeping a range of options open too comes at a cost.

"I always feel like I should be somewhere else," says Magnus Edensvard, a Swedish citizen in Los Angeles. Owner of the successful art gallery Ibid Projects, Magnus initially moved to London to study fine art for three months. He writes:

I left Sweden when I was 17. I had signed up for a three-month course in Art History in London, at Sotheby's Institute. I planned to be in London for one term. I can list the reasons for coming to London as I remember them quite clearly: I wanted to study art history and I wanted to do it in city where I had first-hand access to the works of art I would be reading about. I wanted to study in the English language. I also wanted to experience living in big international city (although it can argued at in the early 1990s London was not nearly as international as it is now). I wanted to experience something new and position myself in what I thought to be a centre of a potential wave of influences, experiences and people that only a large international city can provide. It's a question of statistics, but also the sense of risk-taking that comes with the territory, of being one amongst millions of people. The thought excited me. Will I be seen? And will I meet the most interesting people in the world there? A large city can carry you on its shoulder like a prince, but it can also throw you to the wayside where you can feel like an anonymous National Insurance Number. The challenge is part of the experience, to "make" something out of it. But as much as I was moving to something, I was also getting away from things in my home country: military service, my parents, language, and the familiar, small country values, and culture that, at the time, I felt was limiting, almost claustrophobic. I was idealistic and desperate in equal measures. At the time, I did not see it as a move that would last some twenty years and counting.

Intending to go for three months, Magnus exceeded his intended stay by roughly 8,000 percent. At various junctures in his life, he toyed with the idea of moving to Germany, Los Angeles, or back to Sweden, but he kept London as his home base. After opening a gallery in Los Angeles, Magnus traveled between London and the United States for several years, but in 2016 he finally succumbed to the call of the wild, moving his home base to Los Angeles.

Accidental Migrants aren't always staying abroad for work or studies. Sometimes it's pursuits of an entirely different nature that keep them overseas. Love is a drug, and after a binge, roamers can wake up with a terrible hangover the next morning (or the next decade), wondering, "How on earth did I wind up here?"

"Had I known this is where I'd end up, I don't know if I would have married," says Bianka, a private equity marketing professional in Moscow. Her frank admission is tinged with a smile so that I'm not sure if she's speaking in earnest. Bianka is Hungarian, and her husband, Alonso, is Spanish. They met in London while working in the banking industry, married in Budapest, and now live in Moscow. Both Alonso and Bianka lost their jobs in fallout of the 2008 global financial crisis. Despite having lived in London for five years and owning an apartment there, neither was eager to look for another job in London. "The atmosphere was gloomy in London during the credit crunch," says Bianka. "We wanted a fresh environment where our careers could move ahead, not stagnate like in London."

But where to go next? Alonso's and Bianka's respective birth countries were not on the menu. Bianka didn't see any opportunities in her native Hungary, and Alonso said that he could never work in Spain again. (Incidentally, both were willing to move to each other's country, but not to their own.) So in 2009, Bianka and Alonso set off for Moscow, Shanghai, and Hong Kong, staying with friends while scoping out job opportunities. Bianka found work in a private equity firm in Moscow, and they decided to take the plunge. Alonso found work a few months later, after the move. The couple are now preparing for the birth of their second child, who will be Spanish-Hungarian, born in Moscow to parents who speak English to each other. Despite wishing to be closer to their families, Bianka says that their next move will likely to be to Asia, if they can find work.

Ironically, Bianka and Alonso both went overseas to broaden their horizons, but inadvertently narrowed down their choices. An abundance of options when they were young and single led them to a narrow range of places where they could envisage following their highly specialized careers while still living together—London, New York, Moscow, Singapore, or Hong Kong.

By falling in love, Bianka and Alonso fell into a typical Accidental

Migrant scenario. When they left home to study abroad, neither intended the move to be permanent. After they married, living abroad seemed to become inevitable. Two itinerants rarely agree on one homeland. Instead, they often choose a third, interim destination, thereby pushing the decision of where to settle down further away, sometimes indefinitely.

On the opposite side of the spectrum, several roamers confided that going home was not an option precisely because they *had not* paired up. Fearful of ending up in Bianka and Alonso's situation, they would consider returning to their home country to look for a mate, but all their contemporaries married years ago. As single people, they would feel ostracized at home. Even if they don't meet "the one" where they now live, at least they're escaping their family's pressure and social awkwardness.

Many roamers saw their time abroad as a temporary learning experience; they never meant to turn it into a permanent lifestyle. Some roamers are quickly reconciled to their permanent life abroad, but many experience a cri de coeur when they realize that their path back home is obscured. Going home will be as complex as going abroad was. For plenty of roamers, going home is actually a lot *harder* than staying abroad. Moving abroad is not like going on a vacation; it's like going to Mars.

It's true that a picture can paint a thousand words, but sometimes song lyrics can do the job just as well. English punk rock band the Clash may have unwittingly written the soundtrack to a roamer's life:

> *Should I stay or should I go now?*
> *If I go there will be trouble*
> *And if I stay it will be double*
> *So you gotta let me know*
> *Should I stay or should I go?*

By expanding their horizons, roamers are faced with even more choices than if they had stayed at home. Not only do they worry whether they've bought the right pair of jeans, taken the right career path, or chosen the right partner, they can add a whole list of other doubts like "To which country should I move next?" and "Is it time to move home?" or even "Where is home?" At least roamers can rest in peace knowing that they're not the only ones worried about making the right choice—it's a modern-day curse. So when roamers ask me, as they often do, "Was it wise or foolish to go abroad in the first place?" my educated opinion is: "Yes."

Phase 3: Glocals
Think Global, Act Glocal

"I no longer have the contacts or local knowledge. I don't know if I could go back, even if I wanted to," says Rohinder Singh, a senior accountant in New York. Rohinder spent his whole career working abroad, and now his entire professional network is in London and New York, but that's not the only hindrance. "Because I'm Indian, my work colleagues would expect me to understand the Indian work culture, but I've never worked in India. It would be easier to move anywhere else in the world than to go back to India. I've been abroad for almost twenty years. India has changed in that time." Rohinder has his green card and is married to an American. He intends to apply for American citizenship as soon as he can. Since the Indian government doesn't allow dual citizenship, he will have to forfeit his Indian passport.

Rohinder is a de facto immigrant in America, but like many roamers, he shies away from such a designation.

"Don't immigrants feel like they want to become 100 percent citizens of their new country?" asks Morgan Long, a dual American-British citizen. "Getting my second passport from the U.K. did not make me feel like an immigrant. At the ceremony, though, I was one of the few native English speakers to swear allegiance to the Queen, and I definitely felt like I was amongst immigrants," she says. Morgan has been studying, working, and living in the United Kingdom for almost twenty years, but it was only after she married an Englishman that she began to feel more local, as family ties began to sink into place. "It made me realize that I will settle for the mid-term in the U.K.," she says. Before she met her husband, nothing was set in stone. "Had I been offered a better job somewhere else, even though I was a British citizen, I might have moved," she admits. Even now Morgan adds a caveat: "I would never rule out returning to the U.S. or moving somewhere else. Luckily, my husband has the same spirit." Neither an intentional emigrant from the United States nor a purposeful immigrant to the United Kingdom, Morgan admits, "I don't feel any more British than

I did before. I still proudly feel more American than anything else and always will be. Except of course if we elect another boob as president, in which case I will start denying that I'm American again."

Globally minded locals, or *Glocals*, have settled down "until further notice." Janus-faced, Glocals come in two flavors: *Foreign Glocals* ensconce themselves in a foreign country, and *Local Glocals* do so back home. Foreign Glocals like Rohinder and Morgan are effectively immigrants, but they don't see themselves as such. Perhaps that's because they're not escaping their home countries in a bid for freedom, safety, or a better standard of living. Many didn't deliberately leave their home country "for good." They went abroad, and for whatever reason, they have stayed abroad. Plenty of Glocals didn't deliberately immigrate to their resident country. They simply ended up there because that's where their education, job, love, or purely life took them. Of those who responded to my survey, 9 percent intend to stay put where they live abroad. They may stay in their adopted homeland forever, but a tiny niggling question remains at the back of their minds: "What if...?"

Local Glocals have also decided to stay put, but they have decided to do so in their home country. Having spent such a significant chunk of their lives abroad, however, they no longer have the status of a true local. Their perspective is not just that of a national plus a bit of international experience. They've swapped their national lenses for global ones. When living abroad they didn't consider themselves expats, and although they are not roaming right now, they regularly entertain the idea of doing so again in the future. Currently, 16 percent of roamers are living and working in their home countries.

Pierre A. is a good example of a Local Glocal. He was born in Paris, grew up there, and studied there. He spent semesters abroad in Tokyo and New York. In his mid-20s, he followed his dream to live and work in New York, where he stayed for seven years working as a banker. Pierre eventually left his job, and hoping to bridge the distance between home and abroad, he pursued another line of work that would have required him to travel regularly between Europe and the United States. Unfortunately, the company didn't take off. Instead, Pierre's family business drew him back to a small village in the French region of Brittany. Pierre has now been back for twelve years. He is completely dedicated to his local family business, but his passions and interests remain international. He keeps a network of friends around the world. He subscribes to *The Economist, The New Yorker,* and the French magazine *L'Express.* He follows global trends in arts, science, and contemporary ideas, all while running an agriculture business that is completely dependent on local business partners, local weather conditions, and the local economic climate. Although Pierre is living in a place where his family has been for generations, he has an easier time associating himself with the global than with the local aspect of his life. "When I was in New York, I saw myself a wanderer, as someone who takes planes, works around the world, meets new people, makes himself at home everywhere…and has a girl in every port. Talk about self-delusions!" Pierre laughs. "I worked for a bank in New York where I essentially was chained behind my desk, and now I'm chained to my place in the country."

Pierre is naturally inclined to keeping up with what is happening around the world and struggles to find the same enthusiasm for more local concerns. "I need to become more implicated in the fabric of my local community," he says. "Last week I even considered joining the Rotary Club, which is not something I ever would have imagined before. I'm working on becoming more involved locally now that I've finally reconciled myself to the fact that I'm not living between New York, Paris, and Brittany. I'm living in Brittany." Pierre was instantly attracted to the idea of installing himself in the local milieu when he went abroad, but localizing himself at home requires more diligence. "It's the relationships you have and the patterns you establish that make you a local. It's important to localize yourself wherever you are, whether it's abroad or at home," Pierre concludes.

"I still don't feel at home here in France," says Pierre's wife, writer Héloïse. Like Pierre, Héloïse is a Local Glocal, but with a very different perspective on her homeland. Héloïse "returned" to her country of citizenship, France, where she had never lived, after meeting Pierre at age 29. She was born to French parents, but grew up in Germany and Austria where she attended local schools, international schools, and a French Lycée in Austria. The only time she spent in France was visiting family during school holidays. Despite having now lived in Paris and Brittany for seven years, Heloise says that she still doesn't feel settled. She tells me:

> *Most people I know here are much more "of this place." I feel removed. My make-up is that of a roamer, and you don't shake that off easily just because you settle somewhere. I haven't made this shift yet. You try to become part of the local fabric,*

but I'm not naturally pushed to meet very "local" people. I feel different at a fundamental level compared to the real locals—we don't have a common or shared mental landscape. Being a foreigner and perceived as such has become my default mode and I don't take very naturally to being "home."

Yet, ostensibly, Héloïse is living in her home country. When you arrive in a foreign country, especially if you look or sound different, locals expect you to act or think differently. When you look and sound like a native, locals expect you to fully share their cultural context. The Local Glocal's inner landscape, however, is wildly different. Despite her citizenship and flawless French, Héloïse's natural affinities lie with global, cosmopolitan environment. Now married to a Frenchman, Héloïse plans to stay in France indefinitely. While the transition hasn't been easy, Héloïse ends on a positive note: "At first it was difficult realizing that I was here for the long haul, but I've made peace with this now."

Encountering different cultures broadens your mind, but what is it good for in the long run? When living abroad no longer offers the same returns or family ties beckon, roamers are stuck with a dilemma. Should they, *can* they, return home? Accustomed to many influences, how can roamers return to a less dynamic, less cosmopolitan environment? In an interview with French newspaper *Le Monde*, French mother of four Corine Béquin said, "What helps me keep it together is that I tell myself, one day I will go abroad again." Corine's husband is a director of a large American multinational and had no choice but to accept a posting in France after seven years in Tunisia and four in China. Now back in France, Corine says, "I have the impression that I've aged a lot. In Shanghai it was very easy to make friends. Here, I'm anonymous. I feel like a stranger in my own country." Roughly 2.5 million French nationals live abroad, and most are working on local contracts, so it is not the loss of expat job perks that is troubling the *impatriates*, as *Le Monde* calls the returnees. The difficulties are more diffuse and unexpected. As one *impat* put it, "We have the language, but we no longer have the codes."

By many accounts, going home sounds like a bit of a downer, but a few roamers enthusiastically reintegrate into their familiar birth culture. Some have careers that regularly take them abroad where they can soak up the international scene, keeping one foot at home and the other abroad. Others simply reject the global life altogether. Englishman Christopher

Tanfield lived the life of a high-flying consultant for many years, working in numerous countries, but he finally decided to return back to his native England. Christopher says, "You always have to weigh the positives against the negatives." He gave up his career, which required excessive travel, and became a teacher instead. Christopher has a particularly no-nonsense approach to working abroad: "Over time, the negatives outweigh the positives. When the balance tips, that's when you get out."

Christopher was the only person I interviewed who conducted such a rational cost-benefit analysis and was living back at home permanently without any regrets. Most people I met who had settled down or abroad weren't ex-roamers, but Glocals. They have a supranational mindset that they don't switch off when they finally decide to stay put, and many have a hard time transitioning to a sedentary life. Modern medicine has made some stunning discoveries in the past few decades, but no one has yet come up with a cure for itchy feet. Should you dare to settle down, it might be useful to bear in mind the wise words of one roamer: "Even when you stop moving, you're still a roamer." Unlike Active Explorers, Glocals might not be hardwired to roam, but they've downloaded the app.

Chapter 4
Why Do Roamers Roam?

In *The World Is Flat,* Thomas Friedman describes how technology allows people to work for foreign bosses and clients from their home country as remote accountants, news analysts, call center operators, and virtually any other occupation you can imagine. Friedman writes: "It is much easier and more satisfying for them to work hard in Bangalore than to pack up and try to make a new start in America. In the flat world they can stay in India, make a decent salary, and not have to be away from families, friends, food, and culture." One Indian tells Friedman, "I can work for a multinational sitting right here [in Bangalore]. So I still get my rice and sambar...I don't need to learn to eat coleslaw and cold beef...why should I go to America?"

Roamers take the opposite view: Why participate in globalization from home when they can go to America (or India) for a few years, get intercultural work experience, and try something different? For roamers, "easier" and "more satisfying" are a contradiction in terms. Who wants what's easy? Isn't the greatest satisfaction derived from reaching difficult targets?

So when trying to answer what drives roamers to go abroad when they could easily—in fact much more easily—stay at home, the simple answer is that roamers roam because they want to and because they can.

Take for instance Michael Delfs, an American urban designer who set out to explore the world after graduating from Columbia University in New York City. When considering his options, he looked far and wide. He says, "You look around and ask, 'Where are the opportunities?' If you want to build cities, probably not much will happen in the United States." Michael wanted to build cities, so he packed his bags and set off for India. He had already spent two years working for an ad agency in Shanghai. Michael's mother is Chinese, but despite speaking Mandarin, Michael never felt at home in China. India, however, was different. Michael was instantly attracted to the warmth and openness of Indians. Michael's can-do attitude had landed him a job in Mumbai managing a new city development for 150,000 people—at the tender age of 28. "I worked at levels I could never dream of in a developed market. The opportunities just don't exist," he says. These opportunities exist in India because the country is growing so rapidly that entire cities are sprouting up in the span of a few short years. "The vast majority of worldwide growth for the next ten to fifteen years will come from these new markets," says Michael. "Places that were considered developing countries are no longer outposts." Despite his success in Mumbai, after four years, Michael decided to move to London to do a master's degree at the London School of Economics. I wondered if Michael wasn't taking a step backwards by leaving his great job in Mumbai. "It wasn't easy to reverse-translate my Asian work experience back to the U.S. or Europe," Michael admits. At the same time, he doesn't romanticize the good old days. "I realized back then that I was missing some key components to my training. How do you get project planning through in Europe or the U.S.? In India I learned the soft skills of business like how to look at things differently and how to work in an unclear context where there is no instruction manual, but you're not following an established career path." Now in his fifth year in London, Michael is an urban designer at leading design and engineering firm Arup. He has since married his Indian girlfriend, who in holy matrimony agreed to join in Michael's peripatetic life.

When Vikram Singh finished his undergraduate degree in Bangalore, he moved in the opposite direction of Michael, from India to the United States. This was in the early 1990s, and Vikram wanted to pursue an engineering graduate degree. "Back then, I had to go to America for further education and to pursue my career. The education and jobs just did not exist in India. Today I wouldn't have to leave India to do what I do." When asked if, given all the excellent opportunities in India today, he would still go abroad, Vikram replies, "I definitely would still leave home. Not because I had to, but because I'd still want to have a more international experience." A true roamer, Vikram has no desire take the easy route. So far Vikram has lived in New York, London, and now Munich.

Vikram is one of many who started roaming during their university days. Dr. Teo of the Nanyang Technological University in Singapore says that despite the excellent level of education in Singapore, it's hard to get top-quality local Singaporean Ph.D. students and post-docs because many local students prefer to go abroad for graduate work. Teo says, "Like everywhere in the world, when given the choice, the best and brightest

WHY DO ROAMERS ROAM?

graduates want the opportunity to study abroad. They want some international experience." The Nanyang Business School MBA program has a student body that is only 14 percent Singaporean. The largest segment comes from India (18 percent), followed by 16 percent from Europe, another 16 percent from Southeast Asia, 13 percent from China, 12 percent from Northeast Asia, and 6 percent from the Americas. Likewise, the international students in most of MIT's, Wharton's, and Stanford's graduate degree programs make up over one-third of the student body. More and more graduate students are gladly taking the chance to study abroad even if, or precisely because, they have to learn to eat rice, sambar, coleslaw, and cold beef.

"I spent the morning wondering why we live this way," says Celia Romaniuk. "I decided it's because we can." Celia, an Australian, is married to an Englishman, Dan. Together with their two children, they were living in Treviso, Italy, when I interviewed Celia in 2013. They've moved together several times since meeting each other in London. Instead of dwelling on hardships, Celia and Dan approach moving from country to country with a sense of adventure. They had been living happily in Finland for two years when an Italian company offered Dan a job based just outside Venice. "We loved Finland, but when Dan got his offer to run Benetton's Fabrica, we just couldn't resist. The job itself was too good, but it wasn't our only motivation. We just thought 'Ooh, Italy. That could be fun!'" says Celia. Compared with a generation ago, when travel was complicated and expensive, Celia and her family move seamlessly between countries. "Today the barriers are lower. It's easy to move around the world," she says. That doesn't mean that there are no challenges. After half a year in Italy, Celia's 6-year-old son still misses Finland. "The big hurdles are emotional, not logistical," says Celia. Airplanes might fly at 600 miles per hour, but as the old Arabic proverb says, the soul travels at the speed of a camel.

Personal ambitions and opportunities motivated Celia and Dan to move to Italy, but it's the European Union (E.U.) that allows them to live and work in Italy without the hassle of a work visa. As a British citizen, Dan is allowed to live and work elsewhere in the European Union. Since the 2004 Free Movement of People directive, E.U. citizens are able to move to any other E.U. country and receive the same treatment as local citizens in all aspects of public policy, workers rights, security, and access to public health and education. Over fourteen million E.U. citizens are living abroad in other E.U. states. That's almost 3 percent of the total European population. Germany, Spain, and the United Kingdom are the most popular destinations, with over two million intra-E.U. migrants each. London is so popular with the French that it's now regarded as France's sixth largest city. More French citizens live in London than in Bordeaux or Strasbourg.

Countries within the European Union have the most open "foreign" worker system, but plenty of other governments are enacting laws that allow outsiders in. In 2012, *The New York Times* ran a story about the increasing number of American immigrants' children who are seeking the "American dream" abroad in their ancestral homeland. What is attracting these youngsters is not just personal nostalgia for a homeland they never knew—governments are deliberately enticing them "back."

Take for instance India, which since 2005 has been actively pursuing second-generation Indians whose parents had emigrated. India offers "Overseas Citizen of India" visas to these second-generation Indians, who are "returning" in growing numbers. OCI-card holders are allowed to keep their American, Canadian, British, etc. nationality, but they are also issued a lifelong visa that allows them to live and work in India indefinitely. With a rapidly growing economy of 1.2 billion potential customers—more than the European Union and North America combined—India offers exciting opportunities for those willing to take a chance. Reetu Jain, an Indian-American raised in Texas, says that she and her husband were lured to India by its energy. "We're surrounded by people who just want to try something new," says Jain. The latest figures for the United Kingdom show that 30,000 people left for India in 2010, a figure that is likely to have risen, according to the BBC.

How many of these people, however, are eventually making their way *back* to the United States or the United Kingdom? Are they going to India forever or just for a few years? In response to the *New York Times* article, one reader claimed that the success rate of "repats" is not high; plenty of OCIs are coming to India, but just as many are leaving. For roamers, staying in India (or wherever) isn't necessarily a badge of success. Moving back and forth is a natural part of the process.

The same article mentions Margareth Tran, an American who moved to her parents' homeland, China, after she couldn't find a job on Wall

Street. Tran said that she could imagine staying in Shanghai, moving back to America, straddling the two, or even moving to a totally different country. Tran may or may not consider herself a roamer, but her outlook would resonate with many roamers.

This is a far cry from how previous generations thought about living overseas. If you wanted to work abroad but your company couldn't transfer you out, the bureaucracy was so vast that it would cure almost everyone's itchy feet. Mary and Bern Gardner, however, were undeterred. In the early 1970s, they were young newlyweds with a dream to circumnavigate the globe once in their lives. Mary was a teacher, and Bern was a young engineer. Their employers were unable to offer them jobs abroad, so they decided to go it alone, and they didn't do things in half measures. Instead of staying somewhere closer to home, the Gardners opted to look for work in the farthest corner of the planet—New Zealand. The process, though, was drawn out and full of hurdles, as Bern explains:

You couldn't just work in New Zealand. You had to officially emigrate from England and apply to become a New Zealand immigrant. You could keep your U.K. passport and citizenship, but you couldn't have an English bank account. You had to transfer it to a non-resident bank account. You couldn't tell your office that you would like to take a few months off to travel. You had to quit your job and prove that you were moving to New Zealand permanently. I started applying for jobs through the New Zealand embassy in London in 1974. I sent letters of application to New Zealand, then finally one day I had a response. I had a job interview in New Zealand House in London, and they asked me to bring my wife to prove that I was married!

Two years after Bern began applying for jobs, the Gardners finally boarded an airplane and set off on their Winnie-the-Pooh-style *Most Grand Adventure.*

Picture today's economy class flying experience—security lines, sardine-size seats, and lackluster airline food served by harried airline attendants. It's hard to believe that in the 1960s and '70s, flying was actually glamorous. Because it was a special occasion, people dressed up in their Sunday best before boarding a flight. The passengers were largely businessmen, and the stewardesses were young and pretty. You could smoke on the plane. There wasn't a distinction between economy and first class—flying *was* first class. And prices reflected that. In real terms, airline tickets cost approximately four times what economy class tickets cost today.

"A single, one-way flight to New Zealand cost £600," Mary says, "so the total price for both of us was £1,200," equal to £5,000 or $8,000 today. "I was working as a teacher, and my annual salary was £3,000 before tax, so our flights cost us the equivalent of more than six months of my salary." The couple pillaged their life savings just to pay for them.

Back then, New Zealand was even farther from England than it is today. There was no direct flight, so the Gardners flew from London, stopping in Frankfurt, Bombay, Bangkok, Hong Kong, Sydney, and Auckland before finally reaching Wellington. The Gardners don't even remember how long the journey took, but it's in the ballpark of days, not the still exhausting twenty-four hours it currently takes.

Flying back and forth with ease, roamers today live a life that was the preserve of a few businessmen and diplomats only a few decades ago. As the supply and demand of flights grew, the cost of flying plummeted, making global travel accessible to the masses. So much so that holidays *not* spent abroad today have a special designation—the staycation.

The Gardners enjoyed their time in New Zealand, but after the birth of their first child they began to feel isolated from their extended families. Both Mary and Bern had elderly parents, and suddenly three of Mary's siblings were engaged to be married. "We missed two of the weddings and sent telegrams—that's what you did in those days," says Mary. "Today you'd just hop on a flight, but back then when it was 50 percent of your annual salary, you couldn't just go home for a wedding. It was impossible." After two years, the Gardners decided to move back to England. A few years ago, when their own daughter, Kate, was living in Hong Kong, the Gardners were able to keep in touch daily, seeing Kate's flat via Skype and flying over to visit. They never felt very far away from their daughter. "It was incomparable to our own experience of living abroad," says Mary.

All this easy travel and easy communication can have unintended consequences. In 1997, American Ian Krassek was working in New York when his boss surprised him with the opportunity to start a new desk in London. "I didn't even have a passport when he made the offer," says Ian. Young, motivated, and excited by the prospect of a new venture, Ian took up the challenge and moved to London. Four years later, Ian accepted another job offer and relocated to Milan. After almost eight years in Europe, Ian began considering a move back to New York to live closer to his family. En route from New York to Milan, Ian was switching planes in London's Heathrow Airport when he got a call from his former boss who, by then, was working in Hong Kong. "He insisted that I not board my flight to Milan and come to Hong Kong immediately," says Ian. "It was crazy." Ian finally relented, skipped his flight to Milan, and boarded the next plane to Hong Kong. "It was the first time I heard Chinese," says Ian. Once Ian was in Hong Kong, his former boss made him a tantalizing offer. He gave Ian a few days to decide whether to move back to his home country or to move farther away than he'd ever been before. Unable to resist the challenge, Ian picked Hong Kong. Ian ended up living in Hong Kong for eleven years, a pretty considerable commitment from someone who had never meant to live abroad in the first place.

Aging parents were a key factor in the Gardeners' decision to move back to England, but roamers don't need to make that trade-off today. Families still exert an emotional tug, but regular contact via phone, email, and Facebook alleviate concerns for both roamers and their families. "You want to create a monument to the people who invented Skype," says Monica Araya, a Costa Rican in Oslo. Monica left home before the advent of Skype, so she appreciates the value of keeping in touch with her family for free, apart from the cost of a smartphone and a latte at Starbucks. Almost 18 percent of roamers call or Skype family and friends in another country once a day, and 44 percent use Facebook on a daily basis to reach friends and family, near and far. In the era when the Gardners went abroad, travelers couldn't afford luxuries like calling home every week. A three-minute phone call from London to New York in 1966 cost £3, the equivalent of £15 or $23 today.

All the social, technological, and political changes over the past twenty years are making it feasible for roamers indulge their wanderlust swiftly, easily, and cost-effectively. Roamers go abroad today because they want to and they can. The question is quickly changing from "What motivates people to move abroad?" to "What *stops* people from moving abroad?" Recent research has found a surprising link between mobility and quality of life. The World Migration Report 2013 says that migrants who move from countries in the North to other countries in the North are happier, healthier, and wealthier than those who stay home. North-to-North migrants rate their lives better than if they had not migrated, and financially they fare as well as their native-born counterparts, if not better. The report goes on to say that "83% of North-North long-timers (migrants in destination countries for five or more years) are satisfied with their personal health, vs. 75% of non-migrants who remained in origin countries." Even in terms of family relations, long-term North-to-North migrants are just as likely as native-born citizens to report that they have friends and family they can count on. Overall, North-to-North migrants appear to do better than if they had stayed at home. (If I may poke my head into the frame for a moment, I'd prefer to steer clear of using outdated concepts like "The North" and "The South," but since these terms are still used by the United Nations, the IOM, the World Bank, etc., we're stuck with them. North-to-North migration is roughly fifty million people, and given that most are not moving for socio-economic or political reasons, I assume that a majority of these migrants are roamers.) The European Union has found similar results. Mobile E.U. citizens have higher employment rates than those who stay at home. People who are willing to move simply do better.

Desire and ability aren't always the main trigger for going abroad, though. Increasing instability means that relative opportunity costs decrease. If your job is safe, your country is stable, and the economy is booming, moving abroad might seem like risky business. But if you've just been laid off or if your country's economy is on the verge of collapse, the cost of moving abroad suddenly goes down. In fact, it might seem like a good investment.

In 2014, I met a group of three Spanish women who had moved to Shanghai with their boyfriends after the 2008 Global Financial Crisis. For each couple, either the woman or her boyfriend had been laid off at that time. When one of the women was made redundant at a property company in Madrid, she was distraught, but her partner said, "Don't worry. We'll use this as a chance to go abroad." He still had a job in Madrid, but he was happy to transform this unfortunate circumstance into an opportunity. She said, "We left Spain because we weren't 100 percent happy. There was a stagnation in Europe, and we wanted new energy."

Moving abroad involves both push and pull factors. These three women had numerous pull factors, including the means and the ability to move abroad, a sense for adventure, and entrepreneurial natures. Economic uncertainty in Spain simply provided the final push. Their hunch to leave Europe was proved right. Unemployment in the European Union reached epic proportions over the next few years: In 2013, unemployment stood at almost 11 percent in the E.U., its highest rate since the turn of the century. The 2008 financial crisis spurred one in seven of my survey respondents to move or stay abroad.

Sometimes prosperity, rather than scarcity, drives roamers abroad. Take for instance the one million mainland Chinese who are worth over $1.6 million. According to the findings of a recent study, 16 percent of these wealthy Chinese nationals have acquired foreign residency status, 44 percent are planning to emigrate, over 85 percent are planning to send their children abroad for education, and 33 percent own assets overseas. Only a quarter of those surveyed say that they felt confident about China's prospects over the next two years. These prosperous Chinese citizens are cashing in their chips and leaving while the going is good, before a downturn or a government policy makes their departure more difficult.

It's not only the wealthy who are hedging themselves against an uncertain future. Another study shows that despite China's economic success, middle-class Chinese youths are pessimistic about the future. In 2010, 508,000 Chinese left for the thirty-four OECD countries—a 45 percent increase from the year 2000. Many cited long hours of work, an unhealthy natural environment, and an unstable political situation. China's 2015 stock market meltdown is putting more pressure on an already slowing economy. Those who are living abroad might be asking themselves if now is a good time to go home.

If you moved abroad before a crisis hit your country, moving back has huge opportunity costs. Take for example the case of Italy. Italians who moved to the United Kingdom in 2007 to get international experience and to brush up on their English skills will have a hard time going home today. Italy's unemployment levels, economic growth, and inflation rates were roughly on par with the United Kingdom's when they emigrated, but the balance has tipped. While the United Kingdom's economy is not particularly rosy, Italy's persistent economic recession since 2011 is even more worrying. That may be why almost 120,000 Italian citizens live in the United Kingdom—including over 40,000 in London alone—while only 30,000 British-born citizens live in Italy. This discrepancy is even more telling when you consider that it's mainly young Italians who are making their way to the United Kingdom, while most of the Brits heading to Italy are retired.

Italy is a good place for not only British retirees, but Italian ones, too. Italian employment policies protect those nearing the age of retirement, but they do not provide any protection for those starting their careers, so young Italians struggle to enter the job market. While Italy's overall unemployment rate is comparable to the rest of the European Union, its youth unemployment in February 2015 stood at 42 percent, *double* that of the E.U. average. Because Italy has no minimum wage, salaries can be too low for young people to afford their own place, so many wind up living at home with their parents. German magazine *Der Spiegel* interviewed Italian architect Alessandra Bertolini, 36, who was still living with her parents. Despite a good job managing construction sites, she was forced to look for other work when her employer didn't pay her wages for six months. In 2011, she sent out 200 applications to other Italian companies, but received zero replies. She began applying for jobs abroad, and finally three offers came her way—two from London and one from Dubai. All offered her a salary double her previous (albeit unreceived) wage. Alessandra accepted one of the jobs in London. Alessandra told *Der Spiegel* that she didn't want to leave Italy, but was forced to go. "Italy didn't want me. I have no choice," she said. Young Italians are moving abroad in increasing numbers. For many, it's less the carrot than the stick driving them into the life of a roamer.

Of course Alessandra had a choice whether to leave Italy, but it was a lopsided one. Her push factor—the lack of jobs in Italy—was greater than the pull of adventure or international work experience. Many other reluctant roamers go not because they *want* to, but because they *must*. This is the new global culture of work.

"The modern-day candidate is a global candidate. They don't see geographical boundaries as a limitation," says Simon Walker, managing director of recruitment firm Hydrogen Group. "If you want to progress in your career, at some point, you must be open to a move," Walker tells me. In the past, companies might have held on to their best managers for progression within the headquarters, but today they need them to keep on top of global trends so they understand local conditions when making strategic decisions. Jobs increasingly require employees to be flexible and mobile, but staying globally ready comes at a cost—to the roamer. Companies might still be willing to pay the direct moving expenses, but Walker says that hardship expat packages are a thing of the past. Walker still occasionally meets candidates who expect a typical expat package because this is what they remember from ten years ago, but those who insist should heed a word of warning: "If you want an expat package, what you're saying is that you're not a global candidate," Walker says. He regularly tells candidates to consider their move abroad, above all, as a stepping-stone for their career. There may be some advantages to moving abroad, such as lower taxes or more dynamic markets and opportunities, but candidates should anticipate a similar standard of living to the one they have at home. "If you're in New York or London and don't have a driver, cook, or country club membership, don't expect to have them when you move to Singapore, Hong Kong, or Shanghai," Walker says. My own research indicates that Walker is right. While 15 percent of roamers were asked to move abroad by their company, only 33 percent of those were offered an expat contract in return.

What about the roamers who don't work for a company? Academics, for example, don't have expat packages, and their roaming territory seems to get bigger and bigger. As science becomes increasingly specialized, scholars might be searching for sub-atomic particles, but their job search is global. One of my survey respondents says that she has no idea where she will end up next. "In academia you go where you are hired," she writes. Another academic responds, "I did my [postdoctoral research] in Melbourne. It was only one of a handful of places in the world where I could have done a post-doc."

The requirement to live abroad does not always subside as you move up the career ladder. The founder of international relocation company MOVE Guides, Brynne Herbert, writes in her blog that 74 percent of chief financial officers in the highest pay bracket have international work experience. "Modern careers are no longer drawn by national boundaries," she says. Quoting Kraft China's chairman, Lorna Davis, Brynne says that all senior managers need to engage in a global zigzag. "Moving from country to country for work is no longer considered either a privilege or a hardship, but a basic job requirement," she writes. When I interviewed Brynne, she told me, "Having worked in headhunting, I could see that most human resources departments in multinationals don't get it. They still think they are dealing with expats. This generation of global workers is different. They don't see a posting abroad as a hardship. They've traveled a lot. They've done internships abroad. They speak several languages. They know they need to adapt."

Dane Peter Sorgenfrei agrees. "In the same way that people used to work with one company for twenty-five or thirty years but now we change jobs every three to five years, we will soon see people regularly switching countries." So far, Peter has lived and worked in four countries, but he thinks that this is only the start of the trend. "I believe that my son will live in eight or ten countries before he retires," he says. (Since our interview, Peter has corroborated his statement by moving from New York to London, with his American wife and son in tow.)

Companies increasingly expect managers to have international experience before considering them for overseas positions. In an interview with the *Financial Times*, recruiter Simon Lynch says, "When the economy was booming and there was a skills shortage, businesses were willing to take the risk of hiring a candidate before they landed in the country. Now the marketplace is tighter for jobs. You need to be there for the interview to be taken seriously. They want to see you, shake hands with you, and really get to know what you're like before they commit to placing you in a role." More and more, those lacking the requisite geographical experience are taking the risk, quitting their jobs, and moving to their desired location in hopes of finding something once on the ground. When international experience is a job requisite, as with a university degree, it's up to you to stump up the cash for it.

Whether roamers are lured abroad or pushed by socio-economic circumstances, no one is forcing them to relocate. Plenty of people who can't find a job in their own country switch careers, become entrepreneurs, or just stay unemployed. Those who are looking for adventure, on the other hand, take up skydiving or online gambling instead of moving abroad. And the ones in search of new social circles start online dating or join their local hiking group or table tennis club. Resource scarcity may have forced nomads to move from one pasture to another, but roamers don't have the same impetus today. So why do roamers feel the need to do these things by going abroad? Why do so many of them feel the irresistible itch to see more, explore more?

Scientist Svante Pääbo offers a unique answer that runs deeper than social, economic, or even psychological justifications. A director at the Max Planck Institute for Evolutionary Anthropology in Leipzig, Pääbo is one of the world's leading experts on evolutionary genetics. Named one of *Time* magazine's hundred most influential people in 2007, Pääbo is a popular science hero best known for his sequencing of Neanderthal DNA. This might sound totally irrelevant to modern day roaming, but wait—there is a twist.

Like other mammals, Neanderthals and Homo erectus settled in the Old World, but only our direct ancestors, Homo sapiens, made it to distant islands like Madagascar or Australia 45,000 years ago. "It's only fully modern humans who start this thing of venturing out on the ocean where you don't see land," Pääbo says in an interview with *The New Yorker*. Pääbo puts this partly down to technology—you need bigger ships to sail farther away—and partly down to psychology. He still wonders what drove these early humans to venture far beyond the territory they needed for basic survival. "How many people must have sailed out and vanished on the Pacific before you found Easter Island?" he asks rhetorically. "I mean, it's ridiculous. And why do you do that? Is it for the glory? For immortality? For curiosity? And now we go to Mars. We never stop." Without finding a material basis for our insatiable (and often fatal) curiosity, Pääbo concludes that genes may be to blame. "If we one day will know that some freak mutation made the human insanity and exploration thing possible, it will be amazing to think that it was this little inversion on this chromosome that made all this happen…We are crazy in some way."

It may be that Pääbo is on to something. Since completing the Human Genome Project, geneticists have been busy unlocking the mysteries of what make us tick. It would be trite to argue that human experience can be put down to the flick of a switch on chromosome a, b, or c, but it looks increasingly likely that genes lay the ground for particular physical and psychological tendencies. One gene in particular, DRD4-7R, has been linked to curiosity, movement, and novelty. Numerous studies have suggested that those carrying the DRD4-7R variant are more likely to take risks, to try new foods or relationships, and to welcome change. Found in roughly 20 percent of the world's population, this so-called *restless gene* seems to be particularly prevalent in migratory cultures and in those whose ancestors traveled furthest out of Africa. One study even found that male

African nomads with the 7R variant are better nourished than those without the gene. When they are settled as villagers, however, those carrying the 7R gene fare *worse* than their sedentary peers. This suggests that those with the urge to voyage and explore do better if they heed "the call" instead of trying to squeeze into some sedentary mold that just doesn't fit.

These studies are still rudimentary. Don't jump to the conclusion that you've got to keep moving to stay happy and well fed; human behavior is far more elaborate than that. Roughly 19,000 genes make up one unit of human. You need not only the predisposition, but also the tools and the opportunities (and the interplay of 18,999 other genes) to indulge in this habitus.

Still, a neat answer seems tantalizingly within reach. Is this why we go to such extreme lengths to satisfy our curiosity to see what's *over there?* Is this why roamers have the unstoppable urge to relocate around the planet even though they could *far* more easily stay at home? Could many roamers be carrying this restless gene?

At present, it's impossible to answer these questions, so we'll have to relegate the theory to fireside debates. For now, all we can do is wonder whether Lady Gaga was right—maybe we're simply born this way. Or to paraphrase Svante Pääbo, maybe, just maybe, we're all insane.

PART II:
THE EFFECTS OF ROAMING ON SOCIETY

CHAPTER 5
IT'S THE ECONOMY, STUPID

The greenback has been through ups and downs, and the euro has seen better days, but the Dorothy Dollar and the Pink Pound are stronger than ever. The global spending power of the lesbian, gay, bisexual, and transgender community (LGBT) is estimated to be in the region of $3 trillion. That's equivalent to the entire GDP of Germany. For years, LGBT spending power went unnoticed by the market at large, with gays and lesbians starting most businesses geared to LGBT patrons. This is changing. From political parties to big business, everyone is starting to court this valuable demographic. Swiss bank Credit Suisse launched its American LGBT private banking initiative in 2009, and Morgan Stanley followed suit in 2011. Merrill Lynch, UBS, and Wells Fargo now offer LGBT financial planning seminars. Previously optional, LGBT training is now compulsory in Credit Suisse's MBA training program. The global gay and lesbian community is now too powerful to ignore.

In the same way that the Dorothy Dollar was circulating in the gay community long before a broader audience took notice, roamers have been serving their own community for years, sometimes unknowingly. To my amazement, almost 20 percent of roamers are either self-employed or running their own businesses abroad, further dispelling the myth of the expat corporate lifer on a generous package.

When I asked a few of these entrepreneurs what proportion of their customers are roamers, many were surprised by their own responses. Britt Lintner ran her namesake, high-end fashion label for working women. She says, "Wow. I hadn't thought about it before, but a huge number of my clients would be considered roamers. Somewhere between 60 and 70 percent." Mats Klingberg, owner of Trunk Clothiers in London, also says that most of his clients are international—including visitors to London and non-Brits living in the United Kingdom. Unwittingly, through a network of contacts and referrals, roamers are forming their own internal-international economy.

Because roamers are not yet a recognized demographic, it's impossible to gauge how large this market might be, but more and more businesses are beginning to recognize "foreigners" as a target market. One of the largest and most comprehensive global initiatives is HSBC's expat services and products. It offers bank accounts in multiple currencies, expat mortgages, and financial planning services for globetrotters. HSBC's target audience, however, is still the traditional wealthy expat on a corporate allowance. The evidence can be found in HSBC's Expat Explorer survey, which in 2012 ranked the most desirable places to live according to indexes such as yacht ownership, access to luxurious holidays, and having a swimming pool or domestic help at home. With such measures, it is not surprising that Singapore ranked as the most desirable place to live in the 2012 survey. Few foreigners in London, Tokyo, or New York have a swimming pool in their garden or a yacht moored down the road. Those surveyed in Singapore are also indicative of the results—46 percent of the respondents worked in finance, and 43 percent had a British passport; 67 percent of the respondents were male.

This indeed may be HSBC's ideal target market, but a much larger roamer demographic remains largely untapped. A few farsighted businesses are trying to get their heads around connecting and monetizing this new, burgeoning population. Mainly based in cyberspace, communities like Internations, Move Guides, and Expatica are designed to help foreigners connect and find city-specific information. Expatica even hosts an annual fair in Amsterdam called "I am not a tourist." (Perhaps an enterprising roamer will launch a fair called "I am not an expat.") Despite their global reach, these businesses are accessing only a tiny portion of this thriving roaming community. The potential is huge, and untouched.

One industry is sitting up and taking notice. It shares the roamer's leitmotif: "Location, location, location." The property industry has seen a huge surge in foreign investment over the past two decades. Some of these "foreign investors" are scouring the planet for good deals, acquiring property where they find the best return on investment. But plenty of these customers are not "foreign foreigners"; they are "local foreigners" living in the country where they buy.

I'd be rich if I'd collected a dollar from every roamer who told me, "I should have bought an apartment when I got here." Since roamers by definition don't know how long they will stay anywhere, many are reluctant to make substantial local outlays until their long-term position is clear.

Investment choices are easier for traditional expats—make money abroad and spend it back home. Roamers don't know exactly how long they'll live anywhere, so investing in a particular place can be fraught with indecision. Seemingly normal junctures in life, like deciding whether to buy a car or a house, can send roamers into existential tailspins. On top of the classic shock of realizing that you can't afford to buy in the part of town where you rent, roamers face other crises. They must tackle questions such as: "Should I invest where I live, where I grew up, or in a third location?" "Should I save in the local currency, my home currency, or even in a third currency?" "In the long run, will I stay or will I go?"

Some roamers put off making big commitments and let status quo be their guide because, in accordance with Murphy's Law, the surest way to precipitate a departure is to commit to staying in one place. "After four years in London, we finally bought a car, and now we're leaving," said Stephanie Campbell, an American-Colombian now in Hong Kong. Anne Eckert, an Australian in London, explains that she and her husband aren't taking on long-term financial obligations. "We haven't bought a place here because that would admit that we're staying." Anne's husband is Belgian, and they have lived in five countries in the past decade. Anne says that she can't foresee them staying anywhere for long, but adds, "The rent, however, *is* exorbitant."

Whatever their rationale, only 45 percent of roamers own property. Age, of course, is a significant factor. By the time roamers hit their 40s, their rate of homeownership rises to 69 percent.

Roamers might not know where they'll end up, but when they decide to purchase property, they tend buy where they live, with 49 percent buying homes in their current country of residence. In comparison, only 38 percent get their foot on the property ladder where they grew up, and the final 13 percent purchase in a third location, with some buying in multiple locations.

Some who don't own any property simply are not interested in buying, but others are squeezed out of the market, and they may have other roamers to blame. In global cities, the impact of foreign buyers is unprecedented. In London's prime neighborhoods, foreigners account for 65 percent of all new-build residential property sales and for 34 percent of older property resales. The majority of these buyers are not simply making a financial investment; they live and work in London—66 percent are buying the property as their main residence.

Real estate firm Savills regularly publishes reports comparing the residential property markets of global cities. Savills's 2015 World Cities Index included twelve cities: New York, London, Paris, Tokyo, Shanghai, Hong Kong, Singapore, Mumbai, Los Angeles, San Francisco, Dubai, and Sydney (Moscow has been included in the past). These cities are dotted all over the planet, but they share some remarkable similarities. "Residential markets in our World Class Cities have more in common with each other than the mainstream markets of the countries in which they operate," writes Savills. Sales and rentals in these global cities are indifferent to national property trends. From 2005 to 2010, when the United Kingdom's average house price rose by 6 percent, London prices shot up 26 percent. In the same period, American property values plummeted by 27 percent, but New York's stayed level. Russia's property prices grew 94 percent, while Moscow climbed 104 percent. The prices in all these cities are related to other global trends: London's house prices are correlated to the price of gold and equities, while Moscow's property is coupled to the energy industry. Moscow's property prices jump $200 per square meter ($19 per square foot) when the price of oil rises $1 per barrel. Consequently Moscow's luxury properties have fallen almost 20 percent since oil prices and the ruble plummeted in late 2014.

Vancouver, not a top global city by the usual standards, is home to some of the world's highest disparities between housing prices and the average family income. It is the second least affordable place to live on the planet (just after Hong Kong). With the median family income at 66,527 Canadian dollars and and the minimum income required to mortgage an average-sized family home at 158,475 Canadian dollars, who can possibly afford a house in Vancouver? The answer is simple: the Chinese. Clean and safe, Vancouver is considered a secure place to park your cash. International investors account for half of all luxury home sales in Vancouver, with an estimated one-quarter standing empty year-round. Local interest rates and average incomes have only a modest effect on Vancouver's property market, which is most closely coupled to the Chinese economy.

With locals getting squeezed out of the property market in many cities, legislators are beginning to safeguard the purchasing power of their own citizens. Several governments have imposed a two-tier taxation system, one for locals and another for foreigners. In 2012, the Hong Kong government hoped to slow a hyperactive property market by slapping down a 15 percent levy on property purchases by foreigners. To avoid the tax, foreigners who live in Hong Kong can become permanent residents—if they have lived there for at least seven years. CNN interviewed Jason Leung, a young, mainland Chinese public relations professional who lives and works in Hong Kong. He and his wife had just managed to scrape together the deposit for a tiny, 400-square-foot family flat when the measure came in, and suddenly they found themselves unable to afford the extra 15 percent. After years of hard work and saving, Leung was dejected. "It is unfair," he said, "but I have to accept it. I have to accept it." He and his wife were considering whether to resuscitate their plans to buy a "home away from home" in Hong Kong or to look back home in mainland China.

Justifiably, the Hong Kong government is trying to protect its local citizens from foreign property speculators, but it's the foreigners working *locally* who are getting hit the hardest. Nevertheless, one can't fault the government for trying to dampen prices: Hong Kong's property prices shot up by 20 percent in the first nine months of 2012 while the economy grew by only 1.4 percent. The measure worked for a few years until the underlying problem—a housing shortage—jumpstarted the market again. After plateauing for a year, residential property prices rebounded, rising over 13 percent in 2014.

In January 2013, Singapore's government introduced similar cooling measures. On top of the regular stamp duty, foreigners with no long-term residency rights (such as those on a work visa) now pay a 15 percent surcharge on new purchases, up from 10 percent. Unlike Hong Kong, Singapore also hits foreigners who have obtained permanent resident status. They now pay an extra 5 percent levy on their first property and 10 percent on subsequent purchases. These populist measures impact all foreigners, not just jet-setting millionaires. "Of course it is unfair," says Filipino architect Ram Poyaoan, 48, in an interview with *The Straits Times*. "But what can we do? It's like living in your uncle's house. You don't get the same treatment."

With Hong Kong, Australia, the United Kingdom, and other states putting the brakes on foreign buyers, is it wiser to invest your money back in your country of citizenship? Plenty of people are doing just that.

The word "remittances" typically conjures images of poor migrant workers lining up outside Western Union, sending wire transfers to support their even poorer families back home. Yet again, this is a completely outdated notion. Some of the world's richest countries have the highest inflows of remittances from their citizens living abroad.

In 2013, the twelve countries to receive most remittances in absolute terms were India, China, the Philippines, Mexico, Nigeria, Egypt, Pakistan, Bangladesh, Vietnam, and also France, Germany, and Belgium. The World Bank estimates that the global value of remittances sent home by migrants was $557 billion. Roughly a quarter of that went to "developed" countries.

Most of this money was made in the following dozen countries, in descending order: the United States, the Russian federation, Saudi Arabia, Switzerland, Kuwait, Germany, the United Arab Emirates, France, Luxembourg, Italy, the Netherlands, and Spain. Two countries—France and Germany—appear on the lists for both top remittance inflows *and* top remittance outflows. In Germany, roughly the same came out as went in, but in France something unexpected happened—French citizens sent more money *back home* than migrants in France *sent abroad*. For the economic geeks, France had a net inflow of remittances, just like the developing countries typically associated with this type of income.

As a share of GDP, remittances are more significant in smaller or developing economies. In 2013, Tajikistan, Kyrgyzstan, and Nepal topped the pile with over 25 percent of their GDP coming from remittances. In Peru, remittances play such an important part of the economy that they are equivalent to the second largest region of the country. In wealthier recipient countries, remittances make up only a small fraction of GDP—0.8 percent for France and 0.4 percent in Germany. This might seem small, but remittances still accounted for $25 billion in France and $16 billion in Germany in 2014. In Belgium, remittances make up 2 percent of GDP—higher than in China and Mexico. These are not sums that a government can ignore. (Ironically, despite its worldwide taxation program, the United States receives only $7 billion in remittances from its citizens abroad, *less than 0.04 percent of its GDP*.)

In developed economies like France, Germany, and Belgium, these remittances are not sent back home to support aging parents or a wife and children. They are investments in property, bank savings, and other financial buffers. They are a safe place to park your cash until you go home—or at least until you decide where to go next.

Why are so many people able to make enough money abroad that they can send some of it home? Part of the answer lies in factors you might suspect: They have more work opportunities, earn higher incomes, or pay lower taxes abroad. Sometimes, currency disparities mean that a hard-earned dollar, peso, or krona can go a lot further back home.

But there is another important, silent factor: Those going abroad are *already* making more money and are more educated than those who stay at home. In poor countries, this gap is astonishing. A third of highly educated Ghanaians live abroad. Even before departing, Jamaican migrants earn significantly more than those who never leave home. In wealthier countries, those with a higher level of education are still the most likely candidates for migration. Ash Matouschka in Hong Kong told me that an OE (overseas experience) is effectively requisite in New Zealand. "If you have a tertiary education, you go abroad," he said. New Zealand might be more the exception than the rule, but still 1.2 million tertiary-educated Germans and 1.4 million university-educated Britons live abroad—and that's just within the OECD. There are plenty of Germans and Britons living abroad in countries that are not part of the thirty-four-member OECD club of "most developed" market economies and democracies in the world. Intra-OECD migration among the university educated elite has jumped 70 percent in the past decade, reaching twenty-seven million in 2010 and 2011.

None of these numbers should come as a particular surprise to roamers. An overwhelming 92 percent of roamers have university degrees, and of those, almost 75 percent have a postgraduate degree or a Ph.D. Measured against any national yardstick, this is an extremely educated group. Were they a country of their own, roamers would have the highest percentage of eggheads on the planet. (One wonders, though, who would do all the work?)

Up until now, highly skilled foreign workers have been able to sell their skills abroad because they had specialist knowledge, the right contacts, or simply the most get-go. Roamers, however, are facing a new hurdle. Expat packages are dwindling not only because roamers are willing to go abroad without extra incentives, but also because they're running into a new challenger—the local.

"Forget expats. Western companies doing business in Asia are now looking to locals to fill the most important jobs in the region," writes Leslie

Kwoh in *The Wall Street Journal*. To fill job vacancies in Asia, two headhunting companies—Spencer Stuart and Korn/Ferry International—have started sorting executives in four types: "Asia natives steeped in local culture, but educated in the U.S. or Europe; the foreigner who has lived or worked in Asia for an extended period; a person of Asian descent who was born or raised in a Western country but has had little exposure to Asia; and the local Asian executive who has no Western experience." Because local expertise and contacts are critical, both headhunting firms say that the first category is by far the most coveted. Since they are harder to retain, these locals are paid as much as their expat colleagues, if not more. "Companies now want executives who can secure deals with local businesses and governments without the aid of a translator, and who understand that sitting through a three-hour dinner banquet is often a key part of the negotiating process in Asia," Kwoh continues. Three out of four senior executives hired in Asia by multinationals are now native Asians already living in the region; only 6 percent are noncitizens from outside of Asia. The chief executive of the employment website Monster Worldwide, Sal Iannuzzi says that companies are now looking for equally qualified locals, in part because the cost of deploying expats is too high: "It takes [expats] six months to figure out how to take a ferry, they're there for twelve months, and then they spend the next six months figuring out how to get home."

A partner at a leading investment bank explained to me why the highest paid senior executives in his American bank are not based in New York or London. They are in Beijing, Shanghai, São Paulo, and Mumbai:

> *These markets are all about the connections. You need locals to open doors. You'll still find the top performing people in New York, London, and Hong Kong, but they are largely replaceable because there are so many of them. They're all hungry, and they're all working to a similar global standard. This is not the case outside the major financial centers. For the most part, those in our Beijing and Mumbai offices are not our "highest potential people." They are, however, more important than the rock stars in New York and London if you're trying to grow your business in China, Brazil, and India.*

At least one recent survey corroborates his view. A study by Dasein Executive Search found that company bosses in Brazil received the world's highest compensation. Head honchos in São Paulo received an average base salary of $620,000, compared with $574,000 in New York and $550,000 in London.

These trends might worry roamers who left home long ago because many have lost these "local" connections in their country of origin. Ravi Choudhary, an engineer in San Francisco, says that he'd have a hard time getting a job back home. "Professionally it's tough for me to go back to India. The landscape is totally different. In India you need local expertise, and I don't have that. If you're trying to go home, too much international experience becomes a liability." Even if Ravi could get over the reverse culture shock and learn to reintegrate, his professional network and reputation are now anchored in the United States.

There comes a tipping point when you've spent too much time abroad to still have a network or a real connection to your home country. It turns out that if you want to climb to the very top of the corporate ladder or if you ever intend to return home, you should have a bit of international experience, but not too much. So does this spell the end of international mobility? No, but it does mean keeping on top of your game and getting experience in a region before you can expect to land a job there—whether that be abroad or at home. Specializing and making yourself a linchpin, as marketing guru Seth Godin advises, might become increasingly important.

Companies make the hiring decisions, but behind the scenes it's governments calling the shots. Many countries use a visa point system to encourage international workers with particular skills to fill local labor shortages. Other countries—notably Brazil, China, and India—do not offer a highly skilled migrant visa. Instead, China and India focus on attracting those who already have an existing link to the country—their own diaspora. Attracting talented nationals back from abroad is one way of quashing the impression that foreigners are taking jobs from locals (and the social unrest that comes with it).

Malaysia, for example, is experiencing a shortage of workers to fill mid- to senior-level positions. The economy is growing so quickly that supply cannot keep up with the demand for skilled workers. The government gives permission for recruiting foreign talent, but it is prioritizing its own citizens by setting hiring quotas. The country's Returning Expert Program (REP) offers incentives to bring back first generation Malaysian "repats" with professional and technical expertise who left to study or work abroad. Sweeteners include a flat 15 percent income tax for the first five years, tax-free ownership of two locally made cars, accelerated permanent residency for foreign spouses, and tax exemption for all personal items brought back into Malaysia.

Naturally, economic growth is a key factor to drawing skilled local (and foreign) workers from abroad. Except for a significant dip in 2009, Malaysia's economy has been growing from 5 to 7 percent in the past ten years. Countries with strong economies are more likely to provide the best opportunities for repatriates. For example, the three largest minority groups in the Netherlands are from Turkey, Morocco, and Suriname. Because its economy is booming, Turkey is luring repats back at a far faster rate than Morocco and Suriname.

British medical journal *The Lancet* estimates that there are more Nigerian health care professionals working in the United States than in Nigeria. While most African countries have experienced similar "brain drain" over the past decades, many are witnessing a new trend of "brain gain." Most African governments do not implement programs to lure people back, partly because they don't need to—thriving economies and business opportunities are doing it for them. Strong growth in Africa, along with a slowdown in Europe and the United States, is drawing people back in high numbers. Nigeria's economy has been growing rapidly since 2005. "If you think like an entrepreneur, then Africa is really your paradise," says Fred Swaniker, founder of the African Leadership Academy in Johannesburg. "You can really be the next African Sam Walton or the African Bill Gates or Steve Jobs. No one has done that yet. You can be that person." Ghanaian Swaniker knows what he's talking about. After completing studies at Macalester College in St. Paul, Minnesota, and at Stanford University Graduate School of Business, he made his way back to Africa, and he's not alone. Ghana once ranked 125th for retaining educated workers, and now sits in fifty-third place. African graduates of foreign universities are looking at Africa as a real option, which was unlikely a decade ago. "Even without power, Nigeria is growing at 7 percent a year," says Ghanaian-Brit Solomon Asamoah in an interview with *Time* magazine. "Can you imagine what will happen when most of the country has electricity?"

It's not only Africans going to Africa. Plenty of others from around the world are spotting the opportunities. Take for example 88mph, an early-stage incubator offering seed funding to African web and mobile entrepreneurs. Launched by a Danish IT entrepreneur formerly based in Berlin, 88mph has offices in Nairobi and Cape Town. It employs both locals and people from around the world—Denmark, India, Norway, Estonia, Germany, and the United States, to name a few.

A million Chinese nationals have moved to Africa in the last decade, working in engineering, textiles, and every other industry under the sun. China's demand for commodities, along with its direct investments and loans, has made it Africa's biggest trading partner. China's economy is not growing as quickly as it used to, and its slowdown is sure to have a knock-on effect, but African economies are unlikely to head into a slump any time soon. Africa's growth rate as a whole was 4.2 percent in 2012 and 4 percent in 2013, an entire percentage point higher than the global economy.

China has a long history of migrants going abroad and coming back. Known in China as *sea turtles* because they have one foot on land and another in the sea, these migrants have historically done well upon their return to China, sometimes rising to the highest echelons. Former Chinese President Jiang Zemin once worked in Moscow. University of Buffalo graduate Robin Li co-founded China's leading technology conglomerate Baidu. For the first time in recent history, however, sea turtles are having a tough time reintegrating into a fast-changing China. They take longer to find a job—often in lower positions and with lower salaries—than those who studied in China. Once valued for importing rarefied international knowledge and expertise, sea turtles are finding themselves increasingly marginalized in the market. Locals are now at a premium. So what happened to the sea turtles?

Partly, the quality of sea turtles has declined. In earlier times, only top students received government scholarships to study abroad. Today's newly minted Chinese middle classes can afford to send their middling progeny overseas, often to schools or universities of dubious merit. Due to visa restrictions and the global economic slowdown, these students return to China without work experience and with few local contacts. In contrast, those who stay and study in China are still well traveled, Internet savvy, and buoyed by China's ever-growing influence in global affairs. They have shed the inferiority complex that may have plagued earlier, less bolshie generations who didn't have these insights (or cash). A decade ago, venture capitalists might have invested in Chinese entrepreneurs returning from

Silicon Valley, but today they are more likely to back those who never left because they're up-to-date with Chinese consumption habits and trends.

Despite the pendulum swinging in the other direction, sea turtles don't appear to have any inferiority complexes. In an interview with *The Financial Times*, one employer in China said that he was no longer hiring locals with foreign degrees because his last sea turtle hire was disastrous: "He thought he knew a lot and...he looked down upon clients." Another problem arises when two different business cultures collide in one workplace. "Turtles often cling to quaint Western notions like transparency, meritocracy, and ethics, which puts them at a disadvantage in China's hyper-Darwinian economy," writes *The Economist*.

That said, the world's most populous country is facing a mind-boggling threat: a worker shortage. McKinsey Global Institute estimates that China could have a skills shortage of thirty-five million university-educated workers by 2020. Of the 2.6 million sea turtles who left to study abroad after 1978, only 1.1 million have returned. The vast majority of Chinese nationals with American Ph.D.'s, 92 percent, are still living in the United States five years after graduation. Despite China's booming economy, well-educated, successful Chinese nationals in China are moving abroad in record numbers. In 2010, 508,000 Chinese left for OECD countries, a 45 percent increase from the year 2000. Ian Johnson, a *New York Times* journalist, cites several reasons for the exodus, including political instability, lack of religious freedom, and environmental pollution. Hedging themselves, the Chinese migrants "see a foreign passport as insurance against the worst-case scenario rather than as a complete abandonment of China." That may be, but who knows what happens once they're on the road?

Along with the newly revised two-child policy, China's One Thousand Talents program hopes to redress this imbalance. Inaugurated in 2008, the program aims to recruit top senior academics, scientists, and high-tech entrepreneurs with Ph.D.'s from around the world. The program accepts foreigners, but its sweet spot is those who were born in China and left to study abroad at prestigious foreign universities. The government offers generous research grants, high salaries, living allowances, and a variety of other incentives to attract this sought-after cohort. The program seems to be working. It's enticing skilled professionals to move back to China, but a niggling question remains: Is it keeping them there? The program's officials don't reveal how many recruits of One Thousand Talents have remained in China after their grants ran out. *The Economist* argues that China will have a hard time luring top minds back and keeping them there until the government loosens its grip on academia, stamps out corruption, and improves quality of life indexes such as air quality. If these measures don't work, China will face a great battle for brains. Chinese roamers, for one, wouldn't necessarily stick around after their funding runs dry. They may just as well see it as a stepping-stone to a great job elsewhere.

Why are all these countries doing so much to bring their own citizens back instead of just hiring the right person for the job? With more and more people moving around the world, immigration has become a hot potato for governments the world over. By bringing back "their own kind," governments hope to avoid the social unrest that comes with large-scale immigration. In 2015, this unrest erupted into violence in South Africa, and it's not alone. Most countries in the world experience less explosive, but equally vigorous anti-immigrant sentiments come election time. Yet as China's sea turtles illustrate, just because you're speaking the same language, doesn't mean you're speaking the same language. Roamers, who don't see themselves as immigrants, are unnerved to find themselves so regularly lumped in with this type of migrant.

Opening the floodgates might not make the most political sense, but more and more economists are starting to think that it makes the most economic sense. One report recently cited by *The Economist* claims that liberalizing migration far outstrips the wealth created from liberalizing trade. Abolishing all trade barriers might increase global GDP up to 3 percent, whereas free movement of labor worldwide could boost global output up to 122 percent. Allowing people to move where they want, when they want could kick-start the faltering global economy. But democratic governments, of course, must court domestic voters who often view the labor market as a zero-sum game, as foreigners taking *their* piece of the pie. The debate is not so different from the one after World War I and II when women were asked to go back to the kitchen after working in wartime factories. Keeping women in the workforce would have upsized the pie, but instead it took decades for them to re-enter male-dominated industries. Today the economic rationale for keeping women at home seems absurd. So it may be for the free movement of labor, but like women in the twentieth century, foreign workers may also need to be patient.

But slowly, the times they are a-changin'. Perhaps smaller countries will lead the way because, without a vast internal market, they need to stay dynamic and plugged into the global economy. New Zealand offers a refreshing view on foreign workers. The Ministry of Business, Innovation, and Employment recently issued this vision statement: "Attracting and retaining skilled migrants is vital to New Zealand's prosperity. Migrants add $1.9 billion a year to gross domestic product." Popular politician and former Immigration Minister Nathan Guy says, "New Zealand is competing in a global market to attract good quality people." Unlike many, New Zealanders seem to understand that you can indeed have your cake and eat it too.

So do Chileans. Since 2010, the Start-Up Chile program has offered "world-class, early stage entrepreneurs" a one-year work visa, free office space, and $40,000 in seed funding, no strings attached, to relocate to Chile. The founder of Start-Up Chile, Nicolas Shea, studied at Stanford University before America's policies inspired him to attract world-class entrepreneurs to his home country: "I saw smart people being kicked out of the United States because they couldn't get visas to stay, and I thought: Why not bring some of them to Chile?" Start-Up Chile drew in eighty-seven start-ups from over thirty countries in 2011 and had a record 2,446 applications from fifty-seven countries in 2014. The goals of the program are to make Chile the innovation hub of Latin America, to foster more globally minded Chilean entrepreneurs, and—crucially—to inspire other budding local entrepreneurs. This program is open to Chileans and foreigners, just as long as their project has global reach. The program's website says, "We believe and invest in people, looking at their ideas first and their passports second."

With millions of people hitting the road and many more packing up at this very minute, it's extraordinary that we're still stuck on the question of how to stem immigration instead of how migration can make us better off. For now, everyone is just muddling through. Most national governments favor labor restrictions and erecting barriers (even physical walls) to keep all the immigrants out. Like sheep dogs trying to drive a herd of cats, these attempts are at best difficult and at worst futile. Those who want to live abroad will simply find more inventive ways of jumping the fence. In the long run, governments might realize that their measures are neither in keeping with the times nor good for the economy. If we're lucky, governments won't take long because cats have nine lives, but as the great economist John Maynard Keynes once said, "In the long run we are all dead."

CHAPTER 6
NOT COMING TO AMERICA: A CASE STUDY

On a cold winter's night in December 1773, a disaffected group of New England settlers refused to continue paying taxes to a distant and impervious British Parliament. Just before tipping a load of tea into the Boston Harbor, the revolutionaries protested: "No taxation without representation!"

Americans won the war against Britain and, without any hint of irony, went on set up policies to tax American citizens living far away from an impervious Capitol Hill. Other than Eritrea, the United States of America is the only country in the world to impose taxes on its citizens working abroad. These citizens are not quite on the verge of revolting just yet, but their winter of discontent is in the making.

The seeds of the American Revolution were sown at the Boston Tea Party, and 200 hundred years later, Boston was once again the backdrop for a key event in a different kind of revolution. Founded in a Harvard dorm room, Facebook is one of the great success stories of the Digital Revolution. Today one in every seven people on the planet uses Facebook on a monthly basis. Cloaked in a hoodie and jeans, Mark Zuckerberg doesn't cut the figure of a modern-day Paul Revere, but he'll certainly go down in history as a luminary of the information age. A co-founder of Facebook, Zuckerberg adorned magazine covers all around the world in May 2012 when he took the company public. Facebook's stock debut on NASDAQ was the largest technology IPO in American history. Not bad for a start-up that was founded only seven years earlier.

Legends aren't made without a few plot twists and victorious battles. Zuckerberg's arch frenemy is fellow Facebook co-founder Eduardo Saverin, who provided seed financing for the young company. In the same week as Facebook's IPO, Saverin created headlines of his own when news broke that he was renouncing his American citizenship. Everyone presumed the IPO had something to do with it. Saverin watched his initial Facebook investment of just $15,000 mushroom to roughly $2 billion by the time of the IPO. That kind of capital gain was going to trigger a huge tax liability. The media went into a frenzy. *Bloomberg* attacked with the headline "Why Facebook's Co-Founder Just Defriended America," and a *Forbes* caption just did the math: "Facebook's Saverin May Save $67 Million on U.S. Tax Bill."

When Saverin moved to Singapore in 2009, four years earlier, few took notice. He had not been involved in the day-to-day running of Facebook since 2005, retaining only a small percentage of shares relative to his initial 30 percent stake. Saverin had kept a relatively low public profile compared with Zuckerberg, but now he was setting off a huge storm in Washington. How could an American who helped spawn a quintessentially American company, an immigrant who lived the American dream, do something as un-American as renouncing his citizenship just to dodge taxes? For some American legislators, the dilemma was less abstract—what could they do to stop Saverin or, at least, to punish him?

Two American Senators were so furious that within a week, they had presented an anti-Saverin "Ex-PATRIOT Act." If enacted, the legislation would give Internal Revenue Service (IRS) officials the right to decide whether an American citizen or green card holder is expatriating for tax purposes or for legitimate reasons. If the expatriate is found guilty of tax-avoidance emigration, the IRS will impose an additional 30 percent capital gains tax on future domestic investment gains and will bar ex-Americans from ever entering the United States again. Furthermore, the bill would be retroactive, encompassing everyone who gave up American citizenship in the previous ten years.

The bill has not yet passed, but in the meantime other noteworthy Americans have also handed back their passports. In 2013, the Queen of Rock 'n' Roll, Tina Turner, dropped her U.S. citizenship. Again, Americans were stunned. Saverin's damnation was clear-cut: a hungry, unscrupulous capitalist willing to renounce his country for a few million dollars, but Tina Turner's goodbye proved to be a harder sell for the scandal-hungry media. She had left the United States not for money, but for love. In 1995, she followed her German music-producer boyfriend to Zurich, where they have been living ever since. After twenty years abroad and with no plans to return to the United States, Tina Turner, the *echt* all-American, is now Swiss.

In 2014, almost 3,500 people ditched their American nationality, the highest number since 1996, when the government had began "naming and shaming" those renouncing U.S. citizenship. In some countries, so many

Americans are lining up to turn in their passport that the U.S. embassy has a weeks-long waiting list. So why are Americans abandoning their citizenship in higher numbers than ever before?

Unlike Saverin and Tina Turner, most Americans abroad are neither rich nor famous. The son of a physician, Peter Dunn grew in Alaska. After studying in Seattle, Dunn went on to get a doctorate in divinity from Cambridge University in the United Kingdom. A theologian whose Canadian wife works in her family business, Dunn has lived in Canada since 1986, paying taxes in both Canada and the United States, as is required by American law. Despite having no plans to return to his home country, Dunn spent countless hours and thousands of dollars just to file taxes in the United States for twenty-five years, but in 2011 he finally broke down and handed over his American passport instead. Complex and stringent new tax laws were making compliance increasingly burdensome and costly.

Americans and green card holders have been required to disclose foreign accounts exceeding $10,000 since 1972 (the so-called FBAR rules). In 2013, the Foreign Account Tax Compliance Act (FATCA) went into effect. FATCA has introduced stiff new penalties for under-reporting foreign income. It goes further than any legislation before, requiring foreign financial institutions, including banks, to inform the IRS about any accounts held by American citizens. The IRS says that the new rules are designed to "detect and deter criminal activity," including fraud, tax evasion, and terrorist activities.

Americans must declare and pay tax on all earnings abroad, so they are taxed twice—once in their country of residence and once in the United States. There are tax exemptions for lower wage earners, but regardless of income, all Americans abroad must file taxes. This is much less reasonable than it sounds, thanks to convoluted procedures understood by almost none other than tax experts. The fines and other punishments for honest or seemingly irrelevant mistakes are costly.

Most Americans living abroad are not doing so for tax purposes and have no intention to dodge taxes, but they are worried that the IRS might whack them with huge fines for not complying to regulations that they didn't even know existed. In one case, American Kerry Knoll did not realize that his two teenage daughters, who are dual Canadian-American citizens, needed to file U.S. tax returns. "Suddenly we are being told that my daughter's savings account from her summer job is considered an illegal offshore account by the Americans, something that I find preposterous," Knoll said in an interview with Canada's *The Globe and Mail* newspaper. The price for not reporting an account by mistake is $10,000. The bill for willfully not reporting an account is $100,000, or 50 percent of the account at the time of the violation. Serving a prison sentence is not out of the question. "My daughters might owe thousands out of their registered education savings plans," Knoll continued. "These are not even taxes, these are penalties because it was not reported. And the reason we did not report it is because we had no idea we were required to."

For theologian Peter Dunn, the last straw came when the IRS forced him to pay tax on his Canadian tax-free savings account, even though similar tax-free Roth IRAs exist in the United States. "I could not live with the abuse of America taxing me even though I could not receive any services or benefits of living in the U.S.," he told *Time* magazine. Because Americans must declare and pay tax on joint assets, regardless of their partner's nationality, Dunn decided that, increasingly, "being an American was a liability to my wife."

Dunn has spent countless hours giving interviews and writing responses to journalists who charge that he and other former Americans are unpatriotic. When *The Wall Street Journal* columnist Al Lewis accused former Americans of selling their soul and making a mockery of the country that made them so "unthinkably rich in the first place," Dunn fought back. "Do you think Korea was entitled to tax my grandfather after he moved to Hawaii to work on sugar plantations?" he asked rhetorically. "If my grandfather renounced his Korean citizenship to be able to live freely in America, wouldn't you be proud of him, a new American citizen?" Another woman also retorted, "I can maintain loyalty to both the U.S. and Australia. I fell in love with an Aussie man. That doesn't make me un-American, and it doesn't make paying a 60 percent tax rate right either."

Two weeks later, Al Lewis published a de facto apology for his hotheaded piece about ex-Americans. He interviewed Dunn and others who explained that the typical American abroad was earning between $49,000 and $89,000. They are hardly billionaires on the run. Lewis concluded that America's new laws designed to stop money launderers, tax evaders, and terrorists were in fact hitting the "little guy" hardest. "Imagine having to give up a quarter of your retirement savings because you forgot to fill out a form required on the other side of the planet," Lewis mused. It seems he got the point. Americans handing back their passports are probably not evading taxes, but simply exercising their rights and freedoms, which for them translates to living abroad without penalty. Ronald Reagan once said, "If it moves, tax it. If it keeps moving, regulate it. And if it stops moving, subsidize it." Someone clearly added, "If it moves abroad, tax and regulate it *even more*."

Meghan Lang is a human resources manager in London, where she has lived for almost fifteen years. She has British citizenship and is married to a Brit. But when her salary recently surpassed the U.S. income threshold four years ago, she was flummoxed by the tax reporting process. "I asked my accountant about a thousand questions," she says. For one of the world's most expensive cities like London, Meghan's salary is not excessive. She already pays 40 percent tax in the United Kingdom. Meghan accepts that the American government would like her to contribute to American taxes, but she thinks they go too far. "What I really resent is paying New York State taxes for all the business days that I am working in New York for my U.K. employer. This starts to add up. For 2012-2013, I paid the State of New York about $2,000. I find this unfair. I don't live in New York. Why am I paying for being there on business?" Meghan's business trips already contribute to the economy and the tax coffers of New York State. On top of paying her American taxes, Meghan pays a tax advisor to help her navigate the byzantine tax forms. "I spend about $1,500 just on an accountant to prepare my American taxes because the process is very complicated. It takes me one whole day to fill out the forms."

Perhaps the most prominent American in London is the city's former mayor Boris Johnson, a dual British-American citizen. He was born in New York to British parents and left the United States at the age of 5, taking his passport with him. That sounded like a good idea at the time, but like most 5-year-olds, he was seemingly unaware of the obligations that came with it. In 2013, he famously refused to pay American capital gains tax on the sale of his London home, calling the requirement "absolutely outrageous." At that point, he had not lived in the United States for forty-three years. Although he has since relented, agreeing to stump up the estimated $150,000, one can imagine that he doesn't find the rules any less outrageous.

For years, millions of Americans have observed tax reporting rules without much fuss. FATCA, however, is traumatizing not only Americans living abroad, but also the institutions that are meant to be serving them. Increasingly, banks around the world are turning away Americans because the cost of doing business with them is just too high. Rachel Howard, the director of an investment fund in London, tells me that Americans are not welcome in her company's new fund. "We are no longer accepting U.S. investors because of FATCA rules. The fund is domiciled in Switzerland, and the Swiss don't want them!" she told me. Some banks have even gone so far as to close existing accounts of Americans to avoid the extra costs of observing IRS regulations and the enormous penalties if they fail to comply. American Amy Webster is based in Switzerland and married to a Swiss national. When she and her husband tried to get a mortgage, they had to jump through extra hoops because she was an American citizen. "This was infuriating and humiliating," she told journalists. Webster explained that she appreciates the government's need to clamp down on criminals, but she is "outraged that these regulations have impacted honest and hardworking citizens."

Amy's situation is mirrored on the other side of the Atlantic by the Swiss living in America. Pressure on Swiss banks to tackle foreign tax evasion and money laundering has left Swiss citizens abroad with increased bank fees, red tape, and in some cases, no bank account. The Swiss Broadcasting Corporation interviewed some of those stranded abroad. One baffled Swiss citizen said, "I have been living in the United States for the past four years, and at the end of last year, the Zurich cantonal bank told me all my accounts were being shut down. Now what? How will my clients pay me?" Others asked why current accounts are affected since they are useless for avoiding tax. "I can no longer make payments via Internet. You have to fill out pages and pages of paperwork, and it's too expensive because you have to pay for every single transaction," said another Swiss citizen. Some 700,000 Swiss live abroad. The dramatically heightened security is aimed at closing down routes for money laundering, terrorist activities, and tax evasion, but millions of innocent people living abroad are getting caught in the crossfire.

"There are not enough clear guidelines for Americans living abroad on how to do federal taxes," writes American Gordon G. "It took me forty hours to do my first U.S.A. tax return while living abroad in London." Looking for help, Gordon turned to his state tax office, but the officials were clueless. "They could only answer my particular question if the scenario was that of military personnel." American tax procedures are designed for those living in the United States, and there's precious little support for the rest. Whether he was filing his taxes or renewing his driver's license, Gordon found a roadblock at every juncture.

Meanwhile, Facebook's Eduardo Saverin insists that his move to Singapore was not motivated by the balance sheet: "I did not think once about my position related to tax savings. When you look at Internet growth, mobile growth, [Asia] is the center of where the views and consumer base will be in the future." (That may be why, in addition to Saverin, roughly 27,000 other Americans live in Singapore.) When news of his renunciation made headlines in 2012, Saverin had already lived in Singapore for almost four years. He had surrendered his American citizenship in 2011, many months before a Facebook IPO was in the pipeline. "It is unfortunate that my personal choice has led to a public debate, based not on the facts, but entirely on speculation and misinformation," Saverin said. "If I chose to open a bank account locally in Singapore, most of the banks would not accept me having a fully functional bank account," he told *Bloomberg*.

The interesting point about Saverin's case is that he may in fact wind up paying *more* to the tax man than had he stayed in the United States. As *Bloomberg* points out, few Americans (including those proposing the ex-PATRIOT Act) understand how the current expatriation law works. Many presume that Saverin can move to a low-tax country, renounce his American citizenship, sell his assets, and pay lower taxes in Singapore. In fact, Americans do not reduce their current tax bill by ditching their passport. The United States imposes an exit tax on Americans and green card holders who have a net worth over $2 million or an average tax bill exceeding $148,000 over the previous five years. The levy encompasses not only realized gains (such as property or stocks sold), but the estimated value of *unrealized* gains on all assets. Unlike those who stay in the United States, expats must pay this tax bill immediately, not after you sell your assets. Because Facebook was not trading openly on the stock market when Saverin renounced his citizenship, the IRS will allocate a value to his Facebook stocks. Depending on what value they assign, Saverin may actually wind up paying more taxes (and upfront) than had he kept his American citizenship and paid capital gains tax *after* he decided to selling his shares. It's not cheap to become un-American; in fact it's very, very expensive. Experts estimate that Saverin will pay about $365 million in exit taxes on his Facebook shares alone.

So what does all this mean for roamers? Is Saverin a roamer? Probably. Is Saverin also a tax exile? Maybe. Are all American roamers and therefore tax exiles? No! The media jumps on stories of Americans giving up their citizenship, but more interesting are the estimated six million other Americans abroad who do *not* abandon their passport. If you have lived in the United Kingdom for fifteen years, bought a house in London, and are raising a family there, why on earth are you *not* giving up your American passport despite the double taxation, worries about compliance, and potential penalties?

Americans, like many others, do not take their citizenship lightly. They might be citizens of the world, but they're still American. Despite the huge costs and hassle, these Americans are willing to spend time and money to protect their freedom to return to the United States. They are proof that, by and large, roamers are not living abroad for tax reasons. Robert C., a banker in Hong Kong, makes a substantial donation to the American government each year despite having left the United States almost twenty years ago. He has no plans to return. His wife is British, and their young children have dual British and American citizenship. "I want to leave my children the option of being Americans. Maybe they'll want to study in the U.S. and stay there to work. I want to give them those opportunities." Robert also wants to have the option of visiting his parents if they become ill. "I don't want anyone telling me I can't stay longer than thirty days in the U.S. if my mum becomes ill."

Dylan O. is a management consultant who has also lived and worked in the United Kingdom. Now in Thailand he writes:

I have certainly had endless frustrations with American taxation policies and the general intrusion into every facet of my financial life. That said, I cannot see ever giving up my U.S. passport. I certainly see myself as a global citizen and hate the idea of national boundaries and limitations on free travel and employment, but I'm also a realist and an American. My family is based in the U.S., and I would never want a bureaucrat to tell me I could not return if I needed or wanted, even though I don't see it happening anytime soon.

Dylan still owns an apartment in London, but all his investments and retirement savings plans are based in the United States, so despite the hassle, he has fewer complications than those who have made most of their financial investments abroad. Were Dylan to ever cash in his chips, it wouldn't be for tax evasion purposes: "I suppose I might one day consider exchanging my American passport for a British one, but then again Europe is more likely to raise my taxes to unsustainable levels than America, so I wouldn't do it to avoid paying taxes." Dylan is still tied emotionally to his citizenship, and that's not something he would easily forfeit.

It is bemusing that a country as enamored of civil liberties as the United States imposes these world-wide taxes when no other country deems it correct to tax its citizens living *ex patria*. Nevertheless, like most other Americans abroad, Dylan and Robert aren't ready to give up their American birthright and forfeit the ability to stay in the United States with a sick parent. Their main gripe is with the soul-destroying process. Most Americans abroad aren't quite ready to launch a mutiny, but hunched over coffees in Starbucks around the planet, you can hear Americans murmuring, "too much taxation without representation." Who knows, we might yet witness a Boston Latte Party before the century is out.

Despite the headaches of getting in, getting out, and staying there, brand America™ is still strong. Americans told me again and again that they possess the most valuable passport in the world. America is not only popular with Americans. The United States accepts a million legal immigrants every year. The United States is currently home to almost forty-three million immigrants, more than any other country in the world, followed by Russia, Germany, Saudi Arabia, and Canada. One in seven people living in America today was born abroad.

Australia, Canada, Germany, and Spain have more immigrants as a percentage of their population, but America is the single most sought-after destination for migrants. Each year 50,000 foreigners are thrilled to accept their American green card allocated by lottery, while millions more are disappointed. In 2013, the United States granted 65,000 visas for highly skilled private sector workers and 20,000 for science, technology, engineering, and mathematics (STEM) graduates from U.S. universities. When applications opened in April 2013, these quotas were filled in five days. The United States is an enormously popular destination for migrants.

104

These numbers, however, are misleading because in most cases "immigrants" are simply defined as those who "migrate" to the country. This lumps together those who will stay only for a few years with those who are de facto permanent immigrants who intend to live out their days in America. Although the headlines report that America receives a million immigrants each year, in 2011, only 700,000 foreigners became American citizens. Even the immensely clever finance journalist James Surowiecki conflates highly skilled foreign workers with immigrants, using the terms interchangeably in his thoughtful article about America's immigration policy:

> *The U.S. is the world's most popular destination for foreign students...Many would prefer to stay and put their skills to work here after they graduate, but they can't get work visas...Other countries, meanwhile, have positioned themselves to benefit from the talent we're turning away. Australia allows in almost as many skilled workers annually as the U.S., despite having a fraction [c.10%] of the population...In one famous study, the social scientist AnnaLee Saxenian showed that Chinese and Indian immigrants alone founded a quarter of Silicon Valley start-ups between 1980 and 1998...Immigration is also good for innovation in general. One study found that in 2006, foreign nationals living in the U.S. contributed to almost twenty-six percent of U.S. international-patent applications, and last year immigrants contributed to three-quarters of the patents that came out of the country's ten most prolific research universities.*

It would be interesting to know how many of these "immigrants" see themselves as such and how many consider themselves "foreign nationals living in the United States." Like most people, Surowiecki is trapped in twentieth century paradigms, tossing roamers and immigrants into one bucket. Are skilled migrants going to America because they want to become American? Or are they in America because they want to spend a few years working at MIT, on Wall Street, or in Silicon Valley...and then move on? Have they spotted an unfilled niche in the market, and do they want to set up a business in the United States with no desire whatsoever to become American citizens?

The Eduardo Saverin case is interesting because when he immigrated to the United States as a child, he kept his original Brazilian passport and therefore had a built-in, opt-out clause. Many Americans are angry with

Saverin because he didn't abide by an implicit bargain: When the United States of America welcomes you as an immigrant, your part of the deal is to work hard and join the fabric of society. If you do well, you can retire to Florida.

Some roamers may indeed settle in America permanently, and others will spend productive years working hard, creating value, building businesses…and then move on somewhere else. Why governments are not more welcoming of this type of migration is baffling.

Governments (and many citizens) are still desperately stuck in a 1950s understanding of migration. Immigration is still considered an act of charity, giving those who were born in poverty a new lease on life. There are still millions of people migrating under these conditions. But there are millions of people who are participating in a different type of migration—less permanent, less distressed. They are lured by the carrot, not driven by the stick. They'd likely do as well in their home country (if not better). They are simply looking for the chance to live abroad for a few years or maybe forever. Maybe they want to learn a new language or experience a different work culture. Perhaps their home country is undergoing a temporary economic slump, and they want to go elsewhere to find a better job in their field of expertise. These roamers could simply be after a new challenge. Maybe they want to study abroad, and companies want to hire them when they have graduated. Governments take note: These are citizens of the world. They don't want to be a drain on your resources, and they might not want to become citizens of your country. They are an entirely new breed of migrant.

Take for instance Indian national Kunal Bahl. In 2007 Bahl was a hungry MBA graduate of America's top business school, Wharton. Bahl had ambitions to start a company, but when American immigration officials refused to extend his visa, Bahl headed back to India where he set up shop instead. Today, Bahl's venture SnapDeal is worth $250 million. It has an annual turnover of $400 million, and in 2013 eBay invested $50 million into the company. One in six Indian Internet users is a customer, and SnapDeal is hiring a hundred people a month to keep pace with the demand. Would Bahl have been as successful in the United States? Who knows, but we do know that half of the top fifty American venture-funded companies have at least one foreign founder. Are all these foreigners immigrants, or are some of them roamers? Again, we don't know, and they themselves might not know. We *do* know, however, that foreign talent is contributing to economies around the world, so sending industrious and educated young foreigners "back to where they came from" may not be a wise policy decision. A few American opinion-makers are finally catching on to this idea. Staff writer for *The Atlantic* Conor Friedersdorf wrote this pert rebuttal to the Eduardo Saverin bash-fest:

> *What's the worry here, that [Saverin] will return, create billions more in value within our borders, and then leave again for Singapore? Do we want to prevent that from happening? As far as I'm concerned, America should roll out the red carpet for every proven innovator in the world who wants to come invent things here, pay the taxes they owe under the law, and then depart to reside elsewhere for a while….his contribution to public coffers is orders of magnitude bigger than the services he has used, and America is certainly better off economically for the fruits of his intellectual labor.*

Highly skilled migrants tend to be younger than the general population. Even if they stay only a few years, given that they are contributing to the economy and paying taxes that support the local aging population, shouldn't governments be trying to lure these migrants instead of turning them away?

Immigration has always been a cornerstone of America's economic success. An immigrant or a child of an immigrant founded over 40 percent of America's Fortune 500 companies. Today, though, getting an American work visa is lengthy and costly. In 2004, the government capped the number of employment-based visas for non-permanent residents at one-third of the 2003 rate. The result has been a labor shortage of skilled workers in science, technology, engineering, and math (the so-called STEM industries) mainly because not enough Americans are entering these areas of study and work themselves.

In response to the STEM visa shortage, a cross-party committee of mayors and business leaders in America published *Not Coming to America*, a report explaining why America is losing the race for global talent to the likes of Singapore, New Zealand, and other countries where visas are more accessible to highly skilled migrants. On the one hand, America is not short on foreigners. In 2011, the United States granted more green cards than ever before, except for 1990 and 1991 when it accepted large numbers of permanent residents from post-Soviet countries. The report's authors, however, argue that America is not focusing on the right type of immigration: "The basic policy framework governing immigration in America has remained unchanged for nearly half a century. And while we have stood in place, the world has changed." *Not Coming to America* features Poyan Rajamand, a Stanford business school graduate from Sweden who didn't want to play cat-and-mouse with American immigration officials, so he picked up and moved to Singapore instead. "Unlike the U.S., no companies worry about possible visa complications when interviewing you for positions here [in Singapore]. There's no real doubt that that aspect of things will work out," Rajamand said. Instead of beating his head against a brick wall in the United States, Rajamand did what any roamer would do— he just went elsewhere.

Instead of trying to retain all of the highly skilled foreign graduates educated in American universities like Rajamand and Kunal Bahl, policy makers are pushing them away. Let's look at the business case: If a company's HR department hires and trains a group of smart and eager unpaid interns for two years, you'd expect the management to hire at least the brightest ones at the end of their internship. If instead the management turns around and refuses to retain any of these interns on technical grounds, you'd think they were crazy. These interns will just take their knowledge and expertise to competing companies who are willing to hire them. Isn't America doing just that? Isn't it educating the world's brightest students, refusing to let them work, and sending them back to other countries where they can go on to compete with America?

In contrast, Poyan Rajamand's second choice, Singapore, has consciously developed a policy to attract world-class talent, and the policy seems to be working. Rising from developing country in the 1960s, Singapore now sits at the top of global rankings for life expectancy, health care, and other quality of life monitors. In recent years, however, Singapore has also been looking to strike the right balance on immigration. Of Singapore's population of about five million, 38 percent is made up of non-resident workers or permanent residents (roughly equivalent to America's green card). After a prolonged period of courting foreign talent, public backlash against migrants forced Singapore's government to cut permanent residency allocations by over 60 percent in 2010 and 2011.

At the same time, facing one of the lowest fertility rates in the world and an aging population, Singapore's government is keenly aware that economic repercussions lie further down the road if it stops accepting migrants. Singapore might be closing the door to mass migration, but it's still open to the right type of worker—like Poyan Rajamand, who is now CEO of an energy efficiency consultancy that he co-founded in Singapore.

These issues are universal. Virtually every government at one time or another asserts the need to cut immigration, often responding to popular demand. At the same time, perhaps more quietly, the same governments are setting up policies to make sure that their economies remain dynamic, responsive to the globalized world, and attractive to the right kind of migrant. And they're more than happy to scoop up the bright young things that America™ isn't hiring.

Chapter 7
All Politics Is Local

When Friedrich Nietzsche announced, "God is dead," atheists everywhere trumpeted the demise of religion by the end of the twentieth century. Instead, religion today is a stronger geopolitical force than anyone predicted. Religious attendance is up, once-secular countries and regions are now devout (sometimes radically so), and most religions are growing in numbers globally.

Take for instance the Catholic Church, which has more adherents than ever before. On paper, the Catholic Church has over 1.2 billion members. The means that one in every seven people on the planet is Catholic. As religions go, that sounds pretty successful, but in reality, the faithful are divided. On the one hand, fervent Catholics still join evangelization efforts (the "Jesus loves you" camp). On the other hand, millions confess their doubts (the "you don't really *believe* in that old man in the sky stuff, do you?" camp). Nominally, they're part of the same religion, but the two views rarely reconcile. And it's not just Catholics. Every religion has its devout and secular divide.

Might citizenship be heading toward a similar fork in the road? Are we witnessing the nascence of a split between fervent patriots and agnostic citizens? Just as you've probably heard people say, "I'm a lapsed Catholic," might people one day confess, "I'm American, but I'm not practicing"?

In February 2014, I interviewed a couple from India who are now living in Singapore. Indra works for MasterCard, and Rajesh is an engineer. Both were born in Mumbai, but they moved to Singapore as newlyweds when Rajesh found a job in Singapore's shipping industry. Indra and Rajesh have been in Singapore for over a dozen years.

When I'm in Asia, I like to start off with my favorite question that differentiates the chalk from cheese: "Are you expats?" I ventured out. They looked at each other and shook their heads. Indra said, "No, we don't really see ourselves as such. Besides we've been here in Singapore for a long time."

"So are you locals?" I asked. Rajesh replied, "Well, we weren't born here, and culturally we'll always be Indian. But our daughter was born here, and if we stay, I guess she'll see Singapore as home. Indra has kept her Indian citizenship, so we can own property there, but I became a Singaporean citizen."

"So do you see yourself as an immigrant, then?" I probed.

Rajesh admitted that he didn't. "I wanted to move to Singapore, but I could have easily stayed at home. It's not like we were coming here for a better life or like Indians who emigrated a few generations ago. My siblings who stayed in India have a similar living standard to mine. It's just that I like it here. Singapore is cleaner, less chaotic, and an easier place to live than Mumbai."

I continued the line of questioning: "If you're not expats or immigrants, are you global nomads? Or migrant workers?" Both Indra and Rajesh laughed and shook their heads. Neither had really found a way of describing the life they were living.

Finally, Indra ventured out: "We consider ourselves global citizens."

Ah yes, the global citizen. Like Rajesh and Indra, the people I interviewed said over and over again that they were global citizens. People genuinely may *feel* like global citizens, but their impressions are far from reality.

Citizenship bestows rights and duties. Typical rights include basic infrastructure, sanitation, and the power to decide—at least in principle—who governs you. For these privileges, citizens must pay taxes and abide by the laws of the land. Failure to fulfill these obligations could land you in the slammer.

Roamers like Indra and Rajesh have no such rights or duties on a global scale. Perhaps with the exception of the European Union, these powers still sit squarely in the hands of countries. Roamers might *think* globally, but they can only *act* locally, within the boundaries of their nationality. Despite their higher ideals, roamers still live on a planet carved into nation states. It might sound like a nice idea, but there is no such thing as a global citizen—not, at any rate, until roamers get their way.

For some, more passports just mean more options. Getting a local passport might not pluck at the heartstrings any more than getting a local driver's license. With countries increasingly accepting dual nationality and high-tech weaponry making military conscription largely obsolete, the weight of citizenship is no longer as heavy as it once was. In October 2013, *The New York Times* ran an op-ed piece titled "The End of the Nation

State?" The author questioned the future role of national governments. With the rise of other power centers, such as cities and special economic zones, and with disruptive innovations like bitcoins circumventing traditional central government roles, many people already live as if national borders and legislatures were a mere formality. And this is not just about foreigners. Even former New York mayor Michael Bloomberg regularly admitted, "I don't listen to Washington much."

Some national governments are starting to wonder about their half of the bargain. In 2006, the Canadian government removed 15,000 Canadian citizens from Lebanon during the Israel-Lebanon conflict, at a cost of almost 94 million Canadian dollars. Most were dual Lebanese-Canadian nationals, and roughly half were living permanently in Lebanon at the time, so they were not paying Canadian taxes. The hostilities were short-lived, and an estimated 50 percent of them returned to Lebanon within one month. The incident sparked a furor, and the media quickly dubbed these Canadian-Lebanese citizens "Canadians of Convenience." A huge public debate ensued. Were these citizens simply a product of a globalized world (where cheaper travel options, better technology, and liberalized economies mean fewer people are residing in one country forever), or were they cheating the system? And if you need to point fingers, who is to blame?

On the one hand, governments issue citizenship, levy taxes, and provide services, while on the other they liberalize economies, welcome skilled foreign workers, and build ever-larger airports to facilitate all this moving around. Keeping immigrants in their host country might not be the paradigm of the future, and that's a balance sheet discrepancy that governments need to reconcile. Officials need to start recognizing and legislating for a whole new generation of "not quite" immigrants.

When Edward Snowden leaked classified security data to the public, Americans were outraged about how much information their government secretly collects on them. That may be, but more astonishing is how much information governments *don't* collect about their citizens. The United Nations High Commissioner for Refugees estimates that there are over ten million stateless people living in the world today. Finding out how many people in the world have *dual citizenship*, however, is nigh impossible. Of the two dozen or so countries I researched, only the Netherlands has clear statistics on Dutch citizens with dual nationality (1.3 million). Estimates for the United States range wildly from one million to several million. Australian estimates range from four million to five million. Statistics Canada speculates that four million naturalized Canadians have kept their original citizenship, but the agency doesn't know how many Canadian-born citizens have acquired a second passport elsewhere. Official Hong Kong statistics claim there are 16,000 Canadians living in Hong Kong, but according to the Canadian consulate, the figure is more like 300,000. How can they get it so wrong? Most of these numbers are finger-in-the-wind estimations, and an accurate total global number simply does not exist. Governments are suspiciously mute on (or deaf to) the subject.

Why?

How can the Canadian government blame dual citizens for acting in their best interests (life-saving interests, in the case of Lebanon), and then not even keep track of how many Canadians carry more than one passport? It's easier to find out how many people have two SIM cards than how many people have dual citizenship. Privacy is part of the answer, but so is turning a blind eye. Most "pious" religious leaders refuse to acknowledge that their adherents have a devout-secular divide, and legislators seem to be taking the same tack. Simply ignoring the chasm isn't going to make the issue go away. Governments need to accept that citizenship ain't what it used to be and start legislating on that basis.

"Indians ditch their passports as soon as they can," Vikram Singh in Munich tells me. India does not recognize dual citizenship, so those who become citizens of another country must renounce their Indian nationality. As a management consultant, Vikram must get on a plane with a moment's notice, so he needs a passport that allows him to do so. "It would be impossible for me to do my job with an Indian passport," he says. "An Indian passport is a complete headache. You need a visa to go anywhere." Vikram now has a British passport. He could still be roaming with an Indian passport—indeed countless Indians are doing just that—but he'd have to switch jobs to do so. India's non-resident Indian (NRI) population is about 1 percent of its total population, but that still means that somewhere between ten and twenty million Indian citizens currently live abroad. In the long run, Vikram expects to return to the United Kingdom with his British wife, but for now they are both happily living in Munich. Like many roamers, Vikram got a British passport not to live in Britain as an *immigrant*, but to move more freely living abroad as a *roamer*.

This lack of national conviction makes many people with more nationalist sentiments anxious about globalization, and they may have good reason to worry, too. On any given evening, in any number of global cities, you can peer into apartment after apartment to find the lights shut off—not because the occupants are out enjoying the city life, but because the homes lie empty, their foreign owners living abroad, investing in property around the world to hedge themselves against volatile global markets. These foreigners participate in the local economy by pushing housing prices up, but they're not exactly contributing to the fabric of society. Empty apartments in cities that are facing housing shortages are just a small piece of a bigger issue. Even if these foreigners are contributing to the local economy by paying taxes, how much do they really care about what happens here? If times get tough, if the government raises taxes or restricts their movement, they'll just sell up and fly off. Isn't all this globalization just breeding generations of people with no deep connections, loyalties, or local responsibilities?

It's hard to contradict these nebulous worries, and many situations do indeed fuel the fire of mistrust. One industry—investment banking—is notoriously detached from the society it purportedly serves. That may be why the most glaring examples can be found here. A lack of direct accountability has led to some gobsmacking losses at multinational banks. In 1995, Toshihide Iguchi was working in New York when he confessed to losing $1.1 billion for his mothership in Japan, Daiwa Bank. In 2002, Allied Irish Bank uncovered losses of almost $700 million by U.S.-based currency trader John Rusnak. In 2008, Jerome Kerviel managed to lose a breathtaking $7.1 billion while working in London for French bank Société Générale. In 2011, Swiss bank UBS teetered on the brink of collapse when London-based Kweku Adoboli racked up losses of $2 billion in unauthorized trades. Nick Leeson, however, wins the gold medal in this race to the bottom—his unchecked trades in Singapore bankrupted Barings, one of the oldest and most respected banking institutions in British history. In the understatement of the century, Leeson left a note saying "I'm Sorry" before fleeing Singapore in 1995. These cases are among the worst damages ever inflicted in modern banking history, and they all share one salient feature—each rogue trader was based away from the country of his bank's headquarters.

Does that imply that those living away from their HQ adopt a cowboy mentality? These rogue traders seemed to do just that. That doesn't mean that roamers follow suit (even on a much smaller, less destructive scale). The vast majority of roamers are not transborder property investors or rogue traders, but locals may still have doubts about their social and emotional investments into community life. How accountable are globals given that they're not profoundly embedded in their national environment, or for that matter, any national environment?

Admittedly, roamers can sometimes be faulted with making themselves at home all over the world, expecting to live as they always have, forgetting that their new home country has culturally specific laws and mores. Obviously this can cause friction. "What century are we in?" a friend of mine grumbled when he and his girlfriend were not allowed to share a room during a business trip to the United Arab Emirates. The couple work for the same Emirati company in Europe, and their relationship is not a dirty office secret. They've been together for years and will likely marry, but their office only allows officially married couples to cohabitate during business trips. As a European "global citizen," my friend forgot that he was a visitor in a foreign country with customs different from what he considers a modern norm.

Understandably, locals can lose patience. My Singaporean friend Allan regularly complains that Westerners are disrespectful and rude to locals, cutting lines, and using foul language. Is the offensive foreigner simply from a culture where speaking politely and queuing are not mandatory? Is he or she blatantly racist? Is the foreigner simply a vulgar character—here, there, and everywhere? How is Allan to know the difference? And why should he care? He expects foreigners to adapt to his country's customs and procedures.

Another friend of mine, an ordinarily restrained and polite Englishman, once asked a foreigner to kindly remove an unsightly blot of spit that he'd just deposited on a central London pavement. My friend says, "Such manners are not acceptable in England, and we should not just learn to tolerate it."

Many globals set off into the world with the attitude "the world is my oyster." They might make more friends if they enter a country with the attitude "this world is *your* oyster." In a more perfect world with more perfect humans, we could all approach roaming with the understanding that "this world is *our* oyster." Glance at headlines from all over the globe, however, and you'll likely agree that we're nowhere close to that ideal.

Historically, foreigners have always had a frosty reception. Foreigners sometimes came to trade, but they often came to pillage. Today's roamers aren't exactly out to rape and plunder, but attitudes toward them (and foreigners of every variety) remain cool. I don't need to go into the 2015 South African riots or quote Australian government officials and Texan senators to make my point. Anyone who has passed through border control in an American airport knows what I'm talking about, and I speak as a white woman who travels on a Canadian passport. I don't know what kind of interrogation you face as a young Moroccan or Nigerian man. It's perfectly acceptable almost anywhere in the world to vocalize suspicion of foreigners and to cow them into silence. In almost all political arenas, it's even rewarded. Old-age pensions are more likely to bankrupt the modern welfare state than employed "foreigners," but few politicians are willing to take potshots at granny's retirement. Tackling *that* problem would only lead to a serious backlash, whereas taking aim at foreigners is a reliable vote-winner. It's risk-free.

In the past, immigrants used a variety of tactics to quell suspicions. They gave their children local names, emphasized the local language over their own mother tongue, or made other displays of loyalty to their new homeland. Immigrants still expect a level of antagonism, so they often work demonstrably hard (and quietly) to prove that they are here to make a better life for themselves and their children. Despite their best efforts, immigrants have often borne the brunt of racism from both locals and other immigrant communities.

Expats, on the other hand, have typically sheltered themselves socially and economically from the wider community, which they'll leave in a few years anyway. By sticking to their own kind, they often escape the full impact of local conflicts by staying detached from their surroundings.

So how should roamers approach the local milieu? Should roamers learn the local language and abide by local customs? If they don't, doesn't that prove that they're just expats, whether they like it or not? Or has the world changed so much that the educated urbanites everywhere typically speak English and share a modern set of customs, so "going native" is no longer necessary in a globalized world? Do roamers have the right to challenge unfair local practices or views? And how should locals deal with these "new internationals"? Should they ignore them as they would expats since they'll leave in a few years anyway? What if they stay? Should they expect roamers to acquire local customs, habits, and social mores?

If you're an expat working for a large company, you'll likely get intercultural training before you go abroad. Most roamers, though, rarely get such advice (beyond what a *Lonely Planet* provides). Consequently, even when they're abiding by their own high standards of conduct, roamers may unwittingly offend locals. With a Starbucks, an Indian curry joint, and a Chinese restaurant in every big city on the planet, one can make the mistake of thinking that we are all "same, same, but different."

Ironically, those who are "same, same, but different" can cause the highest irritation. One roamer in Taiwan told me that although the Taiwanese are very warm toward visitors, their polite demeanor sometimes belies their true opinions. She writes, "The Taiwanese respect a few nationalities and don't like a lot of them, but their number one dislike is reserved for ABCs [American-born Chinese], who speak Chinese well, but are boisterous and rude in the minds of the Taiwanese." Because ABCs look and almost sound like locals, they're also expected to behave like them.

Overlooking local conventions can have dire consequences. In Indonesia, countless foreigners rot in fetid prisons, and seven were executed in April 2015 because they didn't fully appreciate the local penalties for drug trafficking, even in small amounts. In Singapore, where damaging someone else's property is a serious offence, a disbelieving American teenager and a Swiss IT consultant were imprisoned and caned for two separate acts of vandalism. Numerous foreign couples working in Dubai have been fined or jailed for sexual intimacy, including kissing and holding hands, in public places. In their home countries, most of these offenders would have received a slap on the wrist, a light sentence, or nothing at all. (Kissing in public is practically mandatory in France.) But their lack of a connection with their new, albeit maybe temporary, home caught these lawbreakers unaware.

All of these are extreme cases, but lesser confusion bedevils even the most earnest roamer. Moving abroad typically involves a few disconcerting months of adjustment, followed by an eventual feeling of familiarity and belonging. Life goes on as the new normal sets in. That's often when most misunderstandings take place. Roamers begin to feel more at ease in their new home, sometimes reverting to old habits that might be at odds with local ways of life. Some foreigners are keen to abide by local rules but are simply caught unawares while others just don't bother (particularly if they don't know if they'll stay awhile or forever).

When intimidated by outside influences, people in every culture worry about losing their identity or cultural values. Few of them, however, are concerned about the impact their own nationals are having abroad. A BBC op-ed piece put these worries into perspective:

> *When we see headlines talking of a city the size of Birmingham worth of immigrants arriving each year, we forget that a city the size of Nottingham leaves each year.*
>
> *When we see headlines complaining about the lack of integration of migrants in Britain, keeping to their own culture, and their inability to speak English, we forget about the 750,000 Brits in Spain, watching EastEnders in the Dog and Duck on the Costa del Sol.*

In this description, British roamers are missing—those living and working in Barcelona, Madrid, and throughout Spain; those speaking Spanish and watching *Cuéntame cómo pasó* as well as *Downton Abbey*; the curators and the teachers; and those going to business school or starting their own businesses. But the point of the BBC article is spot-on. There is a growing transfer of people, back and forth, in every country around the globe. In a 2010 World Bank report, the Top 10 list of *immigrant* destinations included India, Russia, and Britain. India, Russia, and Britain were also on the Top 10 list for the highest number of citizens who have *emigrated* abroad. We are all on the move.

Globally minded roamers are frustrated by national governments who seem to be dragging their feet even as globalization speeds forward. One American, who had lived abroad in London, Hong Kong, and Barcelona for eleven years, had her wings clipped by falling in love with a fellow global citizen from the wrong side of the tracks. She married a green card holder and wrote this in response to my survey:

> *My partner has a green card, but would only be allowed to leave the U.S. for two years maximum in the future. So much for enabling globalization! It seems unfair to basically limit my rights as a U.S. citizen to have the freedom to move my family where best suits us.*

She and her family have been grounded in San Francisco for the past three years. Another respondent to my survey, this time from India, also voiced his frustrations:

> *India mandates that every student who completes a Ph.D. in the United States and works as a post-doc after completing his or her degree for a period of more than five years must either return home for a period of two years or obtain something called a J-1 waiver with no obligation to return back. While they make these decisions on a case-by-case basis, often times, if the applicant is well qualified, they reject the application. This is unfair, especially if the applicants have never studied in a state-funded institution. Not to mention that this violates what I consider a basic human right—the freedom to work wherever one chooses!*

No government on the planet considers "the freedom to work wherever one chooses" a basic human right. Virtually every roamer I met does.

This fundamental rift doesn't look as if it will be resolved any time soon. Likely it will grow, pitting those who eagerly protect traditional national values against those who push for globalism. And make no mistake: This is going to be a grim battle for those with a globalist view. Plenty of roamers lose the right to vote altogether by moving abroad, but even those who don't lose their vote are muted in other ways. Opinion polls are a powerful political tool, and virtually all polls are conducted at the national level, effectively silencing those living abroad. Roamers often have different views and concerns than those living at home, and instead of adding a much needed international perspective to domestic policies, these polls prevent roamers from having any influence on politics anywhere. With politics lurching between left and right almost everywhere on the planet, these roamers' voices could provide a valuable "third perspective," but of course national governments don't want to take even more opinions into account. As David Foster Wallace so insightfully wrote, "the entrenched Establishments…are not dumb. [They] are keenly aware that it is in their interests to keep you disgusted and bored and cynical and to give you every possible reason to stay at home…watching MTV on primary day…tacitly doubling the value of some Diehard's vote." Roamers might not be cynical, bored, or disgusted, but their absence on any political stage certainly does double the value of some Diehard's vote. If they don't intend to take up swords, global citizens had better prepare their pens. The national-global divide will be the greatest social conflict of our times, the great debate of the twenty-first century.

So how do all these global citizens transcend international boundaries? Since there are currently no avenues for living *beyond* national boundaries, the only way to go is *deeper* into cities.

With *urban regeneration* on the lips of every city planner, it's hard to imagine that sixty years ago, *downtown* was a dirty word. Cities were hollowing out, their residents spilling into carefully manicured, safe peripheries where you could drive home from work, park your car in your own garage, and avoid unnecessary contact with strangers. This was the ideal, and for many it still is.

In the midst of this "golden age of the suburb," Jane Jacobs published her powerful book on urbanism, *The Death and Life of Great American Cities*. In a time when driving on the open road was part and parcel of the American dream, Jacobs argued that city planners had it all wrong. Instead of promoting suburbia, they should be advocating high-density, mixed-use, bustling inner-city neighborhoods where one might not even need a car. Rather than mass, anonymous retailers on the outskirts of town, planners should nurture small local businesses that create thriving micro-economies throughout the city. Cities should be designed around sidewalks where neighbors might bump into one another or where perfect strangers might exchange a few words while their dogs sniff each other's private parts. Jacobs pointed out that these seemingly trivial interactions are what create a sense of belonging, accountability, and, ultimately, safer communities.

These truths are now held to be self-evident, but in the 1960s, Jacobs's book was radical, even incendiary. Like many visionaries ahead of their time, Jacobs was vilified. She was branded a rabble-rouser, a housewife, and, worst of all, a Commie.

Today Jacobs is celebrated as one of the great thinkers on city life. Her ideas have percolated down not only to urban planners, but also to individuals and the choices we instinctively make every day: choices about where we live, how we get to work, where we shop, and how we travel. When going abroad, we resolutely want to avoid "tourist" spots despite being tourists ourselves. Instead, we crack open copies of *Monocle* magazine to check out the latest trendy neighborhoods in Manila, Cairo, or Rio. We no longer want to visit Paris only to climb the Eiffel Tower. We want to breathe in the everyday air of Paris. We want to eat at a mom-and-pop café that's been in the family for fifty years, or try a small bistro where a young chef is just making his name. We want to buy berets that have been knit in the Pyrenees for generations and are sold in a small, quirky shop near the Canal Saint-Martin. We don't want to overnight in a soulless chain hotel; we want stay in a little boutique hotel or to lodge with locals via Airbnb so we can see the *real* Paris. Local is cool. Local is authentic. And, ironically, foreigners are important consumers of today's local revolution.

So far, I've mainly been referring to countries. In reality, the roamer's country of residence is less important than his or her city of residence. Few roamers living in London, Moscow, or Shanghai have deep kinship with the countries of Great Britain, Russia, or China beyond the borders of their resident city. If they live in London, they're more likely to spend the weekend in Paris or Barcelona than in Manchester or the Lake District northwest England. One American roamer told me, "We live in London, not Britain. I don't even know if I could locate Leicester on a map. Although we own a house and live here, I still feel like we're floating on the surface." (She shouldn't be too hard on herself, though. I've met plenty of Brits who can't locate Leicester on a map either.)

One can enjoy living in Shanghai or New York without having a similar affinity for China or America. Hsin, a Taiwanese research assistant who lived in Boulder, Colorado, put it this way: "The U.S. is quite big, and people are very different in different parts of the country. I felt at home enough to call myself a Boulderite, but I wouldn't say I felt American." America is a much denser, more emotive concept than Boulder. The United States has a national anthem, a constitution, and an oath of allegiance. It built the American dream. America goes to war; Boulder does not.

The origin of "cosmopolitan" is a compound of two ancient Greek words, *kosmos* (the world) and *polites* (a citizen). So a cosmopolitan is a citizen of the world. But *polites* itself stems from *polis*, or city, and therefore a citizen of the world is actually a citizen of a city. In the same way that the ancients were citizens of city-states, not nation-states, supranational roamers might be going back to the earliest model of *cityzenship*—at least emotionally. Nationals might accuse roamers of fickleness, but whimsy isn't to blame. Forging a new and possibly temporary relationship with a city is simply more accessible than developing a bond with a country.

By focusing on cities, roamers can more easily add "Boulderite," "New Yorker," or "Londoner" to their repertoire of affiliations without having to renounce any pre-existing cultural identities. This may be one reason the tiny city-state of Singapore is consistently voted as the best place to live among foreigners. As one roamer put it, "Unlike Beijing or New York, you can live in Singapore without worrying about what's going on in the backyard." Singapore has no backyard.

Whereas immigrants traditionally built ties to countries, roamers build ties to cities. This shift is happening now because roamers are emerging at a time when cities increasingly matter. As A.T. Kearney's 2012 Global Cities Index puts it, "The world today is more about cities than countries, and a place like Seoul has more in common with Singapore and Hong Kong than it does with smaller Korean cities." *Moscow* is a world away from *Russia*. New York and London's special relationship has earned them the mash-up moniker *NYLON*. New York City Mayor Bill de Blasio and former London Mayor Boris Johnson are as renowned as their national counterparts, President Barack Obama and Prime Minister David Cameron. As cities increasingly become global players and competitors, to put it crudely, the city is *in* and the nation-state is *out*.

For the first time in human history, more than half of the world's population now lives in cities. According to data collected by the World Bank and PriceWaterhouseCoopers (PwC), many cities now generate more wealth than the economies of mid-sized countries. In 2008, Tokyo had an estimated Gross Domestic Product (GDP) of $1,479 billion, while all of Spain had a GDP of $1,456 billion. New York City had a GDP of $1,406 billion, larger than Canada's total of $1,214 billion. Australia had a higher GDP than London ($763 billion versus $565 billion), but not Los Angeles ($792 billion). Osaka, Mexico City, São Paulo, and Philadelphia all have higher GDPs than Belgium, Sweden, and Switzerland. The world's top thirty cities account for roughly 18 percent of the GDP of the planet. Cities are exciting, diverse, and energetic. They are centers of business, innovation, culture, and protest. Cities witness humanity's most breathtaking achievements and most heartbreaking failures. If you can make it there, you can make it anywhere.

So it's no wonder that roamers look to particular cities when considering job opportunities or a move. For most roamers in finance, for example, moving from London to Leeds, the United Kingdom's second financial center, is unimaginable. New York, Hong Kong, or Zurich are far more likely destinations. In an emotional sense, these roamers are living in London, not in the United Kingdom, so they don't consider other opportunities within the country. Part of this emotional shift may do with an increasing importance of cities as geopolitical players in their own right.

Each industry has *sticky cities*, and these vary from industry to industry. For example, if you're an art dealer, your top sticky cities are likely to be London, New York, Venice, Basel, and, increasingly, Hong Kong and Shanghai. Venice and Basel are at the forefront of the global art world, but they're backwaters to high-tech entrepreneurs. Some cities are hubs for many industries, earning the title *Global Cities*. There are several rival Global Cities indexes, but New York, London, Paris, Tokyo, and Hong Kong are typically found among the top five.

According to a recent survey, America is the number one destination for professionals hoping to relocate to a new country. Executive recruitment company Hydrogen reports that 24 percent of professionals would like to move to the United States next. The United Kingdom and Australia come in second and third place with 13 percent of the votes, followed by Singapore with 9 percent.

Part of the problem with this study, along with many others, is that it's still based on countries. Most of the professionals surveyed probably don't want to move to the United States in general, but rather they want to move specifically to their sticky cities. IT specialists hoping to work in the United States likely have their hearts set on Palo Alto, Seattle, New York, Boston, or a handful of other thriving IT hubs. Chicago and Washington certainly have their merits, but the real draw for technology professionals is still the Palo Alto-San Francisco corridor.

What's fascinating about the Hydrogen survey is that Singapore comes fourth in the whole world. The United States is massive, the third-most populous country on the planet, with well over 300 million citizens. Singapore has a total population of five million people. In the survey, Singapore is the number *two* most desired destinations on the planet for finance executives and number *three* for technology professionals. As work becomes increasingly specialized, specific cities, not countries, are industry drivers. Cities offer the most exhilarating jobs, are hungry for more employees, and inspire enthusiastic entrepreneurs. Cities do not, however, issue the work visa.

In my survey, I asked respondents who aren't imminently heading home which two cities are their most desirable destinations. Now the picture becomes more fragmented and reliable. If you add New York, San Francisco, and Los Angeles together, America as a whole gets the top billing at 29 percent. But when analyzing the cities independently, New York, with 16 percent of votes, is the second-most desired destination in the world. Singapore comes in third place with 12 percent, and Hong Kong is fourth at 9 percent. Zurich, San Francisco, Sydney, Paris, Geneva/Toronto/Los Angeles (tied), and Melbourne make up the rest of the top ten. In fact, when you look at individual cities, topping the charts as the single most attractive destination, with 19 percent of the votes, is London.

Beyond the emotional attraction of cities, there are practical considerations as well. Young people throughout the world are questioning the ability of governments and companies to provide adequate social security and pensions to take them through their sunset years. Companies everywhere are slashing or abandoning pension plans for new staff. Practically all advanced economies are facing a shortfall in their worker-to-pensioner ratio because of decreased birth rates and longer life expectancies, not to mention the growing burden of national debts. A survey among people under 30 in America found that 50 percent do not think Social Security will exist when they reach retirement age, and 28 percent think that Social Security will exist, but at much lower levels than today. If countries are an increasingly unreliable source of pensions or social security while global cities offer the potential to earn more money, allying yourself to a city instead of a country makes sense not only emotionally, but also economically.

Cities matter more than ever before because it's not only where people go in search of work, but also where companies go in search of people. Like Alex Ljung, the Swedish entrepreneur who moved his company from Stockholm to Berlin in search of skilled employees, companies sometimes need to relocate to where their employees want to live. Internet search engine Lycos famously moved from Philadelphia because it believed that Boston was more suited to attracting world-class talent. A survey by *The Wall Street Journal* reports that location is only second to salary for those looking to change jobs.

As geopolitical focus increasingly becomes city-centric, perhaps roamers share an outlook that is more appropriately called a *cityview* instead of a *worldview*. When I asked, "Where next?" during my interviews, very few roamers responded by designating a country. No one considering a move to Shanghai or Hong Kong said, "China." Those going to New York didn't say, "the United States." People always had a particular city in mind.

That particular city, however, might not be exactly what you'd expect. When designing my survey, I listed thirty-four cities around the planet where I assumed most roamers would live, places that are listed in the Global Cities Index of the world's most globally connected cities. Almost three quarters of roamers indeed live in these cosmopolitan, global cities. (A large proportion of surveyed roamers live in the cities where I conducted my in-person interviews, with residents of London, New York, Hong Kong, and Singapore making up almost 40 percent of responses.) However, 27 percent of roamers live in places that are not on the map of top-tier global cities—Tashkent, Toulouse, Leamington Spa, Baku, Kiev, Fukuoka, Santiago de Chile, Juba, Bowling Green, Dallas, and almost everywhere else you can imagine. These may be sticky cities for some industries, or indeed it may just show that roaming is a far greater phenomenon than I originally suspected.

For roamers, home is where the heart (of the city) is. But love it or hate it, they still are citizens and residents of a country. As much as Boston, Shanghai, and Barcelona might want them, they'll have to convince the United States, China, and Spain to let them in. Roamers shouldn't forget Socrates, who, long before the age of globalization, proclaimed, "I am a citizen not of Athens or Greece, but of the world." For all their ideals, Socrates' fellow world citizens couldn't stop his fellow Athenian citizens from proving him fatally wrong. The Athenians condemned Socrates to death by hemlock, a classically Greek tragedy to the very end. Without any foreseeable solutions, global citizens who prefer their wine to their hemlock may wish to avoid ruffling the feathers of their fellow Athenians by not issuing too many supranational proclamations. Roamers and others may wish that national governments would just loosen up already, but for now, the score remains Athenians 1, global citizens 0.

When American Congressman Thomas O'Neil said, "All politics is local," he meant that politicians must, above all, listen to the day-to-day needs of the constituents who voted them into office. If that's the case, what happens to constituents who live abroad? Or foreigners who live locally? Who represents globals when all politics is local? Are they slipping through the cracks?

Most countries today allow their citizens to vote from abroad, but an accurate description of the process would involve the phrase "like pulling teeth." You can check your bank balance from anywhere in the world, but except for a few rare cases, teleporting might be available sooner than Internet voting for residents living abroad.

Indians abroad are allowed to vote, but only if they physically return to their constituency in India. Czechs can now vote abroad, but only in person at their embassy, which may be hundreds of miles away or even in another country. Greeks and Turks can vote abroad, but only in specified polling stations, which are few and far between. Even in countries where you can cast your vote through the mail, bureaucratic registration procedures can stymie even the most ardent voter.

Of the twenty-eight countries of the European Union, twenty-two have no restrictions on overseas voters, but British citizens lose the right to vote after living abroad for fifteen years and Germans after twenty-five years. Canadian prisoners have the right to vote, but Canadians who stay abroad for more than five years lose that right. Australians and Danes are some of those worst off, forfeiting their vote after only three years abroad. "This made sense in the 1950s, when you went somewhere by boat and had no news of what was happening back home," said Australian Ed Smith in Beijing. Still, Australians are better off than many. Jamaica, Uruguay, Pakistan, and Vietnam do not allow their citizens abroad to vote at all, along with roughly fifty other countries.

Why all the fuss? Some lawmakers believe that non-residents don't deserve to vote, while others just don't want to bear the extra costs. Some legislators don't think the low numbers merit the hassle, while others think the opposite—those living abroad might swing the election against them. In the latter case, they may indeed be right. In the 2012 election, Venezuelan residents of the United States voted in large numbers against Hugo Chavez. Many had left Venezuela in protest to his policies. In the first round of voting, 99 percent of Venezuelans living in the United States voted for his opponent, Henrique Capriles. Similarly, in the 2013 Czech presidential elections, those abroad voted by a large majority against the eventual winner.

In both cases, however, non-domiciled voters had little effect on the final outcomes. There are fewer of them living abroad, and they have far lower turnout rates than those living within the country itself. For example, of the estimated sixteen to twenty million Lebanese abroad (four times more than the population of Lebanon), 700,000 are qualified to vote, and only 10,000 registered to vote in the 2013 general election. Only 7 percent of Americans living abroad voted in the 2008 presidential election. American high school dropouts are five times more likely to vote than those living abroad. Citizens abroad might grumble that they are not adequately represented, but they have themselves partly to blame.

When citizens abroad first get the right to vote, they passionately engage in the process, but their enthusiasm eventually wanes. In 1976, when Portuguese citizens abroad were first given the right to vote, 86 percent of émigrés participated in the election. By the 2006 parliamentary election, foreign voter-turnout was only 25 percent. This is still a pretty good turnout compared with other countries. In 2008, an intensive campaign persuaded a record-breaking 56,0000 overseas New Zealanders to register for elections, which was about 50 percent more than the previous election. The total number, however, was still under 10 percent of the Kiwi population living abroad.

On the opposite side of the spectrum, some countries mandate expatriate voting. Peru, for example, does not consider voting a right, but rather a civic duty. Citizens risk fines if they do not vote, including those living abroad. Still, only 50 percent of Peruvians abroad voted in the presidential elections of 2011. Brazil has a similar system. Those who don't provide a valid reason for missing an election run the risk of getting fined or losing privileges such as applying for new passport. Yet only 45 percent of overseas Brazilians cast ballots during the first round of voting in the 2010 presidential election.

Part of the problem lies with voter apathy, and part lies with voting bureaucracy. Even if you manage the Sisyphean task of registering for an election while abroad, you can count your lucky stars if you actually receive a postal ballot on time. And despite all the tools available today, there are still real barriers to information, particularly for those who are not plugged into their local embassy, chamber of commerce, or other national clubs. When campaigning for election in 2012, hopeful Julien Balkany said that a quarter of the French citizens he met abroad didn't know that France's overseas constituencies even existed. With ad nauseam pre-election campaigning, it's hard to imagine any person living in his or her home country *not* knowing about an upcoming vote. Living abroad simply makes a difference.

Despite these rather dire statistics, roamers seem to be more civically minded. Of those who have been away from home for more than three years, an impressive 42 percent say that they voted in their country's last national election. The 58 percent who did not vote cited different reasons. Some had been away so long that they'd lost the right to vote, others were unable to reach their embassy to cast a ballot, and others felt that they simply were not knowledgeable enough to endorse a particular party or candidate. "I left Germany when I was 13," says Christiane Bode, a professor in Milan. "I have the right to vote there, but I don't feel qualified to do so." John Terrance, an American in London, has similar misgivings: "It's so weird to be living in counties where you can have a view on politics, but generally can't vote. And then voting in the U.S. just feels bizarre because I don't live there, so I don't really feel like I legitimately should be influencing American election outcomes either."

After living in a few countries, staying informed about your home country can become a monumental task. Ayse Levent is a Turkish and French citizen who lives in New York. "I've lived in Germany, France, the U.K., Turkey, and now the U.S. I try my best to keep up with what's happening in all these places, but by the time I get to the third national newspaper I realize how much I've missed. I become overwhelmed thinking about all that I should know until finally I give up and go to yoga instead." Ayse laughs. She is self-effacing, but in fact, Ayse took vacation time from work to fly back to Turkey to vote in the last national election.

Peter Sorgenfrei, a Dane who was in New York when I interviewed him, has not voted in recent elections. "You have to notify the Danish government once you have been out of Denmark for six months and have settled elsewhere," he explained. "Two years later, your social security number becomes dormant and you can't vote." Because Peter holds only a green card in the United States, he is not qualified to vote anywhere. I asked if that bothered him. "Not really," he replied. "In New York and Denmark, the dominant parties are the ones I would support, so it doesn't matter much. But if I lived somewhere where my vote made a difference, it would bother me."

Voting, of course, is not the only way to be politically involved. "We have no political say, but we also don't have any real social responsibilities," says Stacey Wolpert, a South African editor at an auditing firm in Hong Kong. When you haven't settled permanently in any country, or are semi-permanent in more than one country, it can be hard to know where to be a "socially responsible" citizen. Or like Stacey, you can get involved "politically" just by volunteering with local charities.

"I still read the Montreal news every day," says French Canadian Jean Olivier Caron in Tokyo. "Sometimes I know more about what's happening there than those who live in Montreal." Jean Olivier has been living abroad, in Tokyo and New York, for over a decade. "My childhood dream was to become mayor of Montreal," he says. Today, Jean Olivier doesn't have the right to vote anywhere.

Like Jean Olivier, roamers who would like to engage in state affairs find themselves stuck with the uncomfortable choice between returning home and remaining on the fringes of political life. It's an unfortunate dilemma because their multi-national overview could provide useful checks on irrational national practices.

"Why can't the French learn from the British tax system?" asks an irate Marthe Filliou, a French freelance journalist who has returned to France from London. "It's taken me a good week to do my accounts and tax return, compared to a couple of days in the U.K. If I can see this, why can't the French bureaucrats see it?" Her question is moot because Marthe knows the answer: Bureaucracies run nationally deep, not globally wide. Those who design French tax returns have probably never studied or experienced the tax regimes of other countries. Marthe, on the other hand, has lived in Germany, Austria, Spain, and the United Kingdom. Roamers can be incredibly valuable to governments, but national authorities rarely harness the experience of those who have returned to the homeland. Instead, Glocals like Filliou typically become marginalized from the political process.

France is famous for its political revolutions, but it took a Glocal to launch the first French *capitalist* revolution. Trained as an engineer, Jean-David Chamboredon spent much of the 1990s in Silicon Valley, later returning to his native France to cultivate young start-ups. In 2012, when French President Francois Hollande declared a 75 percent tax rate and proposed to double the capital gains on entrepreneurs selling their businesses, Chamboredon started a quiet rebellion. He wrote a scathing, but measured op-ed piece in a business newspaper explaining why the proposals would choke entrepreneurs and investors. His ire caught flame and other entrepreneurs quickly joined Chamboredon's *résistance* by mounting Twitter, YouTube, and Facebook campaigns. Chamboredon says that until then, the government didn't understand that entrepreneurs and venture capitalists were spending years working hard, often without much income, risking their future to make young businesses successful. In a meeting with government officials, Chamboredon pointed out what many of us would consider blatantly obvious: Venture capitalists invest in companies that are *losing* money or need funds to expand. The officials replied, "Oh, O.K., really? We didn't know that." The government did not intend to choke start-ups; they simply didn't understand that their policies were doing just that. "This political class is mainly professional politicians, and clearly there is a gap in knowledge," said Chamboredon. In many countries, as in France, moving from the public sector into the business world is viewed as "selling out" rather than gaining crucial commercial experience for later use in government.

Similarly, working abroad can carry a stigma. Michael Ignatieff was hoping to become the prime minster of Canada in the 2011 elections when he was relentlessly slammed by the opposition for spending most of his adult life in the United Kingdom and the United States. The smear campaign against him featured jibes like "Michael Ignatieff: Just Visiting" and "He Didn't Come Home For You." (After his train-wreck campaign and his election defeat, Ignatieff didn't attract any more love-ins with the Canadian press when he moved back to Harvard to lick his wounds.)

Around the same time, back in France, Dominique Strauss-Kahn (popularly known as DSK) was getting pelted with soufflés even before officially announcing his bid for the French presidency. Just as opinion polls began hinting that DSK was more popular than the erstwhile president Sarkozy, he began suffering scathing criticism for his international inclinations. Despite two earlier terms in the French parliament, including two ministerial posts, critics lambasted DSK for having spent the previous five years in Washington as the (widely respected) chief of the International Monetary Fund. Before a sexual assault case finally blocked his political ambitions, DSK's enemies were already mounting the barricades. Strauss-Kahn had snacked on too many Freedom Fries and was no longer French enough for the Élysée Palace.

Putting aside the woes of individual politicians, new experiments in democracy mean that while politics might still be local, it's less local than it used to be. Despite short sightedness on some fronts, the French government is at the vanguard of innovative solutions to bring its diaspora back in the national political fold. In 2010, the French government took the extraordinary measure to give the roughly three million French citizens living abroad *direct* representation in the Assemblée Nationale (the national assembly, or parliament). French citizens living abroad can now vote for candidates who represent *foreign* constituencies, that is, electoral districts not based in France. The French government designed eleven new global constituencies by carving up the world along geographical lines (e.g., the United States and Canada are one constituency, Central and South America are another, etc.). French citizens living inside the borders of the global constituency can vote for a candidate living locally to represent them in France's parliament in Paris. These representatives can vote on all laws passed in the parliament and are expected to represent the rights of French citizens living abroad.

When this new system came into existence, opponents argued that the center-right party that had implemented these changes (UMP) stood to gain the most seats. The 2012 election proved these suspicions to be groundless. Swinging to the left, French citizens abroad voted roughly along the same party lines as those in France, with only the Greens finding more support abroad than domestically.

As with most overseas voters, the voter turnout in France's overseas constituencies was low, ranging from 13 to 28 percent compared with 55 percent domestically. Those who abstained had various misgivings. Some said that they didn't understand how one single candidate could adequately represent the interests of a constituency encompassing Russia, Oceania, and most of Asia. On another point, Philippe Marlière, professor of French and European politics at University College London, argued in a British newspaper that French citizens abroad have no right to make decisions for France, such as voting on national tax laws. "I'm politically outside of the national community," he wrote in *The Guardian*. "I don't pay my taxes there. In a way I can't be out of it and at the same time claim rights."

France might feel that it's extending *liberté* to its citizens, but some governments wish that France would keep its *liberté, égalité,* and *fraternité* to itself, or at least where it belongs—in France. In 2012, the Canadian government said that it had no problem with French citizens living in Canada participating in the French presidential election, but drew the line at overseas constituencies. They sent a missive to all diplomatic missions in Canada stating that "the Government of Canada will continue to refuse requests by foreign states to include Canada in their respective extraterritorial electoral constituencies." Having the effect of a deflating balloon, the edict did not stop a single Frenchman from voting for his "local" North American member of parliament.

This was not the first foreign election on Canadian soil that the government had challenged. In 2011, Canadian officials grumbled about the Tunisian election. For the 10 percent of Tunisians who live abroad, about 10 percent of Tunisian parliamentary seats are awarded to overseas constituencies. One of those seats is reserved for the constituency of Canada. "No one should represent Canada—or a part of Canada—as a constituency in a foreign elected assembly," said an angry John Baird, Canada's minister for foreign affairs. "It is a matter of Canadian sovereignty."

His objections have had exactly zero effect. Canada's cousins Down Under haven't had much luck either. In 2006, Australia protested angrily when Italy became the first major democracy to grant its diaspora the right to elect overseas representatives to its national parliament and senate. In Australia, where there is a substantial Italian minority, Italian is the second most common language spoken at home after English. "Italian elections should be conducted in Italy…and not create a constituency in Australia," complained Australia's foreign minister, Alexander Downer, but his criticism fell on deaf ears.

Australia's disapproval did not stop Italy from going ahead with its overseas constituencies, but results of the 2006 election have left Italians themselves doubting their own policies. Candidates for Italian overseas territories must live abroad permanently. This allows overseas politicians, who don't pay Italian taxes or live under Italian laws, to make decisions affecting those living in Italy. Luigi Pallaro is an overseas senator from Argentina, where he emigrated as a child. While he might not be a "real" Italian, he managed to play Italian parties against each other in true Machiavellian style. The only independent candidate elected to parliament, Pallaro managed to use his swing vote in 2007 to coerce the Italian government to spend more money on Italian communities in Argentina than ever before. At the same time, when crucial votes concerning the future of Italy were conducted, such as the vote of no-confidence in the Prodi government, Pallaro was nowhere to be found. Speaking Italian "like a badly dubbed Zorro movie," Pallaro was criticized for being loyal not to Italians in Italy, but to the Italian diaspora in Argentina.

Undoubtedly, overseas constituencies turn the idea of the nation-state on its head. "Canada" and "Australia" may be abstract, cartographic concepts for the French, Tunisian, and Italian governments, but for the Canadian and Australian governments they are very concrete territories with sovereign geographic boundaries. After all, Canada and Australia are in principle willing to go to war to defend these borders. Despite the potential conflicts, Canada and Australia seem to be the only governments vociferously opposed to overseas constituencies.

So is the rest of the world slowly slipping into a post-territorial phase of citizenship? Can we imagine a future where a country is no longer defined by its territory, but by its citizenry? If yes, can we take the next logical step to imagining a self-defined population applying to become a member of the United Nations based on absolutely no territory—i.e., a "country" of citizens who are not attached to any particular piece of land? For now that's an unlikely scenario. The raison d'être for democratic states is the protection of its citizens and the territory in which they live. But if an increasing percentage of citizens live abroad, how far will a state go to protect those citizens?

With more and more people living abroad, governments are realizing that they have more and more voters—and donors—living abroad. In the 2012 presidential election in America, Mitt Romney and Barack Obama received substantial campaign contributions from Americans living abroad. Obama campaigned abroad more than any previous presidential candidate. French presidential candidates François Hollande and Nicolas Sarkozy campaigned in London. How leaders eventually engage these voters is up for dispute. Overseas constituencies are a positive development in the much larger debate about voting rights for foreigners, but the results so far confirm that we still haven't found the right solution.

A few governments are leading the way with other unconventional schemes. Innovation House in Palo Alto is partly funded by the Norwegian government. It offers office space, a network of investors, and

133

other services to fledgling Norwegian tech companies who want to set up camp in Silicon Valley. Innovation Center Denmark runs a similar program just down the road. Because Denmark and Norway have internal markets of only five million people each, their tech start-ups have a hard time scaling up and breaking into larger markets. Both governments hope that they can help their homegrown talent expand abroad while bringing experienced entrepreneurs and investors back home. Unlike venture capitalists, neither government is taking a stake in the companies founded abroad. Obviously some of this talent may stay abroad permanently, but Denmark and Norway don't seem to worry about these details.

The Australian organization Advance is another public-private initiative that acts as hub for talented émigrés living around the world. It brings together Australian thought-leaders by hosting events both at home and abroad. It hosts regular programs in Sydney, San Francisco, Hong Kong, and several other locations. Advance doesn't attempt to entice roaming Australians back to Australia. Instead it focuses on closing the gap between the dynamos at home and those abroad.

Many details haven't been hammered out yet. With one hand these same governments help their citizens to work abroad, and with the other hand they revoke their right to vote after they've been abroad for a few years. The fine print needs refining, but at least these government initiatives are falling into step with the times and are heading in the right direction.

For many of those living abroad, the correct formula includes the right to vote locally. In an interview with *Le Monde*, French citizen in Montreal Noémie G. says, "It would be most rational for foreigners to have the right to vote in the constituency where they currently live and that affects them most." In Europe, the *Let Me Vote* campaign argues that E.U. citizens should have the right to vote where they are living. The secretary general of the French center-right party, Jean-Christophe Lagarde, told *The Local France:* "It makes much more sense to vote in the country where you live than where you are from. If I lived in Germany I would want to have the vote for the Bundestag elections."

Most roamers agree with Noémie and Lagarde. Of those who responded to my survey, 27 percent say that they are *very* interested in participating in the local political life where they live, and an additional 26 percent say that they would like to vote locally, agreeing that "it's important to vote if you have the right to do so." A further 23 percent would only vote if they had a personal stake in a particular election and if voting were made easy. Just 15 percent say that they are not interested in local politics, and 8 percent say that they're not interested in voting anywhere. One survey respondent who admits that she is not a very political person still asks, "If we're disconnected from any form of political participation....shouldn't that bother us?" Well yes, it should bother us.

Most of us think that voting rights are getting broader than a hundred years ago, but that's not necessarily true. Women and blacks now have the right to vote in the United States, but in the early twentieth century, noncitizens were allowed to vote in both local and national elections in almost two dozen American jurisdictions. In the United States, noncitizens were entitled to vote in presidential elections until 1924. All legal residents of Ireland and Luxembourg, including foreigners, have the right to vote in local elections. Foreigners with permanent residency in New Zealand and Chile can vote in both national and local elections. A dozen more countries have various, limited noncitizen voting rights. Perhaps most controversially and most courageously, New York City is drafting legislation to grant all New Yorkers (and taxpayers) the right to vote in local elections, regardless of citizenship. Predictably, this has some American traditionalists at the national level hopping mad. Michael Bloomberg might not have listened to Washington much, and it looks as if Bill de Blasio is following suit.

Democracy isn't exactly predicated on a monetary transaction, but foreign residents pay taxes where they live, so it doesn't take a huge leap in logic to conclude that they should have a political say in how their taxes are spent. Besides, having the right to vote offers a sense of belonging. It says, "You're one of us now and therefore have the right to a voice in our society." Instead of alienating all these intelligent and entrepreneurial roamers, governments would engage them in a broader sense. When you feel part of group, you're more likely to contribute to it. That might mean that we'd see more roamers running for local elections or simply volunteering at their local library or national park.

Roamers are unlikely to draw inspiration from the suffragettes and start chaining themselves to parliament gates until they get the right to vote, but I'll abuse the phone analogy one last time to make my point. Remember the car phone? Before anyone could imagine that a phone

135

could be completely devoid of place and entirely mobile, the landline moved into a location that itself was mobile: a car. Currently, we are in the car-phone phase of citizenship. Governments still want their citizens to be tied to some physical location, but increasingly roamers want the mobile-phone version of citizenship—flexible, portable, relevant to where they live *right now*.

It's not as crazy as it sounds. Even something as seemingly permanent as the passport has come and gone. In 1860, when Sweden revoked passports and allowed anyone to cross into its territory, leading London and New York newspapers published an article lauding the move: "Such an act deserves all praise, and we can only hope, for the sake of civilization, that so good an example may speedily find imitators." And most of Europe did follow suit, until World War I when passports became mandatory. We also should remember that the nation-state itself is an incredibly young political system that has only been around since the nineteenth century. Take for example the Austro-Hungarian Empire, which was one political domain until 1918 when it broke up into eight nation-states. It sub-divided again into thirteen nation-states after the end of the Cold War when Yugoslavia and Czechoslovakia split up. We often think that we are at the end of history, but just as empires that were once considered impenetrable no longer exist, so too the concept of the nation-state is beginning to erode. We live in a world where technology is changing, our lifestyles are changing, and our expectations are changing. National norms and institutions are struggling to keep up. By nature, they are slow creatures. For now, it's up to roamers themselves to either accept nation-states as they are or gently nudge national institutions into change. Sure there are offshore accounts and international schools for those who want to (and can afford to) avoid national systems altogether, but roamers who can't or don't want to opt out of the system are looking for other solutions to how populations should be governed in the twenty-first century.

Will any of this come to fruition in our day, or is it too far-fetched, better suited to science fiction? "Chaos theory" sounds like a word straight out of a William Gibson novel, but in fact it's used by scientists to describe how even the tiniest change can produce unexpected, unlikely, or even seemingly impossible results in a complex system. (The more complex the system, the more difficult it is to predict the result.) In a classic illustration, a butterfly in Brazil flaps its wings, causing minuscule changes in the atmosphere, unleashing a series of changes in weather patterns that eventually trigger a tornado in Texas. This so-called "butterfly effect" is used to explain highly improbable "chaotic" events, such as the global economic meltdown following the collapse of banking giant Lehman Brothers, which, until it failed, was considered too big to fail.

Roamers might seem too atomized and too small in number to make a difference in global affairs, but they are flapping their tiny, little wings. And just over the horizon, you can see the storm clouds gathering.

ROAMING

PART III:
ROAMERS ON THE PLEASURES AND THE PITFALLS OF ROAMING

CHAPTER 8
MI CASA, SU CASA: ROAMERS ON HOME

We can debate roaming's impact on society until we're blue, but as Oscar Wilde said, "Society exists only as a mental concept; in the real world there are only individuals." The last thing I set out to do was to write a rough guide to living abroad, but I can't ignore all the individuals who are looking for answers, tips, or support. During my interviews, the roamers I met were eagerly asking me as many questions as I was asking them. They wanted to know "Can you be a roamer all your life?" "Do most roamers go back home?" "How happy are long-term roamers?" and "What does everyone else say?"

I can't provide simple replies to these thorny questions, but my favorite insight comes from Amine Goraieb, a finance professional who was living in Hong Kong at the time of our interview. He has spent more of his life working around the world than in his native Lebanon. After discussing the pros and cons of roaming at length, Amine finally threw up his hands and laughed. "Everyone has neuroses regardless of where they live or what they do. From the array of options, this is an excellent choice. It's a good complex to have. At least it's interesting!"

We might not all have the same yen to dive headfirst into our own anxieties, but Amine has a point. So if you're a roamer who's not quite ready to confront your own hang-ups, don't worry, you can read about everyone else's neuroses here first. In the following chapters I'll be sifting through my interviews to weigh up how roamers feel about this roaming thing—an emotional cost-benefit analysis if you will. I'll start with the most hopelessly vexed question of all: "Where's home?"

Panic isn't the best way to start a holiday. My friend Anastasia tried not to panic when she got a call from her landlord in London on the first day of our two-week vacation in southeast Asia. It had taken Anastasia forty-eight hours door-to-door to reach our bed and breakfast in Bali. When she answered her landlord's call, she was exhausted, but he was elated. "I've just sold the building!" he announced. Anastasia had thirty days to move out. Searching for a last-minute ticket back to New York was an option, but it was an expensive one. Besides Anastasia really needed a break from her caffeine-fueled media job and other big city stresses. Originally from Greece, Anastasia had studied in London and has been working in New York for almost a decade. She kicked herself for not having bought her own apartment earlier. I empathized with Anastasia's forthcoming moving anxieties. My husband had accepted a job in the United Kingdom, so we would be breaking camp and moving out of Singapore in eight weeks.

Moving house, famously, is one of life's most stressful situations. It's a widespread misconception that the Chinese word for crisis, 危機 (Wei Ji), incorporates the two words "danger" and "opportunity," but it's a useful, if inaccurate, trope that I'm willing to propagate. After scraping the barrel of platitudes to find some opportunity in Anastasia's crisis, I suggested that we meet a local Balinese friend of mine, Wayan. Like many Balinese islanders, Wayan is laid-back and always has a wise word or two to share. When I called, Wayan was with his yoga teacher and guru. He invited us over to his home for a cup of tea, and we readily accepted.

When we arrived, Wayan and his guru were sitting cross-legged on bamboo mats in the terrace-cum-outdoor living room. As gurus go, Wayan's seemed unremarkable. Slight, smiling, and wearing a short-sleeved shirt over his trousers, he didn't look like a monk, but he radiated the same timeless air as the Dalai Lama. He might have been 50, he might have been 80. Wayan invited us to sit down and after the promised cup of tea, the guru offered to read our palms. He assured Irene that everything would be fine when she returned to New York. He gave both of us only one piece of advice: "You need to meditate and do yoga every day." By meditating every morning for half an hour we would sharpen our minds and bring peace into our lives.

That made sense, but I couldn't stop asking myself, "How?" I knew the basics of yoga and meditation, but what escaped me was the supernatural timetable that could tack on thirty minutes to my already hectic twenty-four-hour schedule. How was I going to squeeze in thirty minutes of meditation? For the time being, I filed the guru's advice into my index of other things I've been told I must do for thirty minutes everyday. So far the list includes working out, writing a journal, and shopping. Yes, *shopping*. I once had a colleague explain that my attire was in such a sorry state because I didn't know how to browse. If I would devote just thirty minutes a day to window-shopping, my haphazard forays into fashion could be molded into the semblance of style. Everything from my wardrobe to my soul could be spared the scrapheap of eternal damnation if I could just put in consistent daily effort.

Anyone who has moved house will know that it takes a minimum of four months to pack-up and settle into a new place—that is, if there's no hotel, serviced apartment, or Airbnb sublet in between. Wayan and his guru had no idea what the next few months would look like for Anastasia and me. For my part, I would be pouring endlessly over U.K. property rental websites, selling various bits of furniture on Craigslist, packing boxes, and booking cheap flights for myself, my husband, and our most expensive passenger, our cat. I could foresee the trajectory—I would diligently meditate for thirty minutes each morning until we were down to our last few weeks. Then transatlantic moving headaches (like trying to find a bank that would believe that we were not money launderers) would eke into my shrinking moments of free time. About two weeks before moving day, we'd find ourselves running between frenzied bouts of packing and last minute goodbye dinners. On M-Day, a swat team of movers would descend on us, and siphon the contents of our apartment onto the back of a truck headed for a freighter. Twelve weeks later, and—with any luck—a cat-friendly sublet between, we'd move into our new home and receive our container-load of worldly goods. We would then spend an additional eight weeks settling into our new jobs by day and digging through boxes to find a winter jacket or the Teflon frying pan by night. Yoga? Oh, I'd forgotten about yoga. And shopping.

When I looked to Wayan and his guru as models of serenity, it was because they were. During our conversation, I realized that neither Wayan nor his guru had ever moved house. *Not once.* Their families had lived in their respective homes since, well, forever. For religious and social reasons, families don't sell their homes in Bali. Wayan's father had been born in the family home, so too was Wayan, and twenty-six years later, so was Wayan's son. This cycle would continue without end. When Wayan says, "All life is movement," he means it figuratively, not literally. Seeing the glass half-full when sitting amid twenty half-empty packing boxes requires a higher level of enlightenment than I have so far achieved. Perhaps bad karma from a past life caused me to be born into a life where moving is the norm and repose is found fleetingly between two flights in and out of an island paradise.

143

The average Brit moves five times in his or her life, and the average American moves once every five years. I, on the other hand, would be on my fifth move in five years. Anastasia would be moving into her fourth apartment in New York in six years. "Finding yourself" is an extreme sport when simply pinpointing home on a map resembles a game of pin the tail on the donkey. All roamers are familiar with this constant movement. Even if they themselves are staying put, plenty of their friends and colleagues are doing the *transcontinental shuffle* at any given moment. Those not living the life of a roamer often find this uprooting bizarre, bewildering, and, simply, foreign.

Gianpiero Petriglieri is an associate professor of organizational behavior at INSEAD business school in France. In 2012, he spent a year working and living in Boston with his family. Writing for the *Harvard Business Review* blog, Petriglieri recounts meeting a fellow dad, an "American American," while playing with his kids in the local swimming pool. Upon hearing his accent, the American dad asks Petriglieri the usual opening question: "Where are you from?" He expects his simple question will have a simple answer, but instead Petriglieri's response moves the conversation into uncharted waters:

"We live in Boston," I started, "but we're from Europe. How about you?"

I learned the name of his hometown, where he owned a business, and prepared myself to tack towards our common ground next—the children's age, the local weather, the economic climate. Not quite yet.

"Where from in Europe?"

Fair enough, it's a diverse continent.

"I am from Italy, my wife is British, and we live in France. We are in the U.S. for a year, for work." This explains why the children speak Italian with me, and a very British English with my wife, while sporting an American accent with their little friends—which is what usually sparks these conversations.

"Did you meet her in France?"

I felt the impulse to lie and get it over with. (Isn't Paris the perfect setting for a blossoming romance?) I let it go.

"We met in Switzerland when I worked there." And there it was, the subtle shift in look. My interlocutor had moved me, in his mental filing cabinet, from a folder labeled "foreigner" to one marked "stranger."

The word "stranger" typically implies someone who is unfamiliar to us. In this case, Petriglieri invokes a more disconcerting undertone similar to the ambiguous title of Albert Camus's novel *L'Étranger*, which is translated into English as either *The Stranger* or *The Outsider*. To the American dad, Petriglieri is not just a stranger who might become familiar, but an outsider who will never completely belong in this place—*his* place.

The questions "Where are you from?" or "Where's home?" often imply a secondary sense: "Where, ultimately, do you *belong*?" But as Petriglieri writes, home is often the place roamers *least* belong:

> *A Facebook picture of an old friend's kids on the same beaches where we grew up can be enough to spark that vague unease, the feeling that our bond is made of blood and history but no longer of shared habits, context or enterprise. It is in those encounters, where I am not even a foreigner, that I feel most like a stranger—a misfit by choice…For many years now, I have spent my days in circles where careers and families like mine are the norm….compared with most managers I teach, I have moved infrequently, and not that far. "These are my people," one [student] told me recently, pointing to her classmates. "I feel more at home with them than I do where I was born."*

In *The Wizard of Oz*, Dorothy wants nothing more than to go back home. She clicks together the heels of her magic ruby slippers, repeating, "There's no place like home. There's no place like home." For Dorothy, home is Kansas and Kansas is where she wants to be.

Roamers agree with Dorothy that "there's no place like home," but they don't actually want to *live* there. Mats Klingberg, a Swedish business owner of Trunk Clothiers in London, still "hearts" his homeland, but he doesn't have nagging doubts about having left:

> *We have a digital radio at home, so I often listen to Stockholm-based radio stations. There's something so comforting about listening to Stockholm traffic reports and stories about mushroom pickers when it's mushroom season. It's so cozy. But do I want to go back to living in Sweden? I don't think so. At least not full-time.*

Road works and mycologists might draw a wistful tear to Mats's eye, but this Swede isn't going to shack up in a log cabin outside of Uppsala any time soon. Like the pop duo Simon & Garfunkel, roamers sometimes feel homesick and wish that they were homeward bound, but when their distant gaze snaps back into sharp focus, they often realize that the place at the end of their nose is pretty good after all.

It's not always easy, however, to separate nostalgia from the concrete reality of home. At some point in their lives, many roamers follow Dorothy's lead. Grabbing Toto, they pull on their ruby slippers and make their way back home. More often than not, they reach Kansas only to find that it might be home, but it's no longer where they fit in. Oz is where they truly belong now.

German art consultant Leonie Moschner moved back to Germany, but decided to venture out again after two years. Currently living in London, Leonie says, "I was tired of feeling different at home. I want to live where everyone is like me, where everyone speaks several languages and has lived in different countries." Echoing Gianpiero Petriglieri, Leonie sums it up in one sentence: "In Munich I feel like a stranger."

Although Munich consistently ranks in the top ten of *Monocle*'s Quality of Life Survey, which lists the best cities in which to live and work, it's decidedly less cosmopolitan than New York or Leonie's present home, London. According to the Global Cities Index, New York and London are the two most globally integrated cities in the world, with New York edging into first place. (*The New Yorker* once ran a cartoon with the caption "I've been to cities other than New York. They're cute.")

So if your birthplace no longer fits, where other than New York or London would a roamer want to call home? With unrivaled global connections, copious job opportunities, and cultural offerings to suit every taste, New York and London sound like the perfect terminus for any roamer, no?

Even there, however, roamers don't always unpack their bags, muttering with relief, "Je suis arrivée." Take for instance Danish native Peter Sorgenfrei, who was living in New York when I interviewed him. He and his American wife had decided to expose their young son to different cultures at an early age. When I asked Peter where they might go, he said that they were still debating. "My wife would love to move to Denmark for a few years, but I said, 'No way!' I've had that experience." Despite living in New York for almost a decade and marrying a local, Peter hadn't lost his itchy feet. (Since our interview, Peter has, in fact, relocated to London with his family.)

So if you roam, where is home? After more than a decade of living in London, I began testing the response "London is home," which to me it was. On average, that answer was inadequate for both locals and other foreigners. "No, like where were you *from?*" the person would insist, as if my accent provided some pivotal clue (I've never understood to what). After replying with a one-dimensional but apparently satisfactory "Canada," which is only a small part of my story, I would pose the same question back to my interlocutor: "Where are *you* from?" Locals were often surprised by my question and would frequently reply, "Well, I'm from here!" *Here* seldom meant London proper. As our conversation carried on, we'd often find that I had been in London far longer than "the local," that I knew the city better, and that I was more connected to the fabric of London life. But regardless of how long I stayed, how often I voted, how many episodes of episodes of *Top Gear* I watched, how many taxes I paid, and how much I loved my city of residence, I could never be from *here*.

"The first question everyone in Hong Kong asks is, 'How long are you here for?' I always find it a strange question," says Michelle Mouracade, a Lebanese working in the banking sector and who has lived in Hong Kong for seven years. Michelle's employer allowed her to "localize," which meant forgoing her expat contract for a local one. Now Michelle herself will make the decision whether to leave. "It's impossible to say whether I'll be here for another two years or three. How can you know? You might stay forever," she explains. She pauses and adds, "Or you might leave tomorrow. All I know is that Hong Kong is currently my home."

Like Michelle, 35 percent of roamers say home is "here" when asked, "What best describes your idea of home?" Just over half of this group say that their current city of residence is home, and the other half dance to the tune of Marvin Gaye's "Wherever I Lay My Hat, That's My Home," saying that home is more specifically the house or apartment in which they live.

London-based chefs Yotam Ottolenghi and Sami Tamimi might see the world through their taste buds, but their description of home could resonate with the 23 percent of roamers who say that home is further away, where they grew up. In their cookbook *Jerusalem*, Ottolenghi and Tamimi write:

> *It is more than twenty years since we both left [Jerusalem]. This is a serious chunk of time, longer than the years we spent living there. Yet we still think of Jerusalem*

as our home. Not home in the sense of the place you conduct your daily life or constantly return to. In fact, Jerusalem is our home almost against our wills. It is our home because it defines us, whether we like it or not. The flavors and smells of this city are our mother tongue.

For Ottolenghi and Tamimi, home is as much as place as it is a palate. Home might be where the heart is, but above all it's where the stomach is.

Others are less convinced about their own provenance. "My husband I always argue when someone asks where we are from," says American Sarah Ryan in London. "He always says 'Chicago,' but it makes me uncomfortable because we actually have now lived more of our lives outside of Chicago than in Chicago. I can't ever imagine living there again." Although she was born and raised in Chicago, Sarah's entire professional life has been abroad. "I feel like a tourist at home, but strangely enough I feel comfortable everywhere else in the world." Like Sarah, 12 percent of roamers feel at home everywhere in the world.

Sadly, 4 percent say the opposite—they don't feel at home anywhere. Because the word *home* often implies deep ties to a particular place, these roamers lament their lack of long-term connection to a physical location or simply to a place where they feel they belong.

Some roamers don't mind this dislocation because home doesn't have a set of coordinates, but rather it's a collection of relationships. "Home is where my parents are, although they live in a place I've never lived before," says Swiss national Melanie Teller in Houston. Another survey respondent writes, "Home is where I go for important holidays." Overall, 11 percent of roamers consider home to be where their parents live.

Perhaps American playwright Tennessee Williams summed it up best for the 3 percent of roamers who say that they feel most at home with their partner or family unit, wherever they happen to live:

I don't mean what other people mean when they speak of a home, because I don't regard a home as a...well, as a place, a building...a house...of wood, bricks, stone. I think of a home as being a thing that two people have between them in which each can...well, nest.

"Our children think it's normal to fly twelve hours to see their cousins," says French citizen Gaetane Prinselaar. When I interviewed her, Gaetane and her Dutch husband had been nesting in Singapore for almost a decade. Three of their four daughters were born there. "Our children had their first passports aged 3 weeks and have understood that 'home' is wherever we live at this point of time in the world," she says. Since our interview, Gaetane and her family have moved, and Zurich is now home "at this point of time."

Some find home in a third place, neither where they're from nor where they currently live. James McBride, a South African hotelier, says, "Home is where you are happiest getting into a cab and heading to that place from the airport. My spiritual home from that point is London. Coming out of Heathrow's customs, smelling the aroma from the Costa Coffee shop, heading to the taxi rank and being asked by the cabbie, 'Where are you heading, gov?' is always a moment of true happiness for me. I'm home." Likewise, Taiwanese native Hsin lives and works in Germany, but she longs to return back to where she feels most at home—in Boulder, Colorado. Despite spending the first twenty years of her life in Taipei, Hsin always felt like an outsider. "Even my oldest friends thought I was like a foreigner in Taiwan," she says. When she moved to Boulder to finish her undergraduate studies, something clicked and fell into place. Hsin says, "It was like I was finally back in my own element. I didn't feel Taiwanese when I was in Boulder. I felt more or less just like any other person walking down the street," she says.

Others have more than one home. Jean Olivier Caron says, "Montreal is home with slippers. Tokyo is home with hiking boots. " At the time of our interview in 2011, Jean Olivier had been living and working in Tokyo for almost six years, but he soon moved to New York. I wonder if New York became home with sneakers. (A true roamer, in 2014 Jean Olivier donned his hiking boots and moved back to Tokyo.)

Some roamers have so many homes that their footwear collection would rival Imelda Marcos's. "I have the inherent need to float around the world, but I enjoy, or rather need, to have my Canadian anchor," says Mark Arasaratnam, the London-based advertising executive we met in Chapter 2. Even then, Mark likes to know that there's a place, any place, that he can call home. He says, "Settling down does not mean becoming sedentary, but it does mean having a home base."

I regularly meet roamers like Mark who don't talk about having a *home* or about where they *live*. Instead they say they have a *home base* or describe

149

where they're *based*. That's not surprising. The idea of a base elicits a different emotion from that of a home. *Home base* is where you get if you're really lucky on the first date. *Home* is where you bake cookies.

Experts in semantics, roamers often distinguish between being home and feeling at home. You can't always control the facts, but you can control how you feel about the facts. One survey respondent wrote, "I don't belong anywhere, but I can fit in anywhere."

Writer Pico Iyer might agree. After spending many years wandering around the planet in search of a place he could call home, he finally realized that he'd never be able to hang a watercolor of home in his living room. Iyer said, "Home is not just the place where you sleep. It's the place where you stand...Home is the place where you become yourself." Plenty of roamers have reached a similar conclusion, with 9 percent saying, "Home is a place in my mind that doesn't exist in reality."

When designing my survey, I realized that I could not simply ask, "For how long have you lived abroad?" It seems like a straightforward question, but if you were born in Spain, moved to the United Kingdom where you became a citizen at 7, relocated to your parents' native Morocco at 14, and now live in New York, what on earth does *living abroad* mean to you? If *abroad* isn't a clear-cut concept, then neither is *home*.

In response to my question "How long have you been living away from your home country?" 8 percent of roamers replied, "I grew up living around the world, so I don't see myself as having a home country. I'm a global citizen." For these roamers, expressions like "home sweet home" are unintelligible. They understand the phrase "home country," but it's devoid of meaning. These roamers are both always and never at home everywhere.

Not having a home or a homeland, or even believing in such a thing, is as startling to some people as not having a religion. To non-roamers, it may even sound blasphemous or unpatriotic, but it's not a political statement; it's simply how some roamers feel. If you're one of those roamers, you may at times feel exasperated with trying to explain that your *patria* has neither longitude nor latitude. Rest assured that many others roamers share your sentiments and, as strange as it may seem, they may one day become "the new normal." Perhaps J.R.R. Tolkien said it best in *The Lord of the Rings* when he wrote, "Not all those who wander are lost."

Some roamers decide to stop wandering and set up home in a foreign country. How comfortable should they make themselves? American writer David Sedaris finds out the hard way that while the British government grants him the right to live and work permanently in the United Kingdom, that doesn't mean that he should start to feel at home just yet.

In an article for *Long Way Home*, Sedaris recounts a cascade of misfortunes that beset him after his laptop bag is stolen while on vacation in Hawaii. Losing his computer and stored documents is a disaster, but worse still is losing his passport, which had been tucked inside the bag. Worst of all, Sedaris is stripped of the "Indefinite Leave to Remain" (ILR) sticker glued to a page in his American passport. ILR status grants Sedaris the right to live in the United Kingdom and to call it home, or so he had thought. Sedaris's work as a journalist requires him to travel on a monthly basis, but the process for reissuing ILR stickers (not granting, just reissuing them) can take up to six months, during which the U.K.'s Home Office holds on to your passport, making it impossible to travel outside of the country. Sedaris procures a replacement passport on a stop in Los Angeles, but with a hectic work schedule, he returns to the United Kingdom, but he puts off reapplying for his ILR sticker, which technically is illegal. After returning to the United Kingdom for a second time without his ILR sticker, Sedaris is stopped at the border by an immigration officer. Here is where the real drama begins:

> *[The border official] crossed her arms. "What do you do for a living?"*
> *I told her I was a writer, and she said very sternly that I could write at home.*
> *"Well not about South Korea," I wanted to say, but it's pointless to argue with people like her, so I just stood there, shaking.*
> *"I don't even have to let you in," she hissed. "Do you realize that?"*
> *"Yes."*
> *"Yes, what?"*
> *It seemed she wouldn't be happy until I was crying. "Yes, I realize you don't have to let me in."*
> *I don't think I've ever felt more foolish than I did at that moment. What was I to feel at home in another country, to believe that filling out forms and scoring high marks on a [ILR] test guaranteed me the same sense of belonging I had taken for granted in the United States?*

151

After this border incident, Sedaris realizes that he can no longer wait. He applies for a new ILR sticker and hands in his passport to the Home Office. After two months, the passport is not back, so Sedaris is forced to cancel a work trip to Italy. A few weeks later, the passport is still with the Home Office, so he forfeits a non-refundable Eurostar train ticket to Paris. After four months, Sedaris finally breaks down and asks for his passport back because he simply must fly to the United States for work. Recalling his passport makes the entire four-month process null and void. The lady on the phone reminds Sedaris that there is no guarantee that he'll be let back into the United Kingdom, but he has no choice because he risks losing his job.

"People think it's easy to leave home and resettle in another country, but in fact it's exhausting, and purposefully so," writes Sedaris. "The government hopes to weed out the lazy, though all it really eliminates are those who can't afford an immigration lawyer."

The story has an unexpected twist and a happy ending. One day Sedaris opens his letterbox to find an envelope postmarked in Hawaii. His old American passport, complete with ILR sticker, is inside. The anonymous sender had found Sedaris's computer bag, devoid of the laptop but with the passport still hiding in the pocket. Thanks to the Good Samaritan, Sedaris again has the right to remain in the United Kingdom, but he has learned that home is not always where the heart is.

Ed Smith is on the other side of the planet, but he too knows what it's like to make a home away from home. Ed lived in China for twenty-two years, but unlike Sedaris, he never had the official right to remain; almost no foreigner in China has. Of the 600,000 foreigners living in China, only 5,000 have permanent residence status. Despite starting and running a successful consulting business in China, Ed was not one of the lucky 5,000. Like virtually all foreigners in China, Ed received only a one-year visa. "There are more Chinese permanent residents in Melbourne alone," says Ed, an Australian citizen. Ed's visa was renewed year-on-year, but that never gave him a future guarantee or stability. It was one of several factors that contributed to Ed's decision to return to Australia in 2014.

Mark Kitto also called China home, but after sixteen years, he too decided to call it quits. Married to a Chinese national and with two kids who were born and raised in China, Kitto explains his departure in his widely circulated article "You'll Never Be Chinese: Why I'm leaving the country I loved." A slew of grievances inform Kitto's decision, including the confiscation of his successful multi-million dollar publishing business and a *Groundhog Day*-style seizure of his second smaller business. But as the title of his article suggests, what finally drives Kitto out of China is his realization of one jarring misalignment: Regardless of how much he invests of himself and his family in China, he will always be treated as an outsider.

In response to his article, one person living abroad wrote this to me:

> *I guess you can replace China with Singapore or any other country we live(d) in as global nomads, expats, or temporary guests. To me it raises increasingly the question if adopting your new "motherland" or being successful in a foreign environment is always appreciated by the host country population or if sometimes being completely ignorant (a typical expat who does not know anything about local news, does not try local food, does not mingle etc.) actually is the easier option in terms of expectations and in order to avoid disappointment.*

Whatever your personal experience or ideals, plenty of us are guilty of believing that globalization means we can go anywhere on the planet. In particular, those with the border control equivalent of a black Amex—a "good" passport—have become accustomed to open borders. Yet why should we expect a warm welcome? We all believe that we're not "that" kind of migrant who is here to suck the social security system dry. Why won't the bouncer (a.k.a. immigration officer) let us in? Doesn't he know we have a black Amex?! Doesn't he know that we're here to enrich the club's coffers?

Recently, a friend of mine was irked when the bouncer who had let him into the club was now firmly asking him to leave. My friend holds a "good" German passport, but does not possess a "good" academic degree. Despite holding what the Germans consider a perfectly respectable technical degree and having expertise in his field, my friend couldn't find a way of renewing his Singaporean work visa because he does not have a university degree. Singapore increasingly accepts only highly skilled foreign workers with a university degree or low-skilled temporary workers on the other end of the scale. It turns out that although my friend had the right black Amex, he was wearing the wrong shoes.

The same German friend was shocked to learn that it's illegal for those with Ph.D.'s from Singapore to use the "Dr." title in Germany. Germany permits only those with a doctorate from the United States, Canada, Israel, Australia, Japan, and other E.U. countries to use the title. In an interview with the *Washington Post*, Dr. Gary Smith, director of the American Academy in Berlin says, "It's really an absurd situation in a globalized world." Absurd or not, it is *verboten*. It turns out that the concept of globalization applies more to products than it does to people.

Once you're inside the fold, the United States often offers foreigners another alternative. "I can't vote and I can't be drafted, but otherwise I'm treated as an American," says Norwegian citizen Tor Jakobsen, a green card holder in New York. Built by immigrants, the United States is famously still one of the places where immigrants can make it big. Snug as a bug, Tor may feel at home in the United States, but at fundamental junctures he might be reminded that he's not part of the inner circle. "If my American wife were to die, because we have a child together, I'm considered a flight risk," says Tor. "All our assets would be taxed at 35 percent immediately with the presumption that I will expatriate from the U.S." Even one of the most spectacularly successful and popular American immigrants, Arnold Schwarzenegger, isn't allowed to run for President because he was born abroad (otherwise he'd apparently stand a chance of winning).

Setting up home abroad might be right for you, but don't confuse that with having been born a local. Roamers may live by the generous phrase *mi casa, su casa* ("my home is your home"), but inverting the idiom to "your home is my home" is a lot easier than inverting the sentiment. Even if you promise to make your own breakfast in the morning and to tidy the guestroom, your host may prefer you *not* to stay "until further notice." That might not be particularly generous of your host, and it's not how your family would treat him were he your guest, but there's not much you can do about it.

Despite the emotional hazards of setting up home abroad, most of us would have it no other way. We might not be regulars, but we're here to make the most of it when the bouncer lets us in, particularly if he does it with a smile. (It always warmed the cockles of my heart when, upon returning from foreign travels, Singapore's automated border patrol screen would greet me with the message, "Welcome home PATHA, CM.")

When David Sedaris returns back to the United Kingdom for the first time with the ILR sticker in his passport, he sails through border patrol without incident. He can't remember if the border guard says, "Welcome home," or simply shouts down the line, "Next!" But in the manner of people who are now part of the *in crowd*, Sedaris writes, "I didn't quite bother to listen."

Amin Maalouf is one of France's most respected writers. He won the country's top literary prize, Le Prix Goncourt, and was elected to the hyper-prestigious Académie française. (The closest English-language equivalent might be winning the Pulitzer Prize *and* getting crowned Miss America. It's a big deal.)

There's only one problem—Amin Maalouf is not French. A long-time resident of Paris, Maalouf spent the first twenty-two years of his life in Lebanon before moving to France, where he has lived for over forty years. In his critically acclaimed essay *In The Name of Identity: Violence and the Need to Belong*, Maalouf writes that people regularly ask whether he feels more French or more Lebanese. He rejects the idea altogether:

> *So am I half French and half Lebanese? Of course not. Identity can't be compartmentalised. You can't divide it up into halves or thirds or any other separate segments. I haven't got several identities: I've got just one, made up of many components in a mixture that is unique to me, just as other people's identity is unique to them as individuals.*

Still, the curious ones push Maalouf to choose and explain how he feels "deep down inside." They insist that when push comes to shove, Maalouf *must* feel more pride or more sympathy for one country or the other, no? "Non," replies Maalouf:

> *For a long time I found this oft-repeated question amusing, but it no longer makes me smile. It seems to reflect a view of humanity which, though it is widespread, is also in my opinion dangerous. It presupposes that "deep down inside" everyone there is just one affiliation that really matters, an "essence" determined once and for all at birth, never to change thereafter. As if the rest, all the rest—a person's whole journey through time as a free agent; his own individual tastes, sensibilities and affinities; in short his life itself—counted for nothing.*
>
> *Anyone who claims a more complex identity is marginalised. But a young*

155

man born in France of Algerian parents clearly carries within him two different allegiances or "belongings," and he ought to be allowed to use both. For the sake of argument I refer to two "belongings," but in fact such a youth's personality is made up of many more ingredients. Within him, French, European and other western influences mingle with Arab, Berber, African, Muslim and other sources, whether with regard to language, beliefs, family relationships or to tastes in cooking and the arts. This represents an enriching and fertile experience if the young man in question feels free to live it fully—if he is encouraged to accept it in all its diversity. But it can be traumatic if whenever he claims to be French other people look on him as a traitor or renegade, and if every time he emphasises his ties with Algeria and its history, culture and religion he meets with incomprehension, mistrust or even outright hostility.

Maalouf is worried that this need to choose sides breeds violence. Those who add "roamer" to their growing catalogue of identities are unlikely to take up arms, but they can sympathize with the weariness that this forced compartmentalization brings. We all have aspects that will never change because we can't change them, such as our race and our family ancestry. On the other hand, other things like nationality and religion seem fundamental, but in fact they are acquired. You will always have the same parents and you will continue to be black or white, but you can swap your Kenyan citizenship for American, you can convert from Christianity to Islam, and you can change your allegiance from the New York Yankees to the Chicago White Sox.

Even something as seemingly telltale as an accent means little. When I met beautician Adriana Wong in London and asked where she was from, I half-expected her to say Canada because we share the same accent. Instead she replied, "Hong Kong." Adriana had never lived in Canada or the United States. She acquired her accent from a patchwork of influences: "My dad is from Hong Kong, but my mom is American-born Chinese, so I guess that played a role," she says. "I went to the British School in Hong Kong, but I also spent a lot of time watching American TV shows and listening to American music. Funnily enough, my older sister has a totally British accent even though we had the same parents and the same education." In London, people routinely ask Adriana where she's from, but her sister, who also lives in the United Kingdom, doesn't face the same line of interrogation. "Because of her accent, everyone assumes my sister is from the U.K.," says Adriana. In other words, they presume her sister belongs "here," but Adriana doesn't.

Artist Milena Dragicevic believes that standing apart from the crowd has its advantages. "For me, being an outsider is a good thing," she says. "You have a much sharper perspective. You question things others take for granted." As a child, Milena emigrated from Serbia to Canada with her family. She moved to London in the late 1990s to attend art school. Milena has since married an Englishman, with whom she has a daughter, and continues to live in London. In Canada, Milena is typically described as Canadian-Serbian, but in the United Kingdom Milena's heritage is painted with broader brushstrokes. "Now I'm just Canadian to most people because of my accent. But then curators usually say I'm Serbian because I have a Serbian name and the war seems to give them a more interesting story." Milena did indeed suffer the Yugoslav Wars, but more through the experience of her extended family members who became refugees while her immediate family was safe in Canada. "There's your own reality and the other person's reality or perception of you. People start rewriting your history and then I too start rewriting it to make it more comprehensible," she says. Like a Cubist painting, Milena's three-dimensional past is squashed onto a two-dimensional surface to fit a narrative that others find more accessible.

In some instances, these reductions can lead to surprising but advantageous outcomes. Jana Cooke left the Czech Republic to study abroad in Australia. Famous for its sandy beaches and a great education system, Australia is an increasingly popular destination for foreign students. Jana met her future husband, an Australian, and stayed on after her studies. The couple now has three children, and Jana has since become an Australian citizen. New citizens, however, are not always met with the warmest of welcomes, sometimes finding themselves at the sharp end of barbed comments or sentiments. "Everyone in Australia sees me as an immigrant even though I didn't go there to look for a higher standard of living," says Jana. When Jana moved abroad to Singapore with her husband and children, she found herself in a totally new social situation. "My husband and I are *both* foreigners here in Singapore," she says. "People might call us foreigners, but they don't look down on us." The vast differences between Jana's birth country and her husband's are suddenly wiped out. Oversimplifications can be frustrating, but at times like this, they can be liberating.

You can cook a curry with all the metaphors roamers use to describe their own jumble of races and nationalities:

Bananas: yellow on the outside, white on the inside (e.g., American-born Chinese).
Coconuts: brown on the outside, white on the inside (e.g., Europeans of African origin).
Eggs: white on the outside, yellow on the inside (e.g., Caucasians born in Asia).

Beneath the humor is a sense of not exactly fitting in here, there, or anywhere. Visible (and audible) minorities are regularly asked, "Where's home?" The interlocutors seldom realize that the question implies that they don't belong here. One respondent to my survey writes that he doesn't accept these sorts of ethnic abbreviations:

I believe one's "culture" is where one chooses it to be from. For example, some Indians born in the U.S. will call themselves Non-resident Indians and Americans. I do not. I call myself 100 percent American, even though others would categorize me as American and Indian. A person is their meme: a unit of culture not their genetic make-up (there is no Indian gene, for example).

There's no point in denying that race, color, and creed matter. Prejudice is still deeply ingrained in every culture and society. What matters is how you look at it. The roaming community provides an environment that says, "The devil may care where you're from, but I don't." Roamers don't question the right to a hazy or multifarious national identity and culture. Like Amin Maalouf, they see it in a positive light—it allows everyone to fit in.

Quibblers say that all this ambiguity leads to fickleness and a lack of accountability. Isn't roaming just a gateway drug to the disintegration of societies bound together by common values? Don't globalization and dual nationalities split deep-rooted, and even *necessary*, loyalties?

Maalouf's view is more hopeful: "Globalisation offers a unique opportunity for an inclusive society where everyone is allowed multiple identities instead of boiling identity down to oversimplified monolithic categories, which encourage seclusion." Maalouf's grand ambitions for globalization are, admittedly, rather grand. Still, some of these pipe dreams are seeping into reality. In the summer of 2014, the besieged residents of the Gaza Strip struck up an unlikely alliance with the besieged residents of Ferguson, Missouri. Protesting the police murder of unarmed black teenager Michael Brown, Ferguson rioters chanted "Gaza Strip! Gaza Strip!" when meeting lines of heavily armed police. Gaza residents, who by then had experienced weeks of shelling by the Israeli army, sent back words of support and advice on Twitter. Americans and Arabs often find themselves on opposite sides of the proverbial divide, but amid the fog of tear gas and mortar rounds, these Arabs of Gaza and black Americans of Ferguson became exotic brothers and sisters in arms.

This droplet in the sea of history isn't going to change the course of geopolitics or even local politics, but finding common ground across ethnic, religious, and racial lines—and thousands of miles—shows there's hope yet. (Though I can't argue with the sourpuss who says that the fastest way to create friends is to find a common enemy, in this case the respective authorities.)

In another book, *Origins: A Memoire*, Amin Maalouf rejects the term *family roots* in favor of *family origins*:

> *I don't like the word "roots." Roots burrow into the ground, twist in the mud, and thrive in darkness; they hold trees in captivity from their inception and nourish them at the price of blackmail: "Free yourself and you'll die!"*
>
> *Trees are forced into resignation; they need their roots. Men do not. We breathe light and covet the heavens. When we sink into the ground, we decompose. The sap from our native soil does not flow upward from our feet to our heads; we use our feet only to walk…And we die, just as we were born, at the edge of a road not of our choosing.*

You don't have to roam around the world to espouse Maalouf's philosophy, but roaming makes it easier, or even necessary, to agree. Immigrants plant trees and make a new home in their host country, while expats travel the world knowing that they will eventually go back to their old tree, rooted on home soil. Roamers might be clear about their origins, but they're not going to let themselves be fastened to the ground. They are walking the earth, admiring the forests as they go along, maybe taking a bonsai tree along for company.

I'd love to end on that high note, but the truth is that not all of us are made of such resilient stuff. Roots might shackle trees to the earth, but they also stabilize them. When a storm strikes, shallow roots can spell disaster for a tree. When you're walking the open road, where do you find shelter when a storm hits? Home is more than just a place with a set of particular coordinates. The idea of home conveys security, reliability, and belonging. An unstable base can issue torrents of existential angst. Many roamers are left struggling with questions like "Can I feel grounded without having one particular home?" or "Can I raise stable, non-neurotic children while roaming around the world?" or "Why can't I be like everyone else and have one clearly defined home?" The good news is that you *are* like everyone else, or at least you're like plenty of other roamers who are just as confused.

Some readers may ask, "So what am I supposed to *do* about this?" I'm afraid you'll have to take that question to your shrink, your oracle at Delphi, or wherever you go to request guidance. The only advice I can offer is that if you're feeling lost and adrift without a home, it may be wise to seek counsel. If you haven't yet made peace with your own understanding of home, it may be affecting other areas of your life further up the food chain of emotions. Don't worry too much, though. *Post home-onal stress* may be a new entry in the Dictionary of Psychological Disorders, but from the array of available afflictions, it's a good complex to have.

CHAPTER 9

WE'LL ALWAYS HAVE PARIS: ROAMERS ON LOVE, DIVORCE, AND OTHER JUICY STUFF

"My love life was so colorful that my friends encouraged me to start a blog," says Lana G., an American PR manager in London. "I found that idea utterly depressing. I admit that my adventures were pretty exotic, but I didn't want a blog-worthy love life. I wanted to be normal—well, at least *mostly* normal." Lana laughs.

Excuse the pun, but Lana isn't alone. Relationships are among the most breathtaking, infuriating, humbling parts of our existence. At the best of times it can take a cartographer to navigate affairs of the heart. Roamers have a few extra miles of uncharted territory. How can you find a soul mate or a BFF when you don't know where the fig you'll be in six months? Or even where you *want* to be in six months?

In this case, even Lana's shrink didn't really get to the heart of the matter. "My therapist was really nice, but she really didn't understand what it means to live abroad," says Lana. Eventually Lana herself understood what was wrong in her case. "My parents, my grandparents, and my whole extended family were thousands of miles away. They had grounded me for my entire life, and now it was like a rug had been pulled out from under me. I hadn't fully appreciated how important they were for me. When I looked around, I realized it was the same for many of the men I dated. It was like we were all living in some weird adaptation of *The Lord of the Flies*—there were no adults around to provide some perspective." Hoping to one day make her way back to the United States, Lana tried to date fellow Americans, but as luck would have it, she fell head over heels for a Latvian. Now married with kids, Lana doubts that she'll move back closer to her family, but says that her husband and children now provide the stability she needs.

Lana says that her single friends are asking the same questions she was asking herself a few years ago: "What if I fall in love and my partner won't want to move back to my home country?" or "I love him, but wouldn't it be better to listen to my family and marry someone of my own heritage?"

or "Would we be able to agree on living in a place that will both make us happy and provide a stable environment in which to raise children?"

These are all valid concerns. None have a simple response, so "dinner for one" is a reasonable default option. This may explain why so many roamers—42 percent—are single. You might expect that roamers pair up as they age, but the numbers change very little. Those over the age of 40 may have married and divorced, but 39 percent say that they are single today. Across all age groups, the fairer sex is more likely to be footloose and fancy-free: 46 percent of roaming women versus 38 percent of roaming men are single. It's unclear where the discrepancy lies. Perhaps more gay male couples are roaming or more men are dating and marrying local women.

Many single roamers confess that they are wary of becoming too intimate with a partner for fear of creating heartbreak down the road. "Moving around creates a lot of dilemmas when you're sharing your life with someone," says Jean Olivier Caron, our French Canadian banker in Tokyo. Roamers regularly need to make tough choices about where to work and live, decisions that, for some, are already too fraught and complicated to share with another person. Jean Olivier admits, "With the twenty-first century couple, you have two careers in one relationship, so you worry about starting something and then having to move." Jean Olivier is not fatalistic, but he appreciates the complexities roaming entails: "I initially wanted to share this international perspective with someone I love, but this way of life changes your social canvas."

"Couples need time to grow, and if you're in a transitional lifestyle, it's difficult to get to know each other," says Adriana Wong in Los Angeles. Originally from Hong Kong, Adriana says that her married sister regularly admonishes her to "stop bouncing around so much" if she wants to form a lasting bond. It's tricky to form a lifelong relationship when you're always on the go-go-go.

Not to mention that modern romance is *already* a fraught concept. Some psychologists say that we're asking for too much. Esther Perel, author of *Mating in Captivity*, says:

> *We come to one person, and we basically are asking them to give us what once an entire village used to provide: Give me belonging, give me identity, give me continuity, but give me transcendence and mystery and awe. Give me novelty, give me familiarity. Give me predictability, give me surprise.*

Is that why are so many roamers are single? We ask for what a village would provide and we don't even belong to a village anymore? Bachelor- and bachelorette-hood is on the rise everywhere, but roamers are surpassing national averages. Some psychologists hypothesize that all of us face an internal tug-of-war between deeper intimacy with another human being and deeper emotional isolation. For many roamers, uncertainty about their own future may be tipping the balance in favor of self-reliance.

Then again, roaming might be more the result than the cause. Maybe a large proportion of roamers are single by choice. They have no desire to couple up and have therefore taken to the road. Despite their genuine wish to live alone, they are bombarded by family and peers to couple up, particularly if they live in their home country. Bella DePaulo, author of *Singled Out*, put it this way: "there are social costs to something as innocuous as saying that you are happy, if you are single, and saying that you choose to be single....When single people say they are happy, [others] do not believe them." Studies show that up to 55 percent of singletons have zero inclination to hook up with anyone. Or as one bumper sticker puts it: *I'm not looking for my other half because I'm not a half.*

If you're single at heart, you're lucky because roaming is designed for one. If you're still looking for true love, don't blame yourself. It's not easy roaming *plus one* (or even *plus little ones*). In the meantime, don't fret. A colorful love life might not be what you're after, but as the saying goes, every terrible romance contains the seeds of a wonderful story. Maybe that blog isn't such a bad idea after all.

So for those who want it, is love on the run doomed? Not according to the majority of roamers who have a significant other: 40 percent are married or partnered for life, and a further 18 percent are in a relationship. Of these, a staggering number is found in translation: 67 percent have a partner who was born in a different country. Roamers are the embodiment of the United Nation's goal to "develop friendly relations among nations."

Marrying someone from a foreign country is one of the top reasons for living abroad. A survey of almost 1,000 Americans living in Western Europe found that the largest cohort, nearly a quarter of respondents, is abroad because of a marriage to a non-American living outside the United States.

Emiko and Gonzalo could be the archetypal roaming couple. Emiko was working as an advertising executive in Seoul when she and Gonzalo, a Spaniard, met at a wedding in Thailand. Originally from Japan, Emiko is the daughter of academics, and was raised in the United States, Japan, and Australia. By the time she was 30, she had studied in Sydney, worked in New York, Shanghai, and Tokyo, and had just moved to Seoul for a new job. "Even though I'm Asian, the hardest part was learning how to act like a Japanese or Korean woman," she says. At the office, Emiko needed to be cautious about not coming across as too opinionated or forceful. "Unlike the Koreans and Japanese, I talk with my hands and my face is very expressive. I just couldn't bring myself to cover my mouth when I laugh, as other Japanese women do." Throughout her travels, Emiko enjoyed her time as a single woman: "I dated Americans, Japanese guys, Koreans, Frenchmen, Spaniards...I really had fun."

When Emiko met Gonzalo, he was working in Hong Kong. They began a long-distance relationship, but both privately worried that a commute between Seoul and Hong Kong wouldn't be viable in the long run. Gonzalo made the first move. "Without asking me, he began searching for jobs in New York and Sydney because he knew he wouldn't find a job in Seoul, and he thought I might want to move back to one of those two places." When Gonzalo finally admitted that he was looking for work in a city where they could both be happy, Emiko realized that he was serious, so she offered to move to Hong Kong. New York and Sydney were wonderful, but Emiko wasn't ready to leave Asia just yet. She transferred within her company to Hong Kong and moved into her own apartment. Emiko wanted to be sure that if she was moving countries for love, she didn't lose sight of her own aspirations. "I had heard so many stories of women giving up their high-powered careers to follow their husbands abroad, only for the man to leave them for another woman. These women end up in a foreign country with no close friends and no career. It's a disaster for them." Bearing that in mind, Emiko got her own apartment when she moved to Hong Kong. She spent her first months diligently setting up her own social circle and building her career. "What if we broke up after a year? What would be my purpose in Hong Kong? I didn't want Gonzalo to be my only purpose in Hong Kong. I wanted this move to not only be for him or for us, but also for me," says Emiko. She and Gonzalo have since married and have two young children, but that doesn't mean that the family has settled down in Hong Kong for good.

"We talk about moving all the time," she says. "We're not actively thinking of switching countries, but every couple of weeks the topic comes up." Gonzalo is close to his family in Spain. "Just listen to his accent. He's *so* Spanish!" Emiko chuckles. Gonzalo envisions moving back to Spain in the long run, but Emiko says that they might compromise and eventually move to London. For now, Emiko doesn't worry about it: "We are happy here, but we could be equally happy in New York or London. Spain might be a good option for retirement. I get the feeling that choosing one home is not really going to be the best solution for my fickle moods." Emiko laughs, without covering her mouth.

Like Emiko and Gonzalo, roamers might find their perfect match, but seldom are they the girl or boy next door. If distance makes the heart grow fonder, roamers must be smitten. An astonishing 73 percent have engaged in a long-distance relationship (LDR) or are currently in one. In the film *Casablanca*, Humphrey Bogart tells Ingmar Bergman, "We'll always have Paris." His famous phrase signaled the close of their transcontinental love affair because once Bergman boarded the plane to America, they would never see each other again. Not so today. Roamer couples might not always have Paris, but they'll always have Skype. Technology has radically changed how distant couples can communicate. (Skype sex is a ripe subject of study, but not one for this book.)

Roamers are not the only ones predisposed to LDRs. One American study estimates that 3 percent of all married Americans (3.5 million) live apart for reasons other than separation. The numbers have been steadily increasing since the study began, but there is no reason to worry. Those surveyed report the same levels of intimacy, relationship satisfaction, trust, and commitment as their cohabiting counterparts. They're also not more likely to divorce. Geographically separated couples worry more about their partner having an affair, but statistics show that they are at no greater risk than cohabiting couples. Long-distance couples see each other only 1.5 times per month on average and call once every 2.7 days.

Couples in this American study, however, live an average of 125 miles apart, a paltry distance compared with most roaming couples. When you're countries or continents apart, just scheduling phone calls across different times zones can be a feat of engineering. It's fun to jet off for the weekend with your main squeeze, but sometimes you just want the basics in life, like sharing the flight home together.

Graeme Torre, an Englishman in Hong Kong, is an LDR veteran. He remembers sending blue airmail letters to his girlfriend at home in England when he first moved abroad in the 1990s. The relationship didn't last. "It's hard to feel connected emotionally to a person living 10,000 miles away," he says. Graeme zones in on his fundamental grievance: "In a long-distance relationship you have to act like you're in a couple. In reality you're living as a single person, but you can't act like a single person."

I was once under the impression that couples must at least *live* in the same city to nurture a fulfilling relationship, but I have since met plenty of roamers who have proved me wrong. Take the extraordinary example of Sarah and Patrick Ryan. Sarah and Patrick met in 1997 in their hometown, Chicago, where both were living—for the next two months. They didn't live in the same city for three years. They married in 2001, but shortly after the wedding they again moved apart. The next time they lived together was 2007. So during the first ten years of their relationship, Sarah and Patrick only lived together for two years and traveled together for six months. Sarah explains, "Patrick is a management consultant, so he travels from Monday to Friday. It doesn't matter if we live together or if we travel to see each other every weekend. The time spent together is the same." By living apart, both have managed to pursue fulfilling jobs without either having to sacrifice a career for the other.

In 2007, Sarah and Patrick were finally able to move in together, six years after their wedding. (They lend a new meaning to the seven-year itch.) Sarah was already living in London when Patrick joined her. "At first it was a shock for Patrick," says Sarah. "He came home on Monday to find out that I was at my book club, on Tuesday I had yoga, and on Wednesday I had booked theater tickets with some girlfriends. He felt like he had to book a date with his own wife! On the other hand, I wondered, 'What did he think I'd been doing all these evenings while he was traveling? Sitting at home, pining away?'" She chuckles.

Sarah and Patrick eventually coordinated their schedules so that both were happy with their quality time together, but the story doesn't end there. In 2011, Patrick had a fantastic job offer in Singapore, and Sarah planned to follow until suddenly she too had a fantastic job offer—in London. For the next two years, Sarah and Patrick divided their time among London, Singapore, and Bangkok. In 2014, Patrick decided to move back to the United Kingdom. Still happily married, Sarah and Patrick are currently both living in London—for now.

Roamers can navigate far-flung affairs of the heart with more ease than ever before, but what do they do when love knocks, enters…and then walks out again? When "terms of endearment" nosedives into "not on speaking terms," foreign divorce proceedings can make Iran nuclear negotiations look like an afternoon tea party.

Diego G. is in the middle of a one such romance gone wrong. Diego is Venezuelan. Soon after moving to Austin, Texas, he met his perfect match, a local who had spent time living in South America. Before Diego had even popped the question, the couple decided to buy a house together. Although they both invested in the property, for tax reasons, they decided to put the house in her name only. When she suggested writing up a prenuptial agreement, Diego refused because he was marrying "for life," as he puts it. "I'm a lawyer! I can't believe I did that!" says Diego. After the relationship soured and his wife left (Diego wanted children, but his wife did not), the property became a source of contention. They bought the house in an up-and-coming neighborhood, which is now trendy and expensive. The wife has a new boyfriend, but three years later the marriage is still not officially dissolved because Diego is contesting the divorce. "My ex doesn't even *live* in Austin anymore!" Diego complains. "She lives in Mexico City, and she still wants the house!"

Diego's breakup is unfortunate, but couples with children can find it harder still. Family law varies wildly from country to country. Most roamers don't know the implications of divorcing abroad until proceedings are well underway. In some countries, authorities have the right to revoke foreigners' custody of their own children to prevent them from absconding the country with their kids. In other jurisdictions, the partner who decides to call off the marriage is considered guilty of abandoning the home and has no right to alimony. Women still tend to have fewer assets than men in married life, and in some cases, lawyers have accused husbands of pressuring wives into moving abroad just before calling for divorce in order to protect their wealth in a more lenient jurisdiction.

Husbands also sometimes suspect that they were unfairly tricked into moving to another country. "I'm stuck living in London," says Australia James R., who works in the energy sector. James moved to London from New York with his wife and two kids shortly before their marriage fell apart. His ex-wife is British, and she insisted on moving to Britain so the children could live closer to their grandparents, a.k.a. her parents. James admits prior marital issues, but he hoped that the transcontinental move would bring a new energy into the relationship. Instead his wife requested a divorce. "I don't even want to *be* in the U.K. anymore," James says, "but I have no choice if I want to see my kids." Even in the case of an amicable divorce, deciding where to live with the ex-family can be a huge source of contention, or a fait accompli if one ex-partner refuses or is unable to move.

Destination weddings are wildly popular, but few couples militate against their happy day turning into an unhappy, multi-year divorce. One person hoping to remarry, but whose ex-partner had no desire to help, shared this story:

> *The divorce process has taken me an appalling three years. I don't know when or where we lost the wedding certificate, but it was a nightmare trying to get a copy from the local officials in Bali. I emailed and telephoned our wedding agent, who was utterly unhelpful. I even flew to Bali, visited government offices, but still I had no luck. Finally I looked for help through divorce lawyers in Jakarta. It took me ages to find one who could help. It cost a few thousand dollars, but it was worth it. They managed to get a duplicate of our marriage certificate, and the good news is that in two days my divorce will be officially complete. I did the exact opposite of what I learned in my business classes—I invested into a marriage with low barriers to entry and high barriers to exit. I never imagined it could be this complicated.*

No one wants to fork out thousands for a sheet of paper to prove that you're in a marriage that you no longer want. It helps, though, when you have cash to burn. *Divorce à la mode* while living on a shoestring is a whole other business.

When I met Carolina, a tall, glamorous redhead, I presumed she had it all—a beautiful house, a beautiful husband, and a beautiful child. She did indeed have all that, but she also had an ugly backstory. Carolina was born in the outskirts of New York to an American father and an Argentinean mother. While the family looked like a typical, happy family from the outside, Carolina's father was emotionally, verbally, and sometimes physically abusive.

When Carolina married at the age of 25, she thought her older, worldly husband would save her from it all. She desperately wanted to escape and start her own family, which indeed she did. At 26, Carolina was pregnant. She should have been thrilled, but Carolina's young and fragile marriage was beginning to unravel. Rather than helping her escape domestic violence, Carolina's husband began to resemble her father. After a few happy months following the birth of their daughter, Carolina's husband became increasingly mentally and emotionally abusive. Still hopeful and seeking a solution that didn't involve breaking up the family, Carolina suggested a move abroad to see if a new environment might help. Although neither one had ever lived outside the United States before, her husband agreed, and later that year, he moved internally with his company to Singapore.

Rather than improving their relationship, the move made things worse, and Carolina's husband began mistreating their daughter as well. On her thirtieth birthday, Carolina decided that neither she nor her daughter could continue to live with the abuse, and she resolved to leave her husband. So after only a year in Singapore, without the support of her family or her oldest friends, Carolina garnered the courage to ask for a divorce. Luckily, her husband agreed and moved out.

The ensuing divorce brought a whole new series of traumas. Things had been bad, but Carolina had not realized how bad. "I found out that my husband had engaged in a string of extramarital affairs since arriving in Singapore," she says, still incredulous. "I had to get tested for sexually transmitted diseases." Carolina considered returning to New York, but she eventually rejected the idea. Her own parents had divorced, and her mother had moved back to Argentina. Carolina was no longer in touch with her father, so she would have no family support to look after her daughter in New York, nominally her home city.

Rather than uprooting her daughter, Carolina decided that the sensible decision was to stay put. Shortly before the divorce, Carolina and her husband had been granted permanent residence status, so she had the right to remain in Singapore, even without a job. Besides, Carolina was still on speaking terms with her ex-husband and wanted her daughter to have access to her father, who planned on staying in Singapore. The divorce proceedings were a messy business, but Singapore's laws protect the rights of the mother, so Carolina was relieved when she received full custody of her daughter.

While Carolina received a settlement in the divorce, it was not a windfall. Going from a comfortable setting, Carolina downsized to a much smaller apartment. She considered going back to work, but her qualifications would only lead to a receptionist job, and the modest income would not cover the cost of daycare. Instead, Carolina decided to stay at home with her daughter and tighten her belt. "I couldn't afford to sign my daughter up to activities, so I organized playdates at our apartment to avoid transportation costs. I couldn't afford anything but the basics, so when my closest friend in Singapore would invite me out on a Friday night, she would generously pay for everything."

The stress of the divorce and the new demands of single parenthood in a foreign country were beginning to take their toll. Already slim, Carolina lost a dangerous amount of weight. She thought that she might need counseling, but she didn't know where to look. Websites geared toward foreigners in Singapore offered therapy catering to the traditional expat market, i.e. those with a high income. "When you're a foreigner in Singapore, everyone expects that you're rich. I barely had enough money to eat and pay rent. There was no way I could afford a $200 therapist." One afternoon, Carolina simply collapsed. She was rushed to hospital where the attending nurse pointed Carolina in the direction of AWARE, a local Singaporean organization for women in distress. AWARE offered Carolina counseling services for $20 per session, and she began seeing AWARE therapists once a week. "They helped me understand why I had fallen into such an abusive relationship. They gave me back my confidence. I really don't know where I'd be today without their support."

Carolina was lucky to find the assistance she needed and at a price she could afford, but it took a physical and emotional breakdown to get there. Lower- or middle-income roamers can find themselves in a socio-economic gulf between wealthy international jetsetters and locals with a more extensive network or knowledge base. On most days, that's not a problem. On bad days, roamers can feel alone and vulnerable. In Carolina's case, her story has a happy ending. Six years later, she is happily remarried, with a new baby, and still in Singapore.

Divorce is not always full of doom and gloom. Christine Amour Levar lives by the adage "if you can't fix it, feature it." Like Carolina, Christine, who is half-French and half-Filipina, lives in Singapore with her second husband, an Australian, and her four children in Singapore. Two of her children are from her current marriage, and two children are from her previous marriage, to a Scot.

During the divorce, Christine and her ex-husband consulted a child psychologist to minimize the damage that a breakup can cause. Following the psychologist's advice, they agreed to live in the same condominium, but on separate floors so the children could pop over to see their father several times a day. Nine years later, Christine's ex-husband has moved into a condominium around the block, but the same visiting arrangements apply. "My two younger children often accompany their older siblings to visit their 'uncle' in his apartment down the road," says Christine. "They feel equally at home there and occasionally even share their meals with him. For all of my kids, he is an important member of our family."

Christine's son from her second marriage once declared that, when he grows up, he wants to make a lot of money so he can buy a big house where they can *all* live together. When Christine prodded him about whom he meant by "all," she was impressed by his response. "He included me, his father, his siblings, his half siblings, *and* his 'uncle' and even his step-grandparents," Christine says, laughing. The process of divorce abroad is never easy, but Christine's attitude shows that it can be as damaging or healthy as you make it, if both partners are willing and if they set aside their differences to agree on one thing—putting all the children first.

Closing the dust jacket on *Divorce Tales and other Horror Stories*, now that you and honeybuns have decided to stick it out together, should you add a few little lambs to the fold? An old African proverb says, "It takes a village to raise a child." Of the 27 percent of roamers who have children, several told me that they aspire to live by another dictum: "Give your child both roots and wings." Many parents fret that the global village is good at giving their children wings, but does it fall short in the *roots* half of the equation?

"I'm worried about my children's identity," admits Britt Lintner, whom we met in Chapter 1. Britt is American, her husband is French, and they're raising their children in London. The children attend a French school. "Where will they say they're *from*?" asks Britt. "They're not English." Britt isn't implying that she doesn't want her children to be English, but that they are more decoupled from their place of birth than either she or her husband was.

As a child, Britt never lived outside of the United States, but the family had moved around a lot because her father worked for IBM (employees joke that the abbreviation stands for "I've Been Moved"). When Britt was at university in Wisconsin, her dad was posted abroad and her parents spent several years as expats in Asia before settling back in the United States. Despite living in London for seventeen years, Britt doesn't have that same certainty. "I don't feel like we're completely settled in London," she says. "It's not like my mom who emigrated to the U.S. or like my dad who worked as an expat in Japan and Hong Kong for a few years. We knew my parents were having an international adventure and would move back. My husband and I don't know where we'll end up. We'll probably stay in London or move to France. But we did once toy with the idea of going to Asia." At the same time, Britt doesn't lament the ambiguity. "I don't know what the future holds, but I don't necessarily mind that. In many ways it's liberating not having your future written in stone."

The one thing Britt does regret is the distance between her children and her oldest friends. She had hoped that her friends would act as an extended family, providing her children with deeper roots and more extensive ties. "When my boys were born, I chose my closest friends from college to be godparents," she says. Those friends, however, live and work in the United States and rarely travel to London for holidays. Between a hectic work schedule and holidays visiting grandparents in the United States or France, Britt has little time left to visit her boys' godparents. "In hindsight, I wish I had chosen roamer godparents so my children could meet them more often," Britt says. "Even if the godparents moved away, there would be a good chance they'd be back in town at least once a year."

Children develop their culture not only from their parents and extended family, but also from the schools they attend. In London, both Britt and her husband are foreigners. Like all roaming parents, they had to decide in which tradition to root their children—in the British, the American, or the French culture. London has schools catering to all these options. Brit and her husband selected the French option, but they could have gone completely off-piste. London boasts Japanese, German, Swedish, and Greek primary schools, to name a few. By following the same curriculum everywhere in the world, these offshore schools give parents the freedom to switch countries without disrupting their children's education. Through these international schools, children can form a cultural identity and ties to a country in which they don't live, and in whose borders they may never live (spawning ever more Third Culture Kids).

Some parents are lucky enough to have the choice, but many don't have the income to support an international school, which can cost upwards of $20,000. One worried parent in Singapore told me, "The international schools here cost between $10,000 and $20,000, but you can't get your children into good state-sponsored schools like we can in Australia." Another mother told me that she and her husband were considering leaving Singapore. Despite her husband's well-paying job in finance, keeping three children in international schools was breaking the bank. In Singapore, as in many other countries, state schools are oversubscribed, and local parents often register their children years before they are set to begin. Roamers can find themselves stuck with astronomical school fees that they can't really afford because they're unable to enter into the local school system. International schools themselves can be jam-packed, so getting your child in is not a foregone conclusion even if you've decided to fork over the cash. We all know that children cost a lot of money, but they cost even more on the road.

International education is a booming business, and it's in the business of producing some mind-blowing combinations. I once met a German woman teaching English in a Korean school in Singapore. Diversity is the hallmark of these international schools:

- The American School in Tunis caters to students from over seventy countries.
- The Canadian School in Hong Kong has a student body that is only 40 percent Canadian with over forty nationalities represented.
- The Helsinki International School has students from forty different nationalities. A former resident tells me that a large portion of the student body is made up of local Finnish children whose parents want them to be fluent in English.

Teachers in these schools have to reassess their own worldview. One international school teacher told me, "The hardest subject to teach is history. Math and science are universal, but whose history do you teach?"

How long a family plans to stay in its adopted city or where it plans to go next can affect decisions about education. Heather and Jerry are a Canadian-American couple living in London, where their children were born. Heather and Jerry have both been in London for over a decade, and while they don't exclude the option of moving back to North America, they might also stay in London indefinitely. When it came to deciding about their children's education, they thought global but acted local. "We have a friend who went to the American School in London and as she was growing up, all her friends kept going back to the United States. She was rather traumatized, so the American School was never really an option for us," says Heather. "Our kids are developing English accents," Jerry says, in a distinctly American accent. "It's so weird, but so cute!"

Some parents, particularly those who grew up as Third Culture Kids, are relaxed about cultural roots, focusing on the family unit itself or raising their kids as global citizens. Still others allow their children adapt to the local culture and enroll them in local schools—be it for philosophical, financial, or logistical reasons. Celia Romaniuk is one such parent. Celia is Australian and her husband, Dan, is English. They moved from London to Sydney when their son was 5 weeks old. Their daughter was born in Sydney two years later. When their son was 4, the family moved to Finland, where both children attended local Finnish schools. "It was more by mistake than by design," says Celia. The Helsinki International School was full, so Celia and Dan had no choice but to put the children into local schools. Celia says that she and Dan were not worried because the children were young enough and would pick up the language, which they did. By the ages of 4 and 6, both children were fluent in English and Finnish.

In 2012, Dan had an unexpected and exciting job offer, so despite loving their life in Helsinki, the family moved to Treviso, Italy. Again, the international school was full. Again, Celia and Dan placed their children into local schools, and again they are happy with their decision. The children were settling in well, and after only six months, their teacher reported that both were proficient in Italian. "We believe it's a gift to give our children more languages," says Celia. Celia and her husband didn't have a multicultural agenda when they gave their so many gifts, but they're delighted it worked out that way. "Fate and choice have lead us down a different path," says Celia. "Having kids in the local school connects you to the local community, and we value that."

Some roamers intend to stop moving around when they have kids, but fate also leads them down a different path. Dutch academic Anton is resigned to revising his theories as he goes along. Anton's wife, Susanne, is Swiss and works in international development. Early on in their relationship, Anton and Susanne realized that travel would feature heavily in their married life, but when their two children came along, they prepared to settle down for a longer period for the sake of their kids. They had only one small problem: Where should this *settling down* should take place? By the time their eldest child finished kindergarten at the age of 5, the family had already lived in Bern, Zurich, and London. As their careers progressed and career opportunities came up, Anton and Susanne had to reconsider what was really good for their children. Because Anton and Susanne both were born and grew up in one city, they believed that this type of stable environment was required for a happy childhood. "At first, we were of the firm belief that we were mainly harming our children with each move," says Anton. Their opinion slowly changed. "With the help of friends and family, we began to realize that this moving opens up new opportunities for the children: the gift of learning new languages, getting to know new cultures, and making friends with other nationals." When their eldest daughter was due to start primary school (reception class), Susanne and Anton faced a decision—stay in London, move back to one of their countries of origin, or find a third location. After much soul-searching and considering the impact on each child, Anton and Susanne decided to pursue the third option. They moved to Bern for another year and then accepted an offer by Susanne's employer to take a post in Tunis, where the family now lives. The children go to an American school because it's the only non-francophone school in the city. Realizing that movement and change is an inherent part of their lives, Susanne and Anton are revising the focus of their efforts: "We have switched our approach from *minimizing* disruption to helping our children *manage* these changes and hopefully equipping them with the tools they need to adjust to new circumstances." Susanne and Anton organize playdates and day trips to help the children adjust and appreciate their new surroundings. Above all, their efforts require patience. "Managing these changes can't be rushed," Anton says. "Children require a lot of buffer time."

Susanne and Anton regularly think about the future, but they're not imposing strict timelines about their next move. "We will see how the children are developing and then decide what will be the most enriching experience without unsettling them," says Anton. "Most likely, we will go back to Bern, but it's also possible that the kids will become rooted here in Tunis, and we'll want to deepen their experience here by staying on a few more years. On the other hand, if the kids are stable and robust enough and we feel we would all benefit from going to another country, we'll do that." Taking each day as it comes, Anton and Susanne feel increasingly confident about their skills as roaming parents. Their roaming lifestyle is radically different from how they themselves were raised, but they realize that the world itself is radically different from the one in which they grew up. Anton says, "Our children are gaining many skills that will help them, in the end, become children of a globally connected world."

Roaming doesn't necessarily involve frequent moves, and some roamers may expect to stay put indefinitely. Others may relocate more frequently, but moving internationally doesn't necessarily involve greater or lesser trauma than moving within a city or a region. In all cases, children typically have no choice and can feel helpless unless the transition is well managed by the parents. While adults are better at projecting themselves into their new lives, children tend to understand only what they are losing, such as friends and reassuring routines. Because of this, roaming parents may have an advantage over those working on an expat contract. Companies sometimes give expat families only a few weeks' notice to pack up and transfer to another country, leaving not only the children, but also the parents bewildered. It's hard to reassure your kids when you can't refute the argument "But I don't want to go!" Roaming parents, on the other hand, actively decide to relocate so they may be better equipped to instill a genuine sense of anticipation and confidence in their kids.

As children grow older, the decision-making process changes too. When I interviewed Australian citizen Leanda Lee, she was living in Macau with her husband, daughter, and son. They had moved from Australia when the children were 5. Leanda's husband is Chinese-Malaysian, so when discussions of moving abroad came up, Leanda opted for Macau because she wanted her children to understand the Chinese culture and value system. At first, her children went to a local school with a British curriculum in anticipation of reintegrating into Australia. Leanda and her husband initially told their children that they would stay in Macau for five years, which seemed far enough in the future, but not too far. Five years passed, then six years and seven. After eight years, the family still found itself in Macau with no plans to leave. Leanda decided that it was time to move her daughter into a local Portuguese-language school (Macau's two official languages are "Chinese" and Portuguese). The move prompted some fresh questions. Her daughter's new friends wanted to know how much longer the family would stay in Macau. When her daughter came home with the query, Leanda did not know how to respond. It could be a few more months, or it could be forever. Since her twins were almost teenagers, Leanda decided that they could begin to inform the family's choices. Leanda's husband runs his own international consultancy, and Leanda's career in academia and management is also transportable. When Leanda told her daughter that it was up to *her* how long she wanted to remain in Macau, Leanda was pleasantly surprised. "Her eyes lit up like a Christmas tree! She was ecstatic that she could choose to stay. Even her friends were thrilled." Leanda says that her daughter is now more dedicated to her curriculum, her school, and her friends. "Knowing she has a choice gives her a sense of responsibility and commitment."

Some roaming parents won't move until they have the whole family's buy-in. Others must or want to relocate despite their kids' opposition, so they've got to engage in some pretty heavy negotiations. In the case of refusenik teenagers, this might require motivation in the form of one unequivocal directive: "Suck it up." Those of us with child-replacement pets can resort to the Stockholm syndrome approach: Our pets are forced to adapt to the new environment and may even be drawn closer to us, the perpetrators of their unsettling relocation in the first place. (This strategy may also work with children, but I would be highly suspicious of the psychologist who recommends it.)

Whether you're roaming or sedentary, giving your children both roots and wings is a tall order. Parents who worry about the *roots* half of the parenting bargain might take courage from those who conclude that roaming is actually *good* for their kids, that they're giving them a head start in this ever-expanding global village.

And let's not forget that roaming kids are good for their parents too. As Ryan Kennedy, a Canadian academic in the United States and father of two, says, "Kids are resilient. More than that, they actually help *you* integrate into the local community." Relocation will likely spawn some anxiety, but kids can sometimes adapt better than their parents. Given time, they might have a better sense of humor about it all too. As American actor Rodney Dangerfield once said, "When I was a kid, my parents moved around a lot. But I always found them."

Beyond love, marriage, and the baby carriage, roamers usually have parents and siblings back home who need (and give) some TLC. Parents of roamers might be proud of their kids' achievements, but understandably, many wish that they lived closer to the homestead. Some parents are affronted by their children's choice to live abroad. They dedicated their lives to building a better life for their children. Why do their children now reject this life? These same parents often encouraged their children to travel, expand their horizons, and excel academically or professionally. Little did they know that this heady cocktail of achievement, ambition, and globalization would lead their children to live overseas permanently.

"My parents gave us every opportunity to travel and learn foreign languages, but this is where it leads—both their children are living abroad," says Diana Martin, a Canadian journalist living in New York. "I've married an Australian and my brother works in Paris. His girlfriend is Spanish. We'll probably never live in the same country as our parents again."

Diana's parents are of the baby boomer generation. They settled down and had children when air travel was still a relative luxury. Many baby boomers wanted their children to have opportunities that they themselves never had, such as foreign travel. Diana's parents instilled what they considered to be a healthy wanderlust in their children, expecting them to see the world before settling down…in Canada. With a twinkle in her eye but a twinge of pity for her parents, Diana says, "I think my dad is now getting in trouble with my mom because he encouraged us to travel so much."

It's important to understand how those aggrieved parents feel; the vast majority had no clue that they were ushering their children into a roamer's life. Like home computers, this roaming thing didn't exist when they were growing up, so most parents didn't see it coming. Sure, they wanted their kids to study hard, to learn a foreign language, and to get a good job. Just why do they have to do it so damn far away? These parents couldn't have known that globalization would intervene, sweeping their successful, multilingual, adventurous kids up, up, and away. These parents have become victims of their own parenting success and illustrations of the time-honored warning: *Don't pray too hard, or you may receive what you wish for.*

By and large, parents open the eyes of their children to the wider world, but sometimes it's the other way around. "My life abroad has broadened not only my own perspective, but that of my parents," says American Dana Schwartz. Dana has lived in Hong Kong and studied in Singapore, but her parents have been less internationally inclined. Before 2006, Dana's father had only traveled abroad once. "My father came to visit me in Singapore before going on to a business trip to Holland," says Dana. "He told me he might stay on longer in Europe to take in a bit of Germany. This was unimaginable a few years ago before I moved abroad." Parents who can't persuade their roaming kids to move back home might take inspiration from Dana's dad and adopt the motto "if you can't beat them, join them."

That's the tack that Ian Krassek's parents adopted. Ian is the American banker whom we met a few chapters back. In 2004 Ian was working in Milan but considering a move back to the United States to be closer to his family. Instead, a twist of fate led him in the complete opposite direction to Hong Kong. That didn't stop Ian from seeing his family. For the next eleven years, Ian flew his parents to Hong Kong every November. He called his parents daily and made biannual trips home to Chicago. "My parents say they sometimes see me more than their friends see their kids who live in the same city," he quipped. Ian was happy in his job and his career soared, but he always lamented the distance from his family. "Do I want to be the eccentric relative who flies in once a year?" he asked rhetorically. After Ian had spent eighteen years abroad, this question and many others finally convinced him that it was time to move back home to the United States.

Roamers are living a lifestyle that was largely unavailable to their parents, but let's not forget that parents have changed too. In 1975, the average life expectancy in Europe and North America was roughly 71 years, and in Asia it was only 57. Today Europeans and North Americans can expect to live an extra six years, while Asians have added thirteen years to their average life span. Some cultures still expect children to send remittances home to support the family, but for the most part, roamers and their parents are financially independent. Now that 65 is the new 25, retired parents are often as active as their roaming children. And these active parents don't always want their kids close by, at least not too close by. The 2013 Del Webb Baby Boomer Survey found that 68 percent of American baby boomers would rather lend their children money than let them move back home. Almost 80 percent of retirees are saving for the trip of a lifetime, while only 50 percent are saving for their children's inheritance. We all know that kids aren't what they used be, but then again neither are their parents.

Why do roamers attend more weddings than funerals? Is it because weddings are more fun and if you can avoid staring death in the face, most of us prove to be cowards? Is it because you attend more weddings when you're young and more funerals when you grow older? These theories might all be true, but they're only part of story.

When you don't live in the neighborhood, you can't drop in on a sick parent or grandparent. You can't drive your elderly auntie down to her weekly game of bridge or mah-jongg. You can't attend Sunday lunch with your in-laws. Such family obligations are what drove some roamers away in the first place. Other roamers might love roaming, but miss their families and old friends. They're thrilled to go home for the wedding of their cousin or high school friend, but attending the funeral of an extended family member is a tougher proposition. Funerals aren't usually scheduled events. Taking a few days off to fly to your uncle's funeral might not meet with your boss's approval and might not fit your budget.

On the flip side, when you're new to a country, local friends may invite you to a wedding, but they're unlikely to extend the invitation to a funeral. (Honestly, you would find it a bit odd, no?) Where weddings are inclined to be jovial public affairs, funerals tend to be somber and private (unless you're the Danish prime minister taking a selfie with Barack Obama and David Cameron at Nelson Mandela's funeral).

Extended family members and friends are one matter, but what happens when a member of your immediate family is dying and you live in another country? Italian native Francesca has lived in London for fifteen years. Her family is in Rome. When Francesca's father died earlier this year, none of her London friends attended the funeral, although some had known her father. Two of Francesca's close friends from London offered to fly to Rome for the funeral, but she declined their offer. At the time she couldn't handle the burden of having guests. "Neither of them would have expected me to act as a tour guide, but nevertheless I would have felt responsible for them in my home city. I couldn't handle that extra stress at the time. Had they just shown up without asking me in advance, it would have been amazing to see them."

Instead, Francesca's oldest friends from Rome attended the funeral.

That too elicited mixed emotions. "Friends from high school that I hadn't seen in ten years, but who had known my dad, showed up at his funeral. We had been close as teenagers, but I didn't know what to say to them. You really don't want to catch up on the past decade at that moment. It's hard enough to do so at a school reunion, never mind doing so at your father's funeral. I know they meant well, but it was a bit surreal." When you're mourning and living on autopilot, bolts from the blue can be disconcerting even when they come with the best of intentions.

For those who live in or near their home city, the experience of death is profoundly different. Marc was born in Geneva and lived there most of his life, except for a five-year stint working the United States in his mid-20s. He returned to Geneva six years ago. When his mother died around the same time as Francesca's father, most of Marc's friends, including several new friends who had never met his mother, attended the funeral. The friends were not necessarily there to pay respects to his mother, but to support Marc. Marc didn't have to worry about giving directions to the cemetery or explaining the complications surrounding his mother's death—his friends had all been living through her illness for the past year.

Francesca, on the other hand, had none of her closest day-to-day London friends by her side when she spent two months next to her father's deathbed. Calls and Skype sessions just don't make up for physical presence at such times. Luckily, Francesca's Australian boyfriend works in IT, so he was able to work from Rome and stay with Francesca throughout the ordeal. Francesca returned to London several weeks after her father's death, but she has not yet stopped mourning. "I still have nightmares about my father, and it's strange to talk about it in London. I might be exhausted at work because nightmares have kept me awake for a week, but people won't understand. To them, I was away for four months, and now it's back to business as usual, but it's still very real to me," admits Francesca. "I'm still getting used to talking about my father in the past tense. I'm still processing it." At the same time, Francesca admits that distance from her family has its merits too. "In London, I feel pressure to get on with my regular life, and actually that's also healthy. At the end of the day, that's all you can do."

Regardless how near or far you live from your family, the death of a loved one is always fraught. But once the funeral is over and the loved one is laid to rest, a natural process of grieving and acceptance sets in. For some roamers, however, this sequence of events is not so clear-cut.

Giselle had been working in New York for six years when her mother in Argentina developed cancer. Giselle and her husband took every opportunity to visit Argentina, and when it became clear that the cancer treatments were no longer effective, Giselle took unpaid leave from her job as an accountant to return home and provide her mother with palliative care. Giselle's brother, who works and lives with his family in Barcelona, was unable to join. With the help of a nurse, Giselle became her mother's main caretaker. When her mother passed away six months later, Giselle not only had to face the intense loss, but also had a new burden: deciding where to bury her mother's ashes. Because Giselle's mother had emigrated from Germany to Argentina with her husband, whom she later divorced, she had no extended family or roots in Argentina. Giselle's mother was Protestant but lived in a predominantly Catholic country. She did not belong to a local church, so a default cemetery was not an offer. Giselle was in a fix. Burying her mother in Argentina didn't seem to make sense, but where should she lay her to rest?

Five years later, Giselle has still not decided what to do. "I associate my mother with home and where I belong," says Giselle. "Now that she is not alive, I have no home." Giselle has lived and worked in New York for over eleven years, but she and her husband are not committed to staying for good. Giselle's husband is Austrian, and while he likes to return for holidays, he has no desire to live in Austria again. But Giselle and her husband regularly consider relocating to Europe, and if a good opportunity presents itself, they will likely make the move. This uncertainty makes Giselle reluctant to commit her mother's ashes to any one location. "If I leave my mom's ashes in a fixed place, with my lifestyle, I am worried that I will not be able to 'visit' her. I know it's totally irrational, but because my life is so impermanent, objects and totems acquire a disproportionate importance in my life. I could never bear the thought of scattering my mom's ashes in the ocean or some other non-specific place." Giselle says that she wants to decide about her mother's ashes sometime soon, but without a clear long-term resettlement plan, that sometime just isn't "now."

Just as we're about to finish the interview, I notice a glimmer in Giselle's eye. She leans over and with a conspiratorial whisper lets me in on a secret: "My husband never asked me where I laid my mother to rest. We never discussed it, and I guess he forgot all about it. He doesn't know that my mother's ashes are still lying in a box at the bottom of my wardrobe." After a moment of awkward silence, Giselle and I burst into roars of laughter. I'll be the first to admit that we all have skeletons in our closets, but this one has got to take the cake.

We can't end our whirlwind tour of roamer relations on the melancholy subject of funerals. As Aristotle observed, nature abhors a vacuum. So when old friends and family live way over yonder, new friends sweep in to fill the void.

I was writing in my favorite London café when a couple of guys in their early 30s walked in and sat down at a neighboring table. They struck up a comfortable, intimate, and rather shamelessly audible conversation. I tried ignoring them and drowning them out with music, but nothing worked. Just when I was about to hint that their very private conversation was on very public display, I realized that their accents betrayed a foreign origin. Their conversation swiftly turned to topics covered in this book, so I softened up and instead of trying to beat them, I joined them—by shamelessly transcribing their conversation. Here is part of what they said:

Friend A: *I want someone who cares about me. I wouldn't know anyone or be able to meet anyone in Johannesburg. Here, I'm constantly meeting new people at parties or at work. There, you really don't meet new people. What do I do, go back to Jo'burg and find a job, get an apartment? But I'll have to start again. All my friends and work contacts are in London now.*

Friend B: *You're just at a crossroads in your life.*

A: *I just wish I still had friends back home. We've all moved away and I try to stay in touch, but I can't just ring them up out of the blue anymore. Why is it so hard?*

B: *I don't know, but when we were younger, my mates and I used to chase girls together. We were trying it on with the girls, but it was kind of a bromance between the mates. What about our friend X?*

A: *You know what? I think he's gay. He's gone to New York, and I have a feeling he's now gay. If I think about it, it kind of makes sense. I think in Jo'burg, he just couldn't break out and tell us.*

B: *Anyone has the potential to be anything in the right environment. It's all about context.*

A: *He doesn't stay in touch anymore. But we were good friends.*

B: *Maybe he associates us with a time in his life when he was ashamed to be who he was, and he doesn't want to stay in touch because he has negative associations with that part of his life.*

Conversations just like this one are happening right now in cafés around the world. Friend A considers going back but knows full well what a setback that would be socially and professionally. Meanwhile Friend B, ostensibly in the same boat, tries to look on the bright side, offering nuggets of wisdom. He speculates that "anyone has the potential to be anything in the right environment." I, for one, couldn't be an opera singer in any environment whatsoever, but it's true that a new context might introduce me to a melody that anyone can sing. Without family, friends, and your society implying what you should or shouldn't do, roamers can feel free to explore new or submerged parts of their personality.

Ezra Levy, an Israeli in Miami, says, "In your hometown, everyone knows you since you were a child, and they don't accept or allow you to change as you become an adult. But this is unrealistic—you change all the time. You have to grow as a human." New friends don't have preconceived ideas about who you are or should be; you don't have to endure annoying comments like "My, you have *changed*!" Roamers often tell me they *have* changed—for the better. They're doing things that they could never have imagined doing at home: They're working in a new field, living openly as a gay man or woman, starting a company, or just having friends from around the world. That may be why some 6 percent of roamers say that personal matters, such as meeting new people, was their primary motive for going abroad. And 10 percent say that it was the second greatest influence on their decision to move overseas. Tiffany, a Canadian in Sydney, says, "On one hand I miss my family, but at the same time you develop deep, genuine relationships with friends who become like your family. Normally you wouldn't develop such close friends at this stage in your life." Delphine in India agrees: "When you land in Mumbai, you must make a whole new circle of friends. In France, you have your twenty-five best friends, so you don't need or have time to meet new people."

New experiences, however, can create a cultural gulf between you and your old friends who never moved abroad. Brenna Tinari is an American who was living in Singapore with her South African partner at the time of our interview. She is sometimes surprised by her more stationary friends' view of the world. "When I was back in New York a few weeks ago, a friend of mine was planning her bachelorette party, and she was considering going to Iceland. She asked me, 'Do I need to get a passport to go to Iceland?' I was stunned by the question, but I kept telling myself, 'Don't judge, be nice, be helpful.' So I replied, 'Um…I think you possibly might need one. Maybe you should get a passport, just in case?' Meanwhile, I was thinking, 'Of course you bloody well need a passport to go to Iceland! It's a foreign country!'" Brenna seems to take pleasure in poking fun at some of her fellow citizens (only 41 percent of whom hold a valid passport), but at the same time Brenna is still loyal to her home country. "I'm American and always will be, but I equally feel part of a broader international community. In Singapore I have Singaporean friends, American friends, and friends from everywhere else. It's not about where you're from, it's about who you are."

Some roamers differentiate between their local and their international friends. At least one roamer suggests that this is not a sensible divide. After living and working in half a dozen countries, retired Swiss-American medical researcher Peter Lutterbeck doesn't care where his friends are from, but he does have one criterion: "There are two kinds of people: those that have lived and worked in two or more countries and those that have not," he says. "They don't mix very well, and thus I practice a sort of truncated apartheid."

Whatever their approach, some roamers think that there's a price to be paid for all these new friends: What they're gaining in breadth, they're losing in depth. Lilly Liu, a Canadian-Chinese account manager in Hong Kong, is blunt: "Relationships here are transactional," she says. Roamers shouldn't get too worked up, though. Loose ties aren't just a roaming phenomenon or malaise; they're a growing trend everywhere. As urban guru and author of *The Rise of the Creative Class* Richard Florida writes:

> *Instead of communities defined by close associations and deep commitments to family, friends and organizations, we seek places where we can make friends and acquaintances easily and live quasi-anonymous lives. The decline in the strength of*

our ties to people and institutions is a product of the increasing number of ties we have.

If this is true, roamers are not unique; they're just the vanguard of this trend.

Many roamers say that there are benefits to both kinds of bonds. German-American Dagmar Baeuerle in Hong Kong says, "You miss weddings, you miss birthdays and important holidays. You lose the intensity that you get when you invest a lot of time into people. Then again, you gain a whole new network of friends. I was upset to leave New York, but five years on, I love Hong Kong."

You've got to invest time and emotions into building friendships, so it's not surprising that some people do their due diligence. Meagan, an American in Berlin, says that because she and her husband have seen so many new friends explode onto the scene only to disappear without a trace, they're beginning to conduct social triage. "Anyone we suspect to be leaving within the next six months, or who has already announced their departure, is no longer eligible for choice Saturday night dinner dates," she says. Why build emotional ties to new BFFs knowing they'll likely go MIA? A star is beguiling, until it turns into a black hole.

Milan, a Croatian in Jakarta, knows that no one wants to invest in a sinking ship. He has developed friend-making tactics to make potential investors feel more relaxed: "Whenever people ask me how long I'll be here, I tell them honestly, 'I don't know, maybe forever.' I always notice a slight shift in their attitude toward me. They become warmer, less guarded." Milan says that the same reaction holds true for both locals and other foreigners.

Plenty of roamers are not interested in sticking to their own kind— i.e., other roamers—but it can be difficult to break into the local community. Jean Olivier Caron spent ten years in Tokyo. He learned Japanese so he could understand the intricacies of Japanese life and worked in a Japanese-speaking environment. "Mobility is not just about changing the furniture to meet the same people," he says. Despite his best efforts, Jean Olivier confesses that he was unable to integrate into Japanese life; the best he could do was adapt to it. Even when roamers manage to breach the language barrier, locals may not necessarily want to befriend foreigners because they already have a set social circle, or because they don't want to invest in people who may leave again, and sometimes because they are simply not interested in outside perspectives. They are, after all, the ones who stayed home. Jean Olivier went to Japan to learn about the Japanese culture, but he also gained insight into other parts of the world. He says, "My friends now are from Sri Lanka, Russia, Finland, South Korea, Malaysia, Tunisia—places about which I really knew very little before. This is *my* globalization."

Whether you're a "people person" or an "I prefer animals" person, individuals make up the beauty and the crap of your everyday life. Some of these individuals will inspire you to follow them to the ends of the earth, and others will send you running far beyond their radar. If you've been roaming for a few years, you'll know the joy of discovering new best friends in Hong Kong, followed by the crushing loss of leaving them behind when you move to another city seven time zones away. As hard as you try to stay in touch, it's not the same as popping out for a coffee together. Then again, the friendships that endure across miles offer something really special. Besides, all these ruptures, these new beginnings, help keep us fresh and alive because they give us room to grow. They offer a kind of mental safety net, knowing that you can still make a new best friend at the ripe old age of 40, 60, or 80.

CHAPTER 10
THE BOTTOM LINE: ROAMERS ON WORK, NON-WORK, AND THE TRAILING SPOUSE

Some love their extreme sports, and others love their extreme jobs. Then there are those, like Noa Horvat, who love both. Born in what is now Croatia, Noa has been working abroad for over a dozen years in aviation tax law, and his passion for aeronautics does not stop when he steps out of the office. Whenever he can find a free afternoon, you'll spot Noa with his head in the clouds, either jumping out of a plane with a parachute strapped to his back or piloting a glider. "My motto is work hard, play hard, sleep less," he says.

When growing up in socialist Yugoslavia, Noa always dreamed of going to "The West," the land of blue jeans and rock 'n' roll. In 1996, he got his chance by winning a scholarship to study at the Freie Universität in Berlin. Not satisfied to stay so close to home, Noa managed to land a job in London, and then later in New York and Singapore before finding his way back to London. As with most roamers, Noa's vehicle for living abroad comes in the shape of a cubicle. His price for the privilege of working abroad is long hours, but Noa doesn't mind. "I don't have a life, but it's worth it," he says. "I love my job. I work 100 hours a week, but my colleagues are really interesting, above average, motivated people from all over the world, so it doesn't feel like work."

Noa's work hours are a bit extreme, but he's certainly not alone. Studies show that bankers, doctors, corporate lawyers, and teachers rarely, if ever, experience the mythological forty-hour workweek. Most of us know that trying to stick to a classic 9-to-5 workday is tantamount to career suicide. Most roamers work well above that, with 51 percent saying that they work more than fifty hours per week (and 6 percent saying that they practically live on their phone).

Whether or not we're happily married to the job is a moot point. Most of us don't have a choice—it's right there in the prenup. A few years ago, I was amused to find the following clauses in a job offer:

4.1. You will be required to work a minimum of 40 hours per week, Monday through to Friday, with one hour for lunch each day. Your usual hours are from 9.00am to 6.00pm.

4.2 You will be required to work such hours, in addition, as are necessary for the full and proper performance of your duties, without additional payment.

One little clause and that's a hundred years of hard-won labor rights down the drain. I guess I could have refused to sign it or crossed out the clause, but it would have been pointless. I would wind up working eighty hours a week until burnout anyway.

After the credit crunch, we're regularly reminded how lucky we are to have a job *at all*. Holidays get canceled at the last minute, business trips are considered downtime, and takeout dinners with colleagues are becoming as obligatory as family suppertime once was. These workplace demands are found the world over, but roamers are particularly well suited to meeting them. Why?

If you drew a Venn diagram of the perfect employee, you'd find plenty of roamers in the sweet spot. Besides the obvious factors like high academic qualifications and international experience, roamers have a few secret weapons. For one, roamers have fewer family commitments than locals do. With requisite sixty-, seventy-, and eighty-hour workweeks, who has time for parents and the extended family? Aviation lawyer Noa tells me that he and his wife are now making a concerted effort to spend more time together. "We try to have dinner together at least twice per week," he says. The sad thing about living abroad is that you can't see mom and dad on a regular basis. The happy thing about living abroad is that you can't see mom and dad on a regular basis. If you can't even find time to eat with your spouse more than twice per week, who would have the time?

Roamers have another X factor that many stay-at-homers lack: They speak more languages. Noa is fluent in Croatian, German, and English, and understands basic Russian. Multilingualism isn't just important because you can get the real office gossip when you're standing around the water cooler in Berlin, Moscow, and Beijing. Studies on bilingual children show that they are better than monolingual children at non-linguistic skills such as problem solving, creative thinking, and filtering out information that is not important. *The Economist* reports that bilinguals are better at "executive functions" such as planning and prioritizing. The vast majority of roamers have this edge—32 percent are fluent and able to work in two languages, 30 percent are fully fluent in three languages, and 21 percent are fluent in four or more languages. Just 17 percent of roamers are able to work solely in English. Roamers are better prepared not only to read, write, and speak abroad, but also to think and act in any work environment.

Despite the long hours, changing work cultures, the language barriers, and so on, I met very few roamers who were dissatisfied at work. They might miss their family or old friends or the weather, but most were happy at work and thriving in the creative chaos. This might seem irrelevant, but it's actually pretty extraordinary. Less than half of Americans are satisfied at work, according to the Conference Board's annual survey. According to a Gallup worldwide survey, 63 percent of workers are "not engaged" in their jobs, and 24 percent are "actively disengaged" or slacking on the job. Of course, there's a degree of self-selection—an apathetic, stressed, or unhappy person is less likely to make time for an interview with me. But those I interviewed didn't hold back. Plenty of people expressed frustration with their relationships, life choices, and other subjects, but rarely, if ever, did they grumble about their jobs.

I suspect part of the reason is that roamers are highly career-oriented and make decisions based on what they hope will help them get ahead. That doesn't mean that those who stay at home are unmotivated. Maybe they haven't had the opportunity to go abroad, but perhaps they also don't prioritize their careers enough to follow job opportunities at any cost. They confine their career choices to the local or national arena, even if that means their progression is limited because the company owner will be passing the reins to his daughter, or because the senior professor position won't open for another decade. These stay-at-homers might not want to disrupt their family life, their children's education, or their spouse's career. Some may not want to learn another language or deal with the hassle of moving abroad, or whatever. Sometimes, the idea has never crossed their minds. Roamers, on the other hand, are ambitious enough to look for and follow jobs pretty much anywhere. They want to test their mettle against the world's top dogs, wherever that may be.

And of course plenty of roamers don't just go abroad for the work. They want to experience the country or region they're living in, packing in as many experiences as possible "while they're still here," sometimes to comedic effect. American Sarah Ryan, alumni relations manager for Wharton School, admitted that her desire to have a comprehensive cultural experience reached a feverish pitch a couple of years after moving to London. "I would receive my *Time Out* in the post on Tuesday morning, highlight everything I wanted to see in the evening, and by Wednesday morning I'd have booked half a dozen tickets for the rest of the week. It was exhausting!" Eventually Sarah overdosed. "When I moved to London I felt like I had to make the most of my time here, but after a couple of years I was burning out," she says. She cancelled her subscription to *Time Out* and forced herself into a theater detox. Like Sarah, many roamers are achieving a work-life balance not by cutting down on work, but by ramping up life.

This high-octane combination of work and fun, however, does have a few drawbacks. In the world of physical fitness, the prevailing wisdom is that you are what you eat. In the world of work the equivalent axiom might be *you are what you do…and only what you do.* "Everyone here knows me as a professional," continues Sarah. "My third grade friend 'knows' me better than anyone who knows how I live my life day-to-day." When a friend saw you cry because the school bully punched you or because the principal caught you smoking in the schoolyard, you develop a natural sense of intimacy with friends. But by the time you're polished and professional, there's less scope for letting someone see the more intimate sides of your personality—perhaps even the ones of which you're not so proud. Displaying vulnerability is unprofessional, yet it's often the very quality that brings you closer to others. When your social life centers on university and career-related networks, it can be difficult to get beyond the businesslike façade. South African Adam shares a raw insight: "In Hong Kong, you don't have friends, you have contacts." Adam says that Hong Kong's foreign community is small, so the people are always on their best behavior, especially since most are there for business, not pleasure. "Oh sure, people are friendly…" He hesitates, adding, "but professional." Such utilitarian friendliness never reaches a deeper—and riskier—level of true companionship.

Roamers run the risk of becoming one-dimensional international workers, which might not be a problem until they get laid off. Losing a job is always devastating, but it can be even more distressing for roamers. What's your role now that you're a "highly skilled migrant worker" who is no longer working? Redundancy can mean that you've lost not only your job, but also your raison d'être for living abroad. You can look for another job locally, but what if you don't find one? Without a company sponsoring your work visa, will you be forced to leave the country? But where should you go? Should you go home? It's hard enough to go home when you're flying high, never mind going back with your tail between your legs. That's assuming you're fortunate enough to know where home is.

Those who find another job abroad still must ask themselves, "If time is money, is roaming a good investment?" As roaming becomes more common, it is increasingly roamers, not the employers, who are bearing the cost of living and working abroad. "It took me three years of pushing Citibank to get posted from London to Hong Kong," says British citizen Georgina Hollis when we met in 2013. "I have the same pay as in London, but the cost of living is enormous here," she says. Still Georgina is lucky. Citibank gives her a small rental allowance, which is something most roamers don't get. Even then, it doesn't help Georgina much. "Rents are nearly double that of London. In 2010, the Mid Levels [district] saw a blanket rent increase of up to 25 percent. Imported goods are prohibitive. A pot of Waitrose soup is $70 here [£6], where it is £1.99 in London."

I wondered why, then, was Georgina so keen on moving from London to Hong Kong. "I own property in London and I'm certainly English, but I have more in common with those from abroad," says Georgina. "I've never lived anywhere for more than four years." Born in the United Kingdom, Georgina was only 6 weeks old when she flew to Jakarta, where her father was working. She lived in Jakarta, Hong Kong, Tokyo, Copenhagen, England, and back in Jakarta all before the tender age of 14. Georgina tells me that the move to Hong Kong just felt right. "Asia has always felt like home for me," she says. "It's not home, yet I feel at home."

Georgina even had reverse culture shock when moving "back" to Asia. "I almost fell off my chair when they told me the cost of joining the Aberdeen Marina Club!" she says, laughing. Georgina's dad had been an expat banker in Hong Kong, so when she moved back, she expected to have roughly the same life she'd had the last time around. "My dad had country club memberships as part of his package, and a significant part of our social life revolved around these clubs," she says. "When I moved here, I was astounded by their inaccessibility. They all have seven-year waiting lists. The Aberdeen Club joining fee is over $100,000, and the annual fees are tens of thousands of dollars. There was no way I could afford this!" When I ask Georgina how many foreigners in banking still enjoy the lavish expat packages her father had, Georgina estimates that only the top few percent of the most senior managing directors or partners have a similar deal.

But if the price isn't right, is roaming really worth it? Moving abroad is not cheap. It takes a job offer, a scholarship, savings, a loan, or the support of one's parents to make the costly leap to go abroad. Beyond direct investments, roamers must also weigh the opportunity costs of going abroad instead of scoping out favorable prospects at home.

"In terms of life experience I definitely made the right choice, but looking at my bank account, probably not," says Agnieszka, a product manager in New York. Originally from Poland, Agnieszka got a scholarship for graduate studies in the United States. Only the brightest go-getters from her university in Warsaw headed abroad for further business studies or foreign jobs. "It's funny to go back now," Agnieszka says. "In most cases, it was the less clever students who remained behind in Poland. But while the 'smart ones' were running around the world, our friends in Poland saw new opportunities as the country developed in the 1990s. They started businesses and have gone on to build small fortunes while my husband and I are still living in a tiny two-bed flat in Brooklyn." The stay-at-homers focused on local opportunities instead of spending their income on studying, traveling, and moving as Agnieszka and other roamers have done. Ash Matouschka, a Kiwi in Hong Kong, admits that saving is very hard: "My company paid only minimal relocation costs and adjusted my salary to the higher cost of living in Hong Kong. But many foreigners here live beyond their means because they have a 'holiday feeling' even if they're working really hard."

We all know what it's like to come home from a vacation only to be whacked with a horrifying phone bill at the end of the month. Phone roaming charges are pretty steep, but you don't want to worry about that while you're posting Facebook photos of your fun holidays and your bizarre foreign meals. Unless you're very cautious or your employer foots the bill, using your phone abroad will cost you a bomb. Similarly, roamers only discover the true cost of their international adventures if they decide to go home and open the pile of bills sitting in their mailbox. Tying together pieces of their lives from different countries—bank accounts, pensions, tax returns—are a pain for even the most organized roamer. They might get lucky, but it's impossible to predict exchange rate fluctuations. Careful financial planning can swiftly turn into hopeful financial gambling.

Take for instance Christine and Nicolas, who moved from Canada to London in 2000 for their graduate studies. They stayed on afterwards to work. When they decided to buy a home in 2003, they used all their Canadian savings to fund the purchase. They invested heavily into the property, redoing the kitchen, bathrooms, and floors. In 2008, they decided that it was time to move back to Canada, and they sold the house in early 2009. Despite a steep appreciation, Christine and Nicolas made almost no financial gain from the sale of their house because the Canadian dollar had appreciated against the British pound by almost 40 percent, essentially wiping out any profits. Both academics, Christine and Nicolas didn't have enough savings to leave their British pounds sitting in the bank hoping for the Canadian dollar to decrease; they needed to use the money to purchase another family home in Montreal.

Besides financial and opportunity costs, roamers also make emotional investments. Roaming requires a lot of energy. It takes time to learn local customs, to meet new people, to find a place to live, and to travel back home to visit the family. Getting a local driver's license or making new friends is difficult enough, even when you're not learning a new language to boot. A couple of roamers admitted to asking themselves, "I might be flying around a lot, but am I really going anywhere?"

So when it comes to the bottom line, is roaming a good or a bad investment? Asking yourself that question is about as fruitful as asking a fund manager if putting your money into the stock market is a good idea: There will be winners and there will be losers. If you're seriously averse to losing money, sticking your cash under a mattress is safer than playing the market (or even leaving it in the bank). If you're not the type to take risks, however, you likely wouldn't be roaming in the first place. Roaming offers many advantages, but it comes with hidden costs, and these costs are not paid upfront. They are levied only long after you buy into roaming. As every consumer knows, that doesn't mean you should stop shopping, but *caveat emptor*—buyer beware. Take the plunge, but don't forget to diversify your portfolio.

Shortly before I moved to Singapore, I had dinner with three female friends in London. Among us, there were three master's degrees (Yale, Columbia, and the London School of Economics) and one Ph.D. (Yale). One woman was a director at an Investment Bank, one was a senior policy advisor, a third was an energy efficiency expert, and I was running a start-up. We all had husbands or boyfriends who were taking jobs in different parts of the world—Oslo, Hong Kong, Singapore, and Milan. For all the education, good jobs, and industry contacts, only one of us would stay in London to continue her career while conducting a long-distance relationship. The rest of us were following our partners abroad and had to give up our jobs to do so. It's tricky to figure out if roaming is right for you, and it's tougher still when you're not even the one calling the shots. "We still haven't figured this out," one of my friends commented.

When the animals entered Noah's Ark, two by two, neither partner led, neither partner followed. They just boarded "as God had commanded." Their choice, if they had one, was easy: Get on or drown. Were there a hundred arks, each with a different destination and departure time, the animals might not have had such an easy time agreeing. Which ark should they board? When should they leave? And wouldn't it just be easier to fly?

How do roaming pairs decide which ark to get on and when? Who leads and who follows? When job opportunities come up around the world, it's rare for both partners to receive equally exciting and lucrative offers in a new city. By and large, one roaming partner leads and the other follows. Just under 17 percent of roamers say that their primary motive for moving abroad was following their partner. The majority of these, 67 percent, are women.

Whether male or female, the trailing spouse often has difficulties finding a job abroad. The Brookfield Global Relocations Trends Survey reports on companies that regularly assign people to work overseas. The survey looks at companies that post their employees abroad, so the results reflect a more traditional expat model, but they still offer some interesting insights on the trailing spouse. In the 2015 survey, 71 percent of those going abroad had a spouse or partner. Of the spouses who followed, 59 percent had a job before the international assignment. Only 20 percent continued to be employed during the assignment.

While it might be hard to work abroad, it can be harder to *not* work abroad. Some spouses are happy to stay at home, but the Brookfield study says that when employees refuse an international posting, the top two reasons are family concerns (38 percent) and their partner's career (17 percent). Forfeiting one's career, even temporarily, can put a damper on future prospects and even on the family's long-term income. The report says that there's a "growing concern [that] spouse/partner careers may impact companies' ability to recruit first choice candidates." While the report refers to "spouses" in the generic form, 81 percent of assignees in the study are men. The spouse who follows, then, typically is female.

Roamers who follow their partners abroad and want or need to work must be entrepreneurial. After all, no one has asked *them* to work abroad. They have to come up with creative solutions like telecommuting to their office, asking for an intra-company transfer, or offering to set up a foreign branch for their employer. They might also start their own company or go freelance. Or, like Dagmar Baeuerle, they might actually find a new job in their own field. Dagmar, a German-American, found work in business advisory shortly after landing in Hong Kong with her husband and baby daughter. Although she followed her husband "kicking and screaming," she adapted and to her surprise, began enjoying her new surroundings. "In New York, childcare is expensive and hard to find," she says. "You're constantly running around to relieve the babysitter or arrive at the day care on time. In Hong Kong, domestic help is cheaper and more readily available." Despite her high-powered job, copious charity work, and two young children now at home, Dagmar says that her quality of life has actually improved: "We're so much more relaxed in Hong Kong. We have a great social life, and we spend more quality time together."

Dagmar gets a gold star for her determination, but she's also lucky that she moved to a city where jobs in her field are plentiful and where the language of business is English. Many other roamers are less fortunate because they move to a country where the language of business (and pleasure) is foreign to them. Finding fulfilling work takes a lot of effort, and sometimes the opportunities just aren't there. Many trailing spouses end up taking jobs for which they are overqualified. One American respondent to my survey shared her story:

After studying for years and spending a sickening amount of money on my education, I fell in love with a wonderful man, who just happened to not be

American. We started a family and moved to his home country of Italy. I love Italy, more so than most Italians, but working is nearly impossible. I teach English, a shocking announcement to you no doubt. I hate teaching English. Yes, the money is good, but speaking English does not make me special. I haven't used my brain in any intellectual way in five years. Now that I speak Italian, I am being asked to move again, to Belgium. Do I have to learn French and Dutch now too? My stomach turns and my palms sweat thinking about this. Why did I go to school, why did I study for all those sleepless nights? Why, why, why? I cannot learn two more languages. My emotional state cannot handle the overwhelmingly horrible feeling of stupidity one feels when confronted with these amazing Europeans who rattle off their languages like a grocery list. I cannot compete with them based on this, but I have to believe that somehow, some way my American university receipt, I mean diploma, may actually come in handy someday.

She is not alone. Those who are not able to transfer their work skills abroad must remodel themselves. How well or poorly they manage the transition depends on several factors: the new location (e.g., the language of business, the local work environment, the type of opportunities available, etc.); the roamer's personality and skills (e.g., linguistic proficiencies, professional competencies, ability to adapt, etc.); the support of their partner; and financial imperatives. One's age and stage in family life also play a significant role. For example, if a woman is pregnant, she'll most likely have a harder time finding work after moving abroad (in some countries it's legal to fire a pregnant woman, so fat chance she'll get hired in the first place). Spouses can prepare by taking language classes or looking for work ahead of the move, but you can't do things like taking the temperature of the local job market until you're physically on the ground.

Going abroad can be tough, but going back (or elsewhere) can be equally challenging. What happens to trailing spouses when it comes to tearing themselves away from their new home? "If you're working with one company, then you have one network and it's easier to detach yourself," said Leanda Lee, an Australian in Macau. When Leanda and her family moved to Macau, she worked as an assistant professor at the University of Saint Joseph, Macau. After three years, she left her job but took a huge local network with her. Five years into living in Macau, Leanda was sitting on the advisory committee of a Macau-Australia students association, writing a management column for the *Macau Daily Times*, and even represented Macau in laser sailing at the China National Games in 2013. "When you feel like you're contributing to a community, it's difficult to move. Those connections, those networks make for something very meaningful." Leanda's husband runs his own consultancy with international clients, so he does not have those same local bonds that Leanda and her children have. "He could go at any moment," Leanda says, "but the children have grown up here." Leanda started our conversation by saying she has an umbilical cord to Australia, but she concluded by saying, "Now I have two umbilical cords!"

Most roamers who follow their partner abroad are women, but a substantial 37 percent of them are male. I don't know how many of these men are following male partners and how many are following females, but one thing is certain, the typecast trailing housewife is rapidly becoming obsolete. The gender stereotype, however, still holds sway. Many foreigner-oriented associations like the International Ladies Group and the International Women's Club, along with Facebook groups and Meetups, are geared towards women and moms abroad. These groups sometimes encourage both foreign and local members, but few encourage male participants or dads. Like the photo op of presidents' wives at G20 summits, one wonders where Mr. Merkel is passing his time. A few brave men are breaking down these barriers and signing up to gender-specific groups. The freshly arrived stay-at-home dad might still be a rare breed, but they're growing in number and they too need to find the nearest playgroup and petting zoo.

Whether it's mom or dad, the luxury of a stay-at-home spouse is increasingly rare. More and more, two incomes are required to keep the household afloat. Many trailing spouses would not want the luxury anyway. "I could never be one of those expat wives who plays tennis all day. I would get bored!" says Jana, the Czech-Australian we met earlier in Singapore. In order to keep working, however, Jana had to reinvent herself. She was a paralegal in Australia, but in Singapore she was unable to pursue this line of work, so instead she became an executive assistant. Jana cherishes her family time, but she still wants all the things that come with working, including intellectual stimulation and financial stability. "I had children after I built my career," she says. "I still like having my own money and independence. I don't want to ask my husband for cash."

Happily, like Dagmar and Jana, many spouses are eventually satisfied with their new incarnations. Those who have always wanted to try something different might seize the opportunity to launch themselves into a new career. In my interviews, I met a former marketing executive who opened a swimwear boutique, an executive-turned-fishmonger, a banker who started a jewelry business, and many other entrepreneurs. Most had children and were looking for a more accommodating work schedule anyway. Many were excited about reinventing themselves, despite having put a lot of time and effort into establishing their first career.

Other roamers built flexibility into their jobs from the start. French citizen Inès studied finance in Switzerland, but an internship at Goldman Sachs convinced her that the field did not really suit her interests. While completing a master's degree in history, she began freelancing as a translator in German, English, and French when a friend offered her some part-time translation work. As her studies suggest, she didn't set out to become a professional translator, but she didn't want to be stuck in an office either. Inès quickly discovered her appreciation for having a flexible schedule. "After my first few assignments, I thought this is really great— it provides me with a degree of freedom," she says. "Being mobile is incredibly important for me." Inès has easily transferred her skills from London to New York and now Paris. She divides her time between Paris and Provence, laptop and baby pram in tow.

Sometimes the trailing spouse surprisingly becomes the main breadwinner. I met several roamers who had followed their partners abroad only to find themselves the sole income earner when their partner was fired or was trying to start a new company. Valeria, a Colombian who works in financial services in Shanghai, has been keeping the family afloat for the past three years while her husband is busy getting a start-up off the ground. Valeria says that living abroad is neither a liability nor an asset in her situation. "When one partner is setting up a business, it doesn't matter where you are. It's a lot of work for everyone."

In same-sex relationships, when one partner decides to take a job abroad, the trailing spouse might have difficulties getting a spousal visa or a residence permit. On the flip side, some gays and lesbians are forced to move abroad when their own country will not recognize their union with a foreigner. In 2013, *The New York Times* ran a story featuring American Brandon Perlberg and his English partner, Benn Robert Storey. The couple were forced to move to the United Kingdom when Storey was unable to obtain permanent residence in the United States, despite having lived in New York for seven years and having a local partner. At the time, same-sex marriages were recognized in the state of New York, but the United States would not grant green cards for gay partners. Neither Perlberg nor Storey wanted to ditch their life in New York, but they agreed that a transatlantic commute was not a viable option. Perlberg reluctantly chose self-exile. In New York, Perlberg was an accomplished marriage lawyer, but he was unable to translate his state-specific skills to London. After a year of looking for work in his field, he finally abandoned his aspirations and took a job at an international accounting firm. The move from New York to London hadn't worked to his advantage. "I had a passion for the city and the country in which I lived," he says. "Then in one fell swoop I was just pushed down to the bottom of the ladder." The saddest part is that Perlberg and Story were just slightly on the wrong side of history. Two years after *The New York Times* ran their story, the United States began granting gay couples the same immigration rights as straight couples.

Whether it's an all-male, an all-female, or a mixed crew, getting onto the ark two by two is not easy. That's why some roaming couples are choosing to live apart in separate countries. Others settle in for a long-term commuter marriage. Whatever the solution, a 747 might not exactly be Noah's Ark, but as long as it provides transport during the rainy season, there's still hope for a rainbow at the end.

CHAPTER 11
WHERE DOES IT ALL END? ROAMERS ON GROWING OLD AND UNSETTLING DOWN

So where does the story end? When and where do roamers finally settle down? Do most roamers end up going home? Do they become immigrants elsewhere?

Living around the world is exhilarating, but when the music stops and the lights come on, plenty of roamers stop and ask themselves, "Is this where I want to be?" It's easy to jump on a plane when you're young and all fired up. What's the worst that can happen? If you don't like it, you can always "cut and paste," trying out another place or heading back home. Right? There's nothing wrong with that idea, except this—it's an *idea*. Theory and practice are two very different beasts. Scientists are busy figuring out if we can build a colony on Mars, but plenty of us are still wondering if it's possible to settle down here on earth. Should roamers, *can* roamers, ever truly settle down?

"I want different things now," says Samantha, an American structural engineer in London. She left the United States for graduate studies in the United Kingdom as a single woman in her early 20s. It never once occurred to her that fifteen years later she would find herself married to an Austrian, the mother of two young children, and still living in the United Kingdom. She says, "I felt like I was an all-American girl. Actually I still am one!" Samantha smiles, with an unmistakably all-American smile. A small frown appears when she discusses the future. "It's sort of crazy, but after all these years, I still don't feel settled here. We haven't bought a place in London, and even now, I wonder how long we'll stay. The U.K. is not home for either one of us, although it might be turning into home for our kids."

For some, the idea of "settling down" elicits a warm fuzzy feeling, like falling into your favorite chair with a cup of tea and a good book. For others, the concept is hideous. It's hasty, however, to simply boil these irreconcilable reactions down to personal tastes. The verb "to settle" must accept its share of the blame. It can convey the idea of achieving calm, satisfaction, or ease, as in: "The baby was bawling, but finally settled down." It can also express resolution, as in: "He couldn't choose between getting a cat or a dog, so he settled on a parrot." It can also communicate disappointment, as in: "She was going for gold, but had to settle for silver." These contradictory connotations are built in to the verb, so it's no surprise that roamers approach "settling down" with anticipation and horror in equal measure. That's why *un*settling down is standard protocol for so many roamers. This option, however, can become less attractive the older you get.

They say that the past can teach you about the future. That may be why so many roamers look to their own parents hoping they can shine some light from further up the tunnel. But as much as history repeats itself, it can't be reproduced. Property investment manager Graeme Torre in Hong Kong has compared his life with his parents' and finds them poles apart. "When my parents were single, they lived only three streets apart, so it was easy for them to get to know each other," he says. "When I was growing up in London, my parents spent most of their evenings and weekends together at home. Their lives came together in almost all facets." Graeme's adult life has been decidedly more peripatetic. He first moved from the United Kingdom to Singapore and then Hong Kong in the mid-1990s, and after three years, he decided that it was time to head back home. After two years in London, however, Graeme was struck by wanderlust again and made his way back to Singapore and then to Hong Kong, where he's been ever since. Graeme doesn't know what his future holds. "Will I finish my career here? I don't know. I can't answer that right now. My dad didn't have to think about questions like that."

Because Graeme's dad didn't have to think about questions like that, he didn't have to question where to invest his money, where to buy a house, and where to build his life. He did those things naturally, when the time was right. Roamers have many more variables to factor into their equation. Since many roamers don't know where they'll be in a few years, they often put off important decisions until they feel more settled. This *roamer's dilemma* reminds me of a passage from a story about the Dalai Lama:

> *When the Dalai Lama and his followers fled Tibet to India in 1962, he urged the refugees to plant trees in their new settlement, Dharamsala, but most waved off the idea. The Tibetans said, "We're going to be going back in a few years. Trees take fifty years to grow, what's the point?"*

Like the Tibetans, most roamers leave home thinking that they'll head back after a few years, or that they'll move to another place. So what's the point of planting trees or buying an apartment and settling into a new country when you'll have to leave it all behind in a few short years? Like the Tibetans, however, roamers might be wise to heed the Dalai Lama's advice. If roamers plant a few trees or make other investments in their current place of residence, the worst that will happen is that someone else will enjoy the fruits of their labor. In the words of Warren Buffett, another guru of sorts: "Someone is sitting in the shade today because someone planted a tree a long time ago." If roamers don't invest time, energy, and emotions locally, they might wind up in their new settlement for much longer than expected with no crops to harvest.

Alex Ellsworth, a former New Yorker, learned this lesson the hard way. Responding to a blog post in the former *International Herald Tribune*, he wrote:

> *Studying and living abroad has been a fantastic journey spanning twelve years and three continents. But… expat life has a dark side: getting stuck in limbo, neither here nor there. I've watched as peers back home have married, had children, bought houses, advanced in their careers. Meanwhile, most of us here in Seoul find ourselves living Peter Pan-like existences. I'm entering middle age with nothing tangible to show for it.*
>
> *Except wonderful, rich memories, sure. But the future looms.*
>
> *So should I go home pre-emptively and try to build a life there? But therein lies the expat's problem: there's nothing back home for me now. Home is not "back home"; home is Seoul. My life is here.*

Alex didn't know how long he'd stay in Korea, so he didn't invest. He might have taken the opposite tack—invest in local property, invest in a local relationship, invest in a local career. At worst, he might have had to leave these behind. He might have reached middle age having made a few wrong decisions instead of having "nothing tangible to show for it." Alex's misgivings are not altogether unusual. Spanish citizen Antonio in Manila put it this way: "Sometimes it feels like you've hit pause and I'm waiting to un-hit pause. We're living in a bubble, and you can get spit out the other side many years later and realize that life has continued without you."

Alex and Antonio, though, shouldn't be too hard on themselves. Their conduct comes with the territory. Roamers aren't exactly the settling down types. If they were, they probably would have done so at home. Since roamers didn't want to spend their weekends pruning shrubs in their home country, why should they be expected to plant trees when abroad? Most roamers just don't worry about settling down—at least not in their 20s, 30s, and sometimes well into their 40s. Sometimes never.

The roamers who don't ever settle down still have to face at least one inevitable event that will force them to stop. Several people I interviewed used almost exactly the same cheery phrase: "I don't know where I want to live, but I know where I want to die." One American told me, "I don't know where I'll end up living most of my life, but I know where I'm going to be buried. My parents bought a burial plot near Boston, so at least that much is certain." That lends a sense of security, of sorts.

One thing is certain, though. When you're living in your home country, or at least in one place, things like starting a family or a retirement savings plan come naturally because every society endorses certain age-appropriate behaviors and benchmarks for success. You can either rage against the machine or strive to reach these milestones, but you can't ignore them altogether. Roamers, on the other hand, are living off the grid. They have freedom and flexibility, but they need to work harder at things that most societies consider "normal." Have you missed the boat, or are you doing things when they're right for you? It's up to you to decide. Ayse Levent in New York says, "I don't have kids or a husband, so I'm considered a bit strange in Istanbul." In her mid-30s, Ayse is by no means over the hill, but her contemporaries in Turkey married years ago. "I'm very independent compared to many other Turkish women," she says. By living abroad, outside the accepted conventions of her family and their society, Ayse can set her own standards and choose to live in a place with norms more suited to her own.

Some thrive in this creative chaos, thrilled to set themselves free from traditional boundaries and conventions. Others flail about like astronauts in zero gravity. Roamers might not realize that they prefer solid ground until they find themselves out on the space station. They can get back to terra firma, but they'll have to wait for the next available Soyuz rocket to take them home.

Whatever their preference, most roamers don't intend to stay "here" forever. When I asked survey respondents how long they intended to stay in their current city of residence, the most popular answer, at 31 percent, was between two and three years. I wondered why this was such a popular response. "When we left Paris, we told our friends and family that we would try Singapore for two or three years because everyone wanted to know when they could expect us back," says French citizen Cécile Courbon in Singapore. The time period is both definite and inconclusive. One year is a gap year or a junior year abroad. It's essentially a long holiday, so there's no point in trying something new for such a short time; you can't accomplish much. Four years, on the other hand, is how long you're stuck with a new government or how long it takes to finish a university degree, and that can feel like ages. "We're going on five years now," says Cécile. "We don't know how much longer we'll stay, so we keep saying 'another two or three years' because it's a time scale that people can understand. It doesn't feel *that* far away."

At the same time, it does not suggest an imminent return. To those moving abroad for the first time or moving to a new country, two or three years sounds reassuringly temporary, more like a long sabbatical. Expat and diplomatic postings typically last up to three years to avoid the employee "going native" or losing touch with the mothership. The time frame might also be part of a broader meme percolating through the workforce. Research shows that young American employees expect to stay in a job for under three years (and Europeans are not far off that mark). Since most roamers are abroad for work, it's not unusual that those numbers should coincide.

So where do all these peripatetic roamers go when they decide to leave their current city of residence? When I posed the question "Where next?" to over a hundred people in my interviews, only Michelle Mouracade, our Lebanese in Hong Kong, responded, "I'm here now. Hong Kong has everything I need." Michelle doesn't see herself as an immigrant to Hong Kong, nor she does want to endlessly consider other options. She has committed to living where she is now, in the moment. Like Michelle, 9 percent of roamers expect to stay where they are at present. (Incidentally, since our interview, Michelle has moved to Dubai. Despite their intentions, roamers just never know where life will take them next.)

A further 13 percent of roamers anticipate moving back home after their current stint abroad. American couple Elizabeth Tweedale and Bruce Davison live in London, but they don't intend to stay forever. After I ask when they plan on returning to the United States, two answers simultaneously shoot my way: "Soon!" and "Never!" they reply in unison. A few laughs and sidelong glances later, the couple settle on "ten years." Elizabeth and Bruce have been in London for five years so far. Both have started businesses in London. Their two young children were born there. I wonder why ten years is their magic number. "In ten years," explains Elizabeth, "our kids will have finished their primary education in the U.K., and they'll be able to integrate into an American high school."

Elizabeth and Bruce might not see eye to eye on everything, but at least they can agree on what constitutes "home." That's a good starting point, but how do you take the next step and actually get there? Unlike expats, roamers aren't on a contract that will bring them back home. Some can negotiate intra-company transfers back home, but for most, either they are not working for such a large company or, for whatever reason, their efforts to work back home are met with a cold shoulder. This might be why most roamers are finding themselves living abroad longer— sometimes much longer—than expected. Sixty-two percent of roamers left home expecting to be away for less than five years. Many, if not most, are exceeding their own expectations. Frenchman Alain D. in Bangkok is one of those. He and his Belgian partner have spent almost twenty years living in Asia, but they don't intend to stay forever. "As we get closer to retirement, we constantly ask ourselves where we want to grow old," he says. "It's great to work in Asia, but we don't want to retire here." Knowing how hard it will be to go back to Europe, Alain has a plan. "As a next step, we want to get jobs in France or somewhere in Europe. We want to grow some roots there before we stop working."

Alain works for a large advertising firm and feels confident about getting a job back in Europe, even if it means working for a smaller firm or taking a pay cut to do so. Keeping expectations low is a good strategy because finding work back at home is not an easy task. Many people assume that you understand the corporate and social culture of your home country, but many roamers have never had anything more than a part-time student job in their home country. Like many roamers, Alain has no professional experience at home.

There's a lot of help to be found for going abroad. Alain first went to Japan through a university exchange program. International student groups offered advice and an enthusiastic group of potential friends. When he returned to Japan to work, he could count on the French embassy in Tokyo for help and for regular cultural events where he could meet other French nationals living abroad. But to whom should Alain turn now that he's thinking of moving back to Europe? Alain has family in Lyon, but like many roamers he doesn't have an extensive professional network at home because he built one abroad. There aren't social clubs or "embassies" to welcome this prodigal son back home to France.

In 2013, the Oslo International Club ran a discussion where the question for the evening was "Why do so many repatriated Norwegians find it so hard to return to Norway professionally?" These one-off discussions are helpful, but it's not sustained support for those who are looking to go back to Norway *now* or who are already there but having a hard time reintegrating.

There's precious little assistance for those trying to make their way back home, unless you're one of the lucky ones who want to move back to Toronto. Toronto Homecoming, a social venture, is trying to reverse the city's brain drain by making it easier for talented Torontonians to return home from abroad. Toronto Homecoming runs an annual conference for a hundred Canadians living abroad who are in the early to middle stages of their careers, working in financial and professional services, technology, or retail and consumer packaged goods. I spoke with Eva Wong, co-founder of Toronto Homecoming, about the inspiration for the venture. She said:

> *We were working with Toronto's CivicAction Alliance and considering the future of our city. Author Richard Florida argues that what drives economic growth is innovation and talent. We knew from our own experience that many of Toronto's young leaders and innovators were leaving, so when we considered how to increase our talent pool, we looked for low-hanging fruit. Instead of attempting to draw new people to Toronto or trying to get the younger generation to stay in Toronto, we focused on drawing back accomplished Torontonians.*

Candidates must apply to attend Toronto Homecoming's conference, and only the most promising candidates make it through the selection process. The conference involves seminars, roundtable meetings, and networking events. Forty corporate sponsors attend. "Essentially it's professional speed dating," says Eva.

A big difficulty with coming home is reintegration. Eva says that most people leave for career opportunities and come back for personal or family reasons. But if most of your friends and family stayed at home, you can end up feeling like a complete alien in what is nominally your own home city. Toronto Homecoming provides a new social network for repatriates and other like-minded roamers.

Toronto Homecoming is the most comprehensive reintegration program that I have come across. It's unfortunate that a greater variety and a greater number of them don't exist. Academics, teachers, medical doctors, and others without a corporate background don't have access to headhunters or intra-company transfers (and the popularity of Toronto Homecoming proves that even these routes are insufficient for those in the corporate world). Similar plans could offer a leg up to those without corporate ambitions or to students who have gone abroad for graduate studies. Since recruiting is done during the school year, eager graduate students often end up working where they studied simply because that's where they have access to career fairs and where they get a job offer. Many of these students would have gone home, had they the chance. It's bemusing how many programs exist to help you go abroad and how few exist to help you come home.

A few governments, however, are catching on. Hungary, progenitor of over a dozen Nobel laureates, recently began offering special grants to returning Hungarian research teams. Since 2013, the Returning Singaporean Scientists Scheme has been offering funding and equipment to lure back leading scientists. Projects like China's 1,000 Talents and Malaysia's Returning Expert Programme help to bring the most successful expatriates back home by offering them sweeteners such as tax breaks and living allowances.

Most of these projects have one dangerous flaw: They offer short-term incentives to bring high-value citizens back home but don't necessarily keep them there. The programs may also have one unintended consequence—they may encourage locals to go abroad in hopes of getting bonus rewards for the return journey. If this is part of someone's strategy, it is risky. Once abroad it's hard to predict where opportunities will lead their citizens. Because Toronto Homecoming is a social enterprise and not a government-backed program, it can't offer resettlement packages or treats, but this is to its advantage—it's simply a vehicle for those who *already* want to come back. Still, any government effort is helpful. Most governments, local or national, do nothing at all to help their citizens repatriate. As Stephen Williams in Beijing says, "The Australian government just relies on good beaches to draw us back." The same can be said of the Turkish delight, German beer, and the American dream.

As Eva Wong says, many people want to head home for personal or family reasons, but others are drawn back under less auspicious circumstances. We all know that "early to bed, early to rise makes a person healthy, wealthy, and wise," but it's not easy to adopt that slogan when you live in the city that never sleeps. Elsa was working in New York as a marketing manager and living by the dictum "a balanced life is a latte in each hand" when lightning struck. "I found out I had early stage breast cancer," she tells me. Elsa had lived in New York for five years and had often debated moving back to Finland or elsewhere, but only decided to return to Helsinki after her diagnosis. "I realized how important it was to be near my family," she says. As she faced her own mortality, Elsa's answer to "Where next?" snapped into clear focus.

Elsa's decision was made easier because Finland has one of the world's best universal health care systems and because her family still lives in Helsinki. Were the breast cancer to spread or return in a few years, Elsa knew she would be looked after by her family and by the health care system. Elsa says that she may head out again in a few years, but that next time she'll stay closer to home, in Europe.

Elsa had a choice, and a good one at that, whether to go home, but many roamers do not. Some just don't know where home is. Other roamers who become ill are unable to satisfy their urge to rush back home because they must continue to support their families by working throughout their illness. Sometimes the roamer's partner doesn't have the legal right work in another country or their children have settled into local schools. Some roamers have health issues so their roaming choices have always been limited. (One roamer reports that she had to forgo a Fulbright scholarship to the United States because she had a prior medical condition and her stipend would not cover health insurance. She was unable to pay for the high insurance premium out of her own pocket.) Some roamers are struck by an illness that is so acute that there's no time to think. Still others must come to terms with the fact that they're no longer roamers, they're immigrants—at least for now.

Whatever the circumstances, when tragedy strikes, the roamer's time-space continuum crashes back onto a very hard, very linear earth. No longer a quick call or a simple flight away, 10,000 miles once again becomes 10,000 miles. When a loved one is gravely ill, a twenty-four-hour flight is endless. When you need a hug from your dad, a Skype call simply won't do.

Whether you choose to go back or have it foisted upon you, there is a dark side to going home. As Heraclitus famously said 2,500 years ago, "No man ever steps in the same river twice, for it's not the same river and he's not the same man." Two centuries later, his words still ring true, but how on earth are you supposed to apply them to your daily life? Almost every roamer who moved home since our first interview has told me that she or he is having a tough time readjusting. The comments ranged from "It feels very weird to be in my country of origin...it's tougher than roaming!" to "I am having good days and bad days" and "I miss it dreadfully." How can roamers deal with the reverse culture shock that they'll almost certainly experience upon re-entry?

There's no easy answer to this, and each of us will have different responses and coping mechanisms. There are many deep and complex psychological factors involved that can't be dealt with in this book. At best, it may help to know that you're certainly not alone and that most people feel deflated upon re-entry. If you can muster the enthusiasm, it can help to apply the same sense of curiosity and pluck to your return home that you had on your way out. This might mean approaching home as if you're a foreigner, such as joining expat groups or searching out other *Glocal* roamers. It may mean wandering aimlessly through streets you know in hopes of finding a new cool café or a hole in the wall. It may mean buying a Zagat or a Lonely Planet for your home city and trying something completely new. For some of us, the greatest challenge is staying open not only to foreign cultures, but also to our own. Cosmopolitan Americans will lambaste the narrow-mindedness of people from small-town America, but they'll seek to connect with "real local villagers" in India, who may share similar views to those living in Smalltown, U.S.A. Roamers might applaud the Bhutanese for protecting their culture by limiting tourist visas to those who will spend over $250 per day, but call their own fellow citizens close-minded or conservative when they raise concerns about the loss of traditional British, French, or whatever else culture. Going back to your home country is as disorienting as going back to your parents' house and finding that your old bedroom has been turned into your mom's office. It's not how you expect your homecoming to pan out, but then roamers aren't typical homebodies and you can't have it both ways. If you approach home as a foreigner would, you'll not only reduce your expectations, but you may also discover great new things your home now has to offer. So don't take off your roaming hat just yet because you're embarking on a new adventure and you might need something to complement those rose-colored glasses.

So is this how it all ends? Do all roamers eventually become immigrants or return home and go Glocal? Not by a long shot. The vast majority of roamers intend to carry on exploring. In fact, 58 percent of survey respondents anticipate moving to a new destination next, and 12 percent want to move back to a city where they once lived, but not where they're from.

Take for instance Priya and Sandip, who moved back to India after studying and working in San Francisco for ten years. They wanted their children to be closer to their grandparents and to learn about their own culture. After a decade of adventure, it was time to reintegrate back home. Luckily, Sandip found a job in his hometown, New Delhi, but he was surprised by how difficult he found the transition. "My colleagues never saw me as a peer," he says. Sandip's ways had become too American. "I was no longer one of them. Their style of work was very different," he says. The joys of the New Delhi lifestyle, which had felt so homey to Priya and Sandip when they visited once a year, also fizzled out. They'd become accustomed to jogging by the bay in San Francisco. "When's the last time you tried jogging around New Delhi?" Sandip quips. "It's hot, it's crowded, it's polluted. You have to dodge monkeys." Having family in close proximity had its share of advantages, but it came with its share of burdens too. Family members began showing up at the doorstep unannounced...all the time. Sandip had enjoyed this when growing up, but he and his wife had become accustomed to having a different schedule, their *own* schedule. They no longer wanted to follow the traditional Indian family program. New Delhi was still familiar, but they themselves were vastly different. In total, Sandip and his wife lasted in Delhi for twenty-four months. Now in Toronto, Sandip says, "We're thrilled to be back in North America. Will we stay? We don't know. We may try going back to San Francisco."

Some roamers struggle with unsettling down. As Julia, a Canadian in Shanghai, says, "You need to be mindful. Are you keeping yourself busy, distracted, working, traveling, and moving to keep yourself occupied from facing other, more difficult questions about your life? Or are you actively engaged with your family, friends, and community, as well as with yourself and your longer-term goals?" Such sophisticated self-awareness is a pretty tall order, whether you're moving around the world or just living around the corner from your parents. Julia finally decided to start a family after a psychologist asked her some prodding questions, including whether she preferred living in Shanghai or Taipei, her previous city of residence. "For the first time in four years, I said I preferred it here in Shanghai, and I was surprised that I meant it. I finally felt like this might be home after a decade of wandering around Asia, trying to be one with it all." This realization gave Julia the confidence that she and her husband could provide a good home for a child, even if that home wouldn't be in her own birth country (or even in one fixed place).

Others approach this cycle of moving with a sense of adventure, even gusto. Kevin Brennan works as an environmental finance portfolio manager in San Francisco. Born in Canada to Irish parents, he grew up in the United Kingdom and describes himself decisively as "British-ish." Britain, however, isn't on his travel itinerary. He says, "If San Francisco doesn't work out, I reckon I will end up basing in Vancouver rather than back in London, realizing that overall lifestyle is more important than work alone, and accepting that I may have to start again there, and as a entrepreneur. Who knows, but I am becoming more comfortable with that by the day, and recognizing that as a positive quality rather than something to worry about!" He stops to think and adds, "Though the endless movement is sometimes challenging, you end up valuing freedom and agility more than continuity and playing it safe. Comfort and security aren't as healthy for us as we think." For Kevin, roaming may never end.

So how do Kevin and other long-term roamers deal with the one question that vexes so many: "How do you grow old as a roamer?" The answer is simple: You don't.

Two friends of mine were recently having an acrimonious breakup. Both were in their early 40s. Fed up with their heated dispute, a friend of ours barked at them: "Grow up! You're middle-aged. Get over it!" We were all shocked. Not by her command—only Russians can be so delightfully direct—but by her allegation that our friends were middle-aged. We were fast approaching the age where we could begin buying stupid cars and playing the "midlife crisis" card to excuse any number of misdemeanors. But the very idea of middle age—*our* middle age—was, like the opening crawl of *Star Wars*, receding into a galaxy far, far away.

By no means are we alone. *Time* magazine editor at large Catherine Mayer has identified a new trend in aging, or rather anti-aging. In her funny, page-turning book *Amortality*, Mayer argues that people are increasingly refusing to grow old. We no longer accept that life has set phases, each one ushering in age-appropriate behaviors:

> *One phenomenon blurs definitions of age more than any other: the significant—and burgeoning—number of people who live agelessly. They don't structure their lives around the inevitability of decline and death because they prefer to ignore it. They continue to chase aspirations, covet new products, marry, divorce, spawn, learn, work, assume all options are open, from youth into old age.*

You don't need to look hard to find proof of this. Madonna still looks 40 (she was born in 1958; you do the math). Mick Jagger fathered his latest child at the ripe age of 57, some 29 years after the birth of his first child and long after he was already a grandfather. Sexually transmitted diseases have doubled in the past decade among 50-to-90-year-olds. At the same time, world leaders seem to be getting younger and younger—Barack Obama, David Cameron, and Dmitri Medvedev were all elected in their early to mid-40s. In the same way that politics seems to be ever-converging at the center, age seems to be ever-converging in the midlife. With women giving birth well into their 40s, anti-aging potions to keep us eternally fresh, and health regimens to make us feel like a million bucks, who determines what is "age appropriate"?

Catherine Mayer's vision of eternal youth (or perhaps midlife crisis) sounds promising to those of us who don't want to grow old, but it can't be applied to roaming, can it? It's too far-fetched. When you get older and have kids or grandkids, you must settle down *somewhere*, no?

Believe it or not, no, you don't. Take for instance Nora, who could easily serve as a role model for future generations of roamers (or Mayer's amortals). Nora is an intelligent, attractive, vibrant Iranian woman in her early 60s. If the phrase "yummy granny" doesn't yet exist, I'm coining it and applying it to Nora now. Nora moved to London from Los Angeles six years ago to participate in the raising of her grandchildren. Nora isn't originally from Los Angeles. She was born in Iran and, newly married, Nora left for the United Kingdom with her husband in 1975 to do a master's degree. She intended to go back to Iran, but suddenly her world collapsed. "The [Iranian] revolution happened without me," she says. Nora became a roamer by default. She says, "For years afterward, I was captured in the inner prison of 'Why?' Why was the choice taken away from me?" Nora and her husband left the United Kingdom for the United States, where their three children were born. After several years in Michigan, they eventually "settled" in Los Angeles. Many years later, when Nora's daughter moved to London, married an European, and gave birth to her first child, Nora, by then divorced, moved to London to be on hand. After four years in London and a second grandchild, Nora was still settling into her new life when another tornado struck. Nora's daughter announced that she had an irresistible job offer in Hong Kong, so she and her young family were moving to Asia. They were all packing up and leaving in six weeks. Her daughter assumed Nora would join in the move, but Nora was at a loss for what to do. The thought of another move issued a whole new storm of conflicting emotions and logistical complexities. Despite the many miles under her feet, roaming had not become second nature to Nora. Nora decided to stay behind in London to digest the news and reflect on what she wanted to do next. She considered going back to Los Angeles where many of her friends and family members live, but after visiting Los Angeles, she came back with a fresh insight. "After 30 years of life in L.A., it is not home—at least not at the present time," she said, adding, "Nowhere is home and everywhere is home." When I caught up with her two years later, Nora was still in London and still unsettling down, unsure whether the British government would grant her permanent residency. Even after witnessing firsthand the emotional hazards and traumas associated with moving around the world, Nora still encourages roamers to take the long view:

> *Maybe roamers are the pioneers in taking the notion of connection further in the world. They are developing a wider perspective and connecting more with the present and what is at hand—the person next to you—and not the person chosen according to your family, bloodline, or nationality. Maybe roamers are creating a more sane,*

more widespread, and inclusive culture than a nationally created one. Are we, the first generation of roamers, sacrificial lambs then? No. We are the avant-garde with all the challenges and rewards that come with it.

As Nora so vividly demonstrates, roamers shouldn't feel compelled to "finally settle down" if the time isn't right or it's not in their nature. Long-term roaming might not make life easier, but it can make it richer and more edifying.

So for those stuck in what I call "The Long Middle," somewhere along the continuum of roaming for the first time and whatever end there might be, the best course of action might not be to worry about which milestone you may have missed, what socially accepted norm you may have defied, and whether you'll settle down. Compared with the first time you move abroad, roaming seems to have decreasing marginal returns, but then again, what doesn't? *The Economist* reports that people express decreasing levels of happiness with every passing year—that is, until they hit the seemingly uneventful age of 46. Regardless of our nationality, station in life, employment status, or gender, after 46, people's happiness makes a U-turn and keeps going up until old age. We should feel shoddier the more dilapidated we become, but instead, the older we get, the brighter our outlook.

The take-home lesson for roamers in all is this, then, is *keep calm and carry on.* You won't find a simple happiness formula telling you when, where, or if to settle down, or if it's even possible to do so. There is no roaming road map, and it won't necessarily get easier with time. According to *The Economist*, though, it will all sort itself out. And if it doesn't, after the age of 46, at least you will *think* it has sorted itself out.

CHAPTER 12
CONCLUSION: THE WORLD IS YOUR LOBSTER

At the end of an interview, I mentioned that I was likely moving continents again. The interviewee said, "Let me know where you end up." I laughed and replied, "You know it doesn't work that way." When you're roaming, there is no train conductor to announce: "Last stop. All passengers please get off here." There is no last stop. It's all part of an ongoing journey.

French writer Héloïse reminded me why I had started this book in the first place. During our interview she said, "Narratives are essential for all of us. It's how we approach life. It's why we dream. At a very basic level, it's how we explain things to ourselves." By listening to the stories and concerns of many other roamers, I have explained a few things to myself, in particular that I am not alone. There are probably millions of us, first-generation global roamers muddling our way through, paving the way for those who will learn from our mistakes or make them all over again.

If nothing else, at least I've realized that there's a cosmic disconnect between the ideal of eventually settling down and how a roamer's life actually unfolds. The vast majority of roamers don't start roaming with an exit strategy in mind, and even if they do, it rarely works out as intended. Should they plan an exit or just wait until the right moment presents itself? Have they gone past the point of no return and is this country now their new home? Will a third option become home? Many of those who have settled down, at least for now, continue to ask themselves these questions. Postponing difficult decisions until your situation is more resolved simply doesn't work. The autobiography of a twenty-first century roamer is punctuated by a few periods and exclamation points, but far more by commas, ellipses, and question marks.

My crystal ball stops short of divining how the great divide of the twenty-first century between nationals and globals is going to pan out. As physicist Niels Bohr famously once said, "It's difficult to predict, especially about the future." It's clear, though, that people will increasingly move from country to country for work, play, retirement, or any number of other good and bad reasons. In a global economy where speed and agility are key ingredients, those who are flexible will be the most successful. Most roamers have this trait built in, and those who don't will have it thrust upon them. Some roamers, like Svante Pääbo's early Homo sapiens, will set sail into the unknown and fall off the edge of the earth. The rest will discover Madagascar or Australia.

Roamers are the great *other* living around the world today. They see themselves as global citizens and are bound to ruffle the feathers of national governments that, as the present sole purveyors of citizenship, can't or don't want to imagine a different future. Instead, they continue to legislate on utterly anachronistic understandings of where and how their citizens live. Unless governments start taking roaming and this "permanent impermanence" way of life seriously, they'll continue to create a greater rift between those living globally and those living nationally. Legislators may wish to turn the clock back to simpler times, but that's not how this future thing works. Tomorrow's debate is not about immigration, but about *migration*.

Roamers themselves almost always set out in high spirits, firmly believing the slogan "the world is your oyster." As we all know, oysters sometimes hold the thrilling surprise of a perfectly formed little pearl. Roamers reach their hands deep into the ocean of life hoping to find an oyster and its treasure, but often they end up yanking their hand out, yelping in pain. Instead of a delightful oyster, they've have found themselves at the sharp end of a lobster's pincer. They shouldn't despair. You can find a hopeful metaphor in there yet.

The life of a lobster is more appealing than you might at first think. Lobsters don't technically live forever, but they're forever young. Lobsters can live to be well over a hundred years old, but they don't weaken or shrink with age and never lose their ability to reproduce. Lobsters continue to grow until they die, usually from disease or attack. Because their shells don't expand, each growth spurt means that they must shed their old hard shells, which is when they're particularly vulnerable to attack. When their roomier new shell is ready, however, lobsters are bigger and stronger than ever.

So every time the world hides its pearls and brandishes its pincers, roamers should remember the lobster. Every time roamers move, they shed their old hard shells, becoming vulnerable to whatever ills and difficulties might come their way. But with time, a new, roomier shell will be ready, making them stronger and better prepared for whatever the globalized world throws their way.

Since I started to write this book, countless people have asked me, "Do you think this globally itinerant lifestyle is good or bad?" After all my research, I have only one response: It just is. And it will become ever more prevalent in the twenty-first century. Let's all grow a new shell and get used to it.

* * *

To get a better picture of roamers and others living abroad, I'm launching a second survey. Please contribute your thoughts and ideas by going to:
www.smartsurvey.co.uk/s/XADTY/

ROAMER STATISTICS
516 PEOPLE SURVEYED WORLDWIDE…

WHERE DO SURVEY RESPONDENTS CURRENTLY LIVE?

Total number of respondents: 516
Female respondents: 50%
Male respondents: 50%

Other (25% of respondents)
Auckland / Basel / Beirut / Boston / Buenos Aires / Cairo / Dallas / Doha / Dublin / Gabarone / Geneva / Houston / Jakarta / Juba / Kiev / Lagos / Los Angeles / Macau / Madrid / Melbourne / Milan / Moscow / Munich / New Delhi / Rotterdam / Stevenage / Stockholm / Soeul / Treviso / Toronto / Ulaanbaatar / Vancouver / Vienna / Washington D.C. / etc

Figure 1

WHERE ARE THEY FROM?

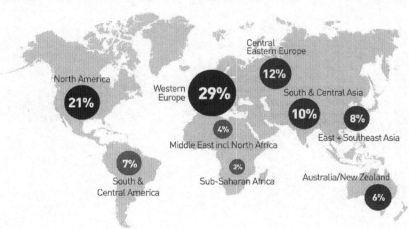

Figure 2

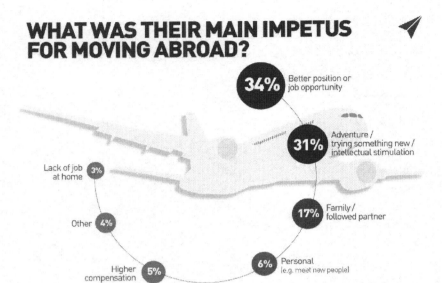

Figure 3

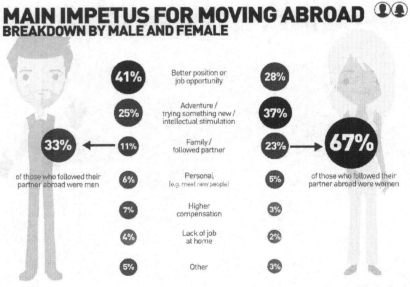

Figure 4

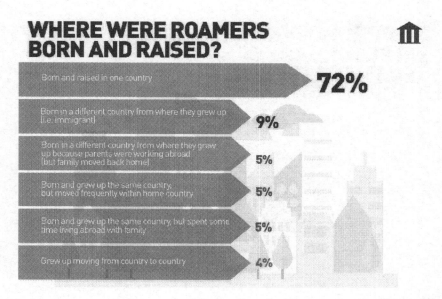

WHERE WERE ROAMERS BORN AND RAISED?

Born and raised in one country — **72%**

Born in a different country from where they grew up (i.e. immigrant) — **9%**

Born in a different country from where they grew up because parents were working abroad (but family moved back home) — **5%**

Born and grew up the same country, but moved frequently within home country — **5%**

Born and grew up the same country, but spent some time living abroad with family — **5%**

Grew up moving from country to country — **4%**

Figure 5

DID THEY GROW UP IN THE COUNTRY WHERE THEIR PARENTS GREW UP?

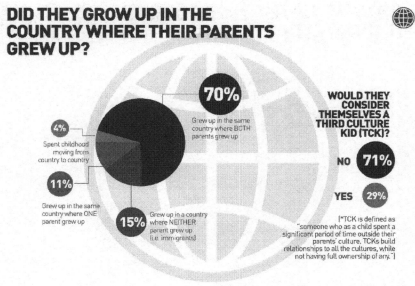

70% Grew up in the same country where BOTH parents grew up

4% Spent childhood moving from country to country

11% Grew up in the same country where ONE parent grew up

15% Grew up in a country where NEITHER parent grew up (i.e. immigrants)

WOULD THEY CONSIDER THEMSELVES A THIRD CULTURE KID (TCK)?

NO **71%**

YES **29%**

[*TCK is defined as "someone who as a child spent a significant period of time outside their parents' culture. TCKs build relationships to all the cultures, while not having full ownership of any."]

Figure 6

221

WHAT KIND OF HIGH SCHOOL OR SECONDARY SCHOOL DID THEY ATTEND?

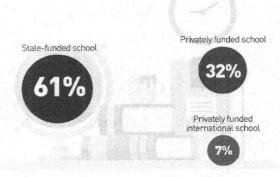

State-funded school

61%

Privately funded school

32%

Privately funded international school

7%

Figure 7

DID THEY STUDY ABROAD IN UNIVERSITY?

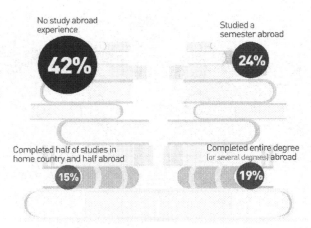

No study abroad experience

42%

Studied a semester abroad

24%

Completed half of studies in home country and half abroad

15%

Completed entire degree (or several degrees) abroad

19%

Figure 8

222

WHAT IS THEIR LEVEL OF EDUCATION?

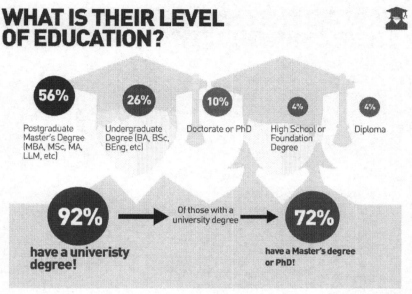

56%

Postgraduate
Master's Degree
(MBA, MSc, MA,
LLM, etc)

26%

Undergraduate
Degree (BA, BSc,
BEng, etc)

10%

Doctorate or PhD

4%

High School or
Foundation
Degree

4%

Diploma

92%

have a univeristy degree!

Of those with a
university degree

72%

have a Master's degree or PhD!

Figure 9

UNDER WHAT CONTRACT TYPE ARE THEY EMPLOYED?

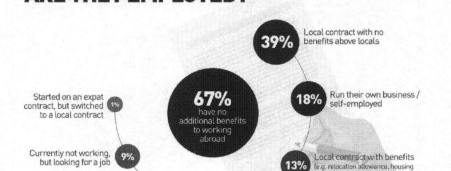

39% Local contract with no benefits above locals

Started on an expat contract, but switched to a local contract **1%**

67% have no additional benefits to working abroad

18% Run their own business / self-employed

Currently not working, but looking for a job **9%**

13% Local contract with benefits (e.g. relocation allowance, housing allowance, cost of living adjustment)

Expat contract (free housing, family benefits, etc) **10%**

11% Local contract with small benefits (e.g. relocation allowance or taxation advice)

Figure 10

HOW DID THEY FIND WORK IN THEIR CURRENT CITY?

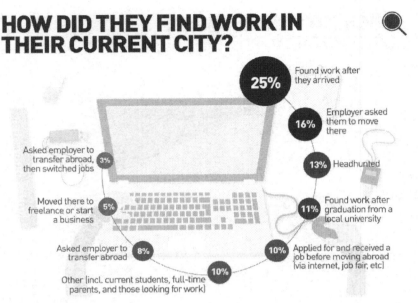

- **25%** Found work after they arrived
- **16%** Employer asked them to move there
- **13%** Headhunted
- **11%** Found work after graduation from a local university
- **10%** Applied for and received a job before moving abroad (via internet, job fair, etc)
- **10%** Other (incl. current students, full-time parents, and those looking for work)
- **8%** Asked employer to transfer abroad
- **5%** Moved there to freelance or start a business
- **3%** Asked employer to transfer abroad, then switched jobs

Figure 11

DO THEY HAVE MORE SPENDING POWER NOW THAN BEFORE MOVING?

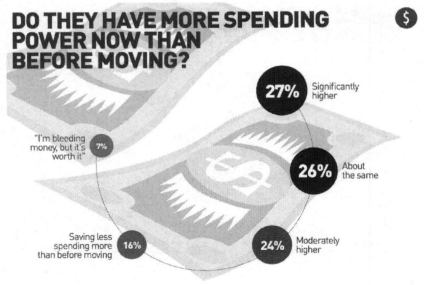

- **27%** Significantly higher
- **26%** About the same
- **24%** Moderately higher
- **16%** Saving less spending more than before moving
- **7%** "I'm bleeding money, but it's worth it"

Figure 12

WHAT IS THEIR RELATIONSHIP STATUS?

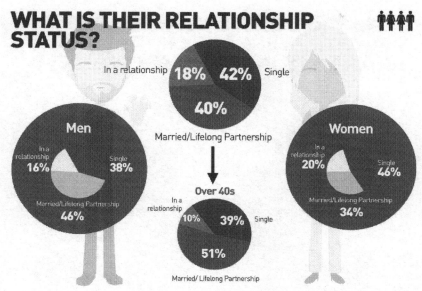

In a relationship **18%** **42%** Single

40%

Married/Lifelong Partnership

Men
In a relationship **16%**　Single **38%**
Married/Lifelong Partnership **46%**

Women
In a relationship **20%**　Single **46%**
Married/Lifelong Partnership **34%**

Over 40s
In a relationship **10%** **39%** Single
51%
Married/ Lifelong Partnership

Figure 13

HAVE THEY EVER BEEN IN A LONG-DISTANCE RELATIONSHIP?

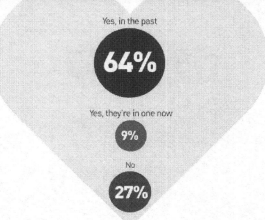

Yes, in the past

64%

Yes, they're in one now

9%

No

27%

Figure 14

IF MARRIED OR WITH A LIFE-LONG PARTHER, WERE THEY BOTH BORN AND RAISED IN THE SAME COUNTRY?

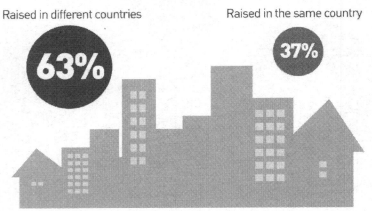

Raised in different countries

63%

Raised in the same country

37%

Figure 15

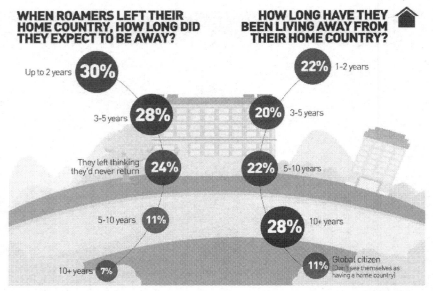

WHEN ROAMERS LEFT THEIR HOME COUNTRY, HOW LONG DID THEY EXPECT TO BE AWAY?

Up to 2 years **30%**

3-5 years **28%**

They left thinking they'd never return **24%**

5-10 years **11%**

10+ years **7%**

HOW LONG HAVE THEY BEEN LIVING AWAY FROM THEIR HOME COUNTRY?

22% 1-2 years

20% 3-5 years

22% 5-10 years

28% 10+ years

11% Global citizen (Don't see themselves as having a home country)

Figure 16

WHERE DO THEY INTEND TO GO NEXT?

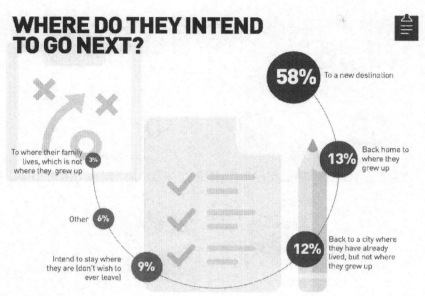

58% To a new destination

13% Back home to where they grew up

To where their family lives, which is not where they grew up **3%**

Other **6%**

Intend to stay where they are (don't wish to ever leave) **9%**

12% Back to a city where they have already lived, but not where they grew up

Figure 17

WHAT BEST DESCRIBES THEIR IDEA OF HOME?

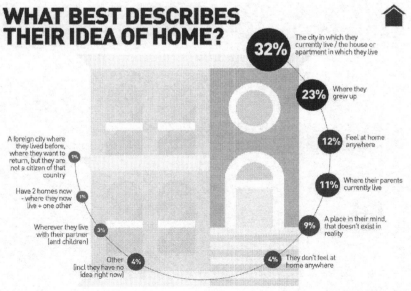

32% The city in which they currently live / the house or apartment in which they live

23% Where they grew up

12% Feel at home anywhere

11% Where their parents currently live

A foreign city where they lived before, where they want to return, but they are not a citizen of that country **1%**

Have 2 homes now - where they now live + one other **1%**

Wherever they live with their partner (and children) **3%**

Other (incl they have no idea right now) **4%**

9% A place in their mind, that doesn't exist in reality

4% They don't feel at home anywhere

Figure 18

OTHER THAN ENGLISH HOW MANY LANGUAGES DO THEY SPEAK FLUENTLY?

English +1	English +2	English + 3 or more	0 - only fluent in English
32%	**30%**	**21%**	**17%**

*Defined as a language in which they could work.

WAS ENGLISH THE MAIN LANGUAGE SPOKEN AT HOME?

Yes	No
39%	**61%**

Figure 19

HOW MANY VOTED IN THEIR COUNTRY'S LAST ELECTION*

Did not vote	Voted
58%	**42%**

[*Those living abroad longer than 3 years]

IF THEY COULD VOTE IN A NATIONAL ELECTION OF THE COUNTRY WHERE THEY CURRENTLY LIVE, WOULD THEY DO SO?

Yes, they're very interested in participating in the political life of wherever they live	Yes, because it's important to vote if they have the right to do so	Maybe, if there was an issue that interested them and if it was made easy	No, they're not interested in local politics	No, they're not really interested in voting anywhere
27%	**26%**	**23%**	**15%**	**8%**

Figure 20

228

IN WHICH INDUSTRIES DO THEY WORK?

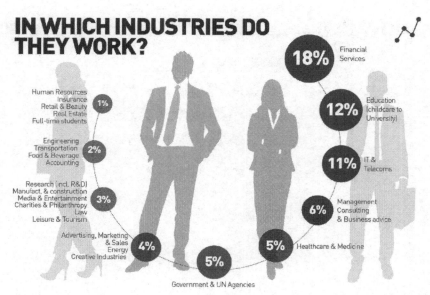

Financial Services **18%**

Education (childcare to University) **12%**

IT & Telecoms **11%**

Management Consulting & Business advice **6%**

Healthcare & Medicine **5%**

Government & UN Agencies **5%**

4% Advertising, Marketing & Sales / Energy / Creative Industries

3% Research (incl. R&D) / Manufact. & construction / Media & Entertainment / Charities & Philanthropy / Law / Leisure & Tourism

2% Engineering / Transportation / Food & Beverage / Accounting

1% Human Resources / Insurance / Retail & Beauty / Real Estate / Full-time students

Figure 21

HOW MANY PASSPORTS DO THEY HAVE?

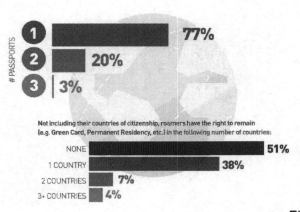

PASSPORTS

1 — **77%**
2 — **20%**
3 — **3%**

Not including their countries of citizenship, roamers have the right to remain (e.g. Green Card, Permanent Residency, etc.) in the following number of countries:

NONE	**51%**
1 COUNTRY	**38%**
2 COUNTRIES	**7%**
3+ COUNTRIES	**4%**

Figure 22

HOW OLD ARE THEY?

20-24	5%
25-29	23%
30-34	27%
35-40	24%
40-44	11%
45-50	6%
50-65	5%
65+	<1%

Figure 23

DO THEY HAVE CHILDREN?

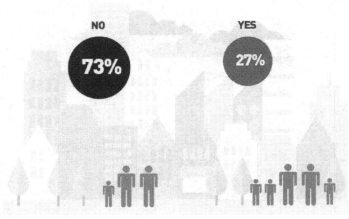

NO 73% YES 27%

Figure 24

ACKNOWLEDGEMENTS

Thank you to all of you who helped make this book possible—those who filled out surveys and passed it on to your friends, those who engaged in hours of conversation over lattes on a rainy Sunday afternoon or between meetings at work, those who pointed out inconsistencies, and all those whose encouragement kept me going. It's thanks to all of you that this book now exists.

Thank you to Rich for painstakingly editing the final two versions of *Roaming*. Your insight and tenacity made this a better book. Thanks to Peter Gelfan, associate editor at The Editorial Department, who helped me see the forest for the trees. Thanks also to Elliott Krause, my sharp and invaluable copy editor.

Thank you to the early adopters and those who encouraged me to write this book, including Maud d'Aboville, Britt Lintner, Sasha Silver, June Miller, and Antoine de Spoelberch.

Thanks to Maud d'Aboville and Sarah Ryan for commenting on early versions of the book and for your relentless cheerleading.

Thanks to Ilan Solot, Mark Arasaratnam, and Will Finn, who were all on different continents when our emails were flying back and forth about the right name for all these "global citizens." Your thoughts helped me shape my ideas and to finally settle on the term *roaming*.

Thanks to Petra Freddi for putting me in touch with half of Singapore and to Amine Goraieb, Will Finn, and Nyree Hu for introducing me to their networks in Hong Kong (and beyond). Thanks to Kerry Ryan for her great introductions in New York. My interviews wouldn't have happened without all of you. Thank you to all of those who have sent emails to friends, who have forwarded my survey to friends and contacts, including Gaetane Prinselaar, Harry Hoster, Irene Gallou, Mark Parkin at the Goodenough College, Claudia Mayer, Alex d'Aboville, Edward Balke, Nina Laarman, and Oliver Trianto.

Thanks to the generous and supportive Christine Amour Levar who guest wrote an article on the first six months of moving abroad. *The First Six Months* appears at the end of the e-book and Kindle versions of *Roaming*. Segments have also been published in Glamomamas.com.

Thanks also to all those who let me interview them for this book, including those whose quotes didn't make it through the final edit and those who just let me bounce ideas off them. I'm grateful to you for your time and candor. You all wrote this book as much as I did: Britt Lintner, Donna Worrall, Zou Bing, Cécile Courbon, Andrea Illescas, Judith Andreassen, Erin Sandral, Brenna Tinnari, Liu Ying Mei, Dana Schwartz, Monica Araya, Ilan Solot, Susan Lee, Kirsten Durward, Dagmar Baeuerle, Iain Henderson, Samuel Kolehmainen, Tuck Meng Yee, Sarah Ryan, Antoine Massoud, Mark Arasaratnam, Michelle Mourcade, William Finn, Nyree Hu, Karin Majdalany, Ayse Levant, Kate Barrette (Kate Menihan), Magnus Edensvard, Morgan Long, Christopher Tanfield, Michael Delfs, Celia Romaniuk, Mary and Bern Gardner, Ian Krassek, Brynne Herbert, Peter Sorgenfrei, Mats Klingberg, Anne Eckert, Stephanie Campbell, Amol Naik, Ash Matouschka, Stacey Wolpert, Christiane Bode, Jean-Olivier Caron, Amine Goraeib, Leonie Moschner, Ed Smith, Milena Dragicevic, Adriana Wong, Graeme Torre, Heather Lyons, Jerry Wattenberg, Leanda Lee, Ryan Kennedy, Fleur De Koning, Elizabeth Tweedale, Bruce Davison, Eva Wong, Kevin Brennan, Nora Ghodsian, Martin Micklemayer, Davide Elia, and Alex Marquez.

Thank you to the 516 generous and open-minded people who took the time to answer all sixty-five (!) of my online survey questions. I never met most of you, so thank you for helping an unknown writer and researcher. Thanks also to Ryan Kennedy for helping me write my online survey and for editing my Monocle essay.

Thanks to Seyed Reza Yousefi at The World Bank and Paul Tostevin at Savills for tirelessly answering my endless questions. Thank you to my first, multi-talented research assistant, Savitri Lopez-Negrete.

Thanks to Heather McGregor, a.k.a. Mrs. Moneypenny, whom I never met but who kindly gave me advice to self-publish via Brynne Herbert. You were an inspiration. Thanks to Lisa Gallagher for her helpful advice on book agents.

Thank you to those who provided back-end support at www.SmartSurvey.co.uk.

Thanks to Bo, Van, and all the other guys at Ginger 'n Spice cafe in Hampstead who kept my teapot full, found my missing laptop, and generally added order to the chaos of my life in the early stages of writing this book.

Thank you to those at *Monocle* who read my unpublished manuscript and asked me to write an essay about roamers and cities for the 2016 Monocle Forecast issue. Thanks in particular to Megan Gibson, Andrew Tuck, and Tyler Brûlé.

Finally, words cannot express my gratitude to my bighearted and long-suffering lifetime supporters, Harry Hoster and Rich Patha. I couldn't have done it without you.

ROAMING

Appendix

Survey methodology

When I closed my survey to responses, 516 people had responded. I used numerous online discussion groups, online forums, and alumni networks to reach foreigners living abroad to solicit survey responses. Respondents were unpaid. The percentage breakdown of where survey respondents live can be found in figure 1.

I conducted face-to-face interviews in four cities: London, Singapore, Hong Kong, and New York. I conducted Skype and written interviews with respondents in other cities around the world including Shanghai, Tokyo, Kuala Lumpur, San Francisco, The Hague, Treviso, Brussels, and Macau.

Where to find help

Since this isn't a *How To* book, some of you might be left with more questions than answers. You'll likely find location-specific groups and information where you live, but here's a short selection of sources that offer broad international information and advice:

www.meetup.com
www.internations.org
www.moveguides.com

Resources for parents:

tckworld.org (website for Third Culture Kids)
Raising Global Nomads
Emotional Resilience and the Expat Child

ENDNOTES

CHAPTER 1
THE WORLD IS YOUR OYSTER

9   Britain still has a store with the anachronistic name Carphone
    Warehouse. Teenagers today must have no idea what that means.

**12-13 All statistics related to the number of people living abroad by
country are from the following sources:**

- Urs Geiser, "Tax disputes spill over to expat community," *Swiss Broadcasting Corporation*, March 24, 2012. www.swissinfo.ch/eng/politics/swiss_abroad/Tax_disputes_spill _over_to_expat_community.html?cid=32351662 (accessed April 30, 2013).

- The British Broadcasting Association, *Brits Abroad: World Overview*, http://news.bbc.co.uk/2/shared/spl/hi/in_depth/brits_abroad/ html/ (accessed April 29, 2013).

- "Canada needs to engage its citizens living abroad," *The Globe and Mail*, August 24, 2012. www.theglobeandmail.com/news/national/time-to-lead/canada- needs-to-engage-its-citizens-living-abroad/article598965/ (accessed November 27, 2013).

- *Te Ara — The Encyclopedia of New Zealand*, www.teara.govt.nz/en/kiwis-overseas/page-1 (accessed April 30, 2013) and Delegation of the European Union to Australia, http://eeas.europa.eu/delegations/australia/eu_australia/key_fact s/index_en.htm (accessed December 5, 2014).

- Statistics Netherlands, *Immigration and emigration hit new record high in 2011*, January 11, 2012, www.cbs.nl/en- GB/menu/themas/bevolking/publicaties/artikelen/archief/2012 /2012-3547-wm.htm (accessed July 28, 2013).

- Bureau of Consular Affairs, U.S. State Department, *CA Fact Sheet*, January 2013, travel.state.gov/pdf/ca_fact_sheet.pdf (accessed November 28, 2014).

- "Paris-on-Thames," *The Economist*, February 24, 2011, www.economist.com/node/18229536 (accessed November 28, 2014).

- Mark Deen and Alan Katz, "French making themselves at home in London," *New York Times*, February 8, 2008, www.nytimes.com/2008/01/25/style/25iht- afrench.1.9495133.html (accessed November 26, 2014).

**Statistics about the total number of people living abroad are from
the following source:**

- "Number of international migrants rises above 232 million," United Nations Department of Social and Economic Affairs, September 11, 2013, www.un.org/en/development/desa/news/population/number-of-international-migrants-rises.html (accessed June 8, 2015).

13   **Statistics about the growth of migration compared to the growth of world population are derived from the above and the following source:**

- United Nations Department of Economic and Social Affairs/Population Division, *International Migration Report 2013*, 2013, www.un.org/en/development/desa/population/publications/pdf/migration/migrationreport2013/Full_Document_final.pdf (accessed June 8, 2015).

The number of roamers is likely much higher than 23 million.

- The International Organization for Migration's *World Migration Report 2013* estimates that 22 percent of global migration, or 51 million, is "North country to North country migration." Much of what constitutes the North and the South are eliding, but I don't want to get into the politics of these statistics, so please use these numbers with caution. Roamers are coming from all over the planet and they're going to all over the planet. Without any clear statistics about the group I call "roamers," I simply must use the data at hand.

15   **Numbers about rural to urban migration are from the following sources:**

- "The World comes to Town," People and the Planet, February 2012, www.peopleandtheplanet.com/index.html@lid=26729&section=40&topic=44.html (accessed December 4, 2014).
- Neil Shah. "Smallville, USA, Fades Further," *The Wall Street Journal*, March 27, 2014, http://online.wsj.com/articles/SB1000142405270230332520457946376163210 3386 (accessed December 5, 2014).

17   **The number of SIM cards on the planet is taken from the following article:**

- "Mobile Devices Now Outnumber Humans: Report," *Tech Times*, October 8, 2014, www.techtimes.com/articles/17431/20141008/mobile-devices-now-outnumber-humans-report.htm (accessed December 3, 2014).

CHAPTER 2
HOW TO SPOT A ROAMER IN THE WILD

22   **Statistics on Dutch East India Company are from the following source:**

- M.W. Van Boven. "Towards A New Age of Partnership (TANAP): An Ambitious World Heritage Project (UNESCO Memory of the World — reg.form, 2002)." VOC Archives Appendix 2, 14.

Etymology of "expat":
- "Is 'expat' domesticated?" *Grammar Phobia*, www.grammarphobia.com/blog/2014/03/expat.html (accessed September 12, 2014).

23   Singapore's Chinese population:
- O.K., 75 percent of Singapore's population is ethnically Chinese, but as any Chinese or Singaporean citizen will tell you, culturally they're worlds apart. First off, most "Chinese" Singaporeans are more fluent in English than in any Chinese language.

27   For more on Thomas Friedman's three phases of globalization, see
- Thomas L. Friedman. *The World is Flat: A Brief History of the Twenty-first Century.* London: Penguin, 2006, 10-11.

30-31   For all of Prof. Hans Rosling's statistics, see the following:
- Hans Rosling. "Hans Rosling shows the best stats you've ever seen," June 2006, www.ted.com/talks/hans_rosling_shows_the_best_stats_you_ve_ever_seen.html.
- This is at least in part due to racial discrepancies within America, where blacks in high-crime urban areas have a life expectancy of 70.8 years, lower than that of Vietnam, Egypt, and Sri Lanka. Of all urban areas in the U.S., Washington, D.C., has the highest life expectancy disparities between blacks and whites—13.8 years for men and 8.6 years for women. See Justine R. Lescroart's "U.S. Life Expectancy Gap Widens," *The Harvard Crimson*, September 13, 2006 and US News, "Life Expectancy for U.S. Blacks Is Shorter Than for Whites," March 1, 2012, http://health.usnews.com/health-news/news/articles/2012/03/01/life-expectancy-for-us-blacks-is-shorter-than-for-whites (accessed October 15, 2013).
- Hans Rosling. "Let my dataset change your mindset," TED, August 2009, www.ted.com/talks/lang/eng/hans_rosling_at_state.html. Statistics available at Hans Rosling's not-for-profit foundation, *Gapminder*, www.gapminder.org/labs/gapminder-china-india-eu-usa (accessed October 14, 2013).
- Hans Rosling. "Asia's rise—how and when," *TED*, November 2009, www.ted.com/talks/hans_rosling_asia_s_rise_how_and_when.html.

The Economist's 2013 Quality of Life Index is from:
- "The lottery of life: Where to be born in 2013," *The Economist*, November 21, 2012, www.economist.com/news/21566430-where-be-born-2013-lottery-life (accessed October 30, 2015).

32   Comparing the cost of living in different cities:
- Expatistan, www.expatistan.com/cost-of-living (accessed October 7, 2013).

34   **Gen Y poll can be found here:**
- "Gen Y and Global Mobility," *MOVE Guides*, 2013, www.moveguides.com/global-mobility/gen-y-insights?confirm=true (accessed October 26, 2013).

Statistics on first-time mothers are from the following sources:
- Mireille Vézina and Martin Turcotte. "Forty-year-old Mothers of Pre-school Children: A profile," September 17, 2009, Component of Statistics Canada Catalogue no. 11-008-X Canadian Social Trends, Canada.
- Livingston, Gretchen, and D'Vera Cohn. *The New Demography of American Motherhood*, Pew Research Center, August 2010, Washington, D.C., U.S.A.

36-37   **Alex Ljung's story is quoted from the following article:**
- Mark Scott. "Companies Born in Europe, but Based on the Planet," *New York Times*, June 11, 2012, http://dealbook.nytimes.com/2012/06/11/companies-born-in-europe-but-based-on-the-planet/?_r=0 (accessed October 17, 2013).

39   **Trying to track down statistics on highly skilled workers, beyond my own survey, leads to finger-in-the-wind estimations.**
- Although governments regularly set immigration targets for particular professions, they are not keeping good track of which highly skilled professionals are coming and going. The BBC has been trying to compile such figures, but it reports that even the head of the OECD's international migration division, Jean-Christophe Dumont, admits a lack of proper figures: "Several groups have been trying to develop comprehensive datasets about the migration of professionals, with no success so far." Quote taken from "Global migrants: Which are the most wanted professions?" *BBC*, March 26, 2013, www.bbc.co.uk/news/business-21938085 (accessed June 17, 2013).

45-47   **For more information on cosmopolitanism, see the work of Ulf Hannerz:**
- Ulf Hannerz defines cosmopolitanism as "a willingness to engage with the Other" and "the concern with achieving competence in cultures which are initially alien." "...an aesthetic stance of openness toward divergent cultural experiences, a search for contrasts rather than uniformity. To ...turn into an aficionado, to view [cultures] as art works." Ulf Hannerz, "Cosmopolitans and Locals in World Culture," *Theory Culture Society*, July 1990: 239-40.

For more on the theories of Creative Class, see
- Richard Florida. *The Rise of the Creative Class* (New York: Basic Books, 2004), 68.
- Those who make the most money are the superstar Creatives like movie stars, football players, entrepreneurs and other A-Listers. Just like most of the real winners of the Gold Rush weren't those

digging for gold, but those who sold them their (Levis) jeans, the creative sector workers raking in the most money consistently are the support team—the bankers, lawyers and management consultants.

- Richard Florida. *The Rise of the Creative Class* (New York: Basic Books, 2004), 90.
- Florida, 78.

The Economist's tongue-in-cheek advertorial can be found here:

- "Intelligent Life," The Quarterly from The Economist, Volume 3, Issue 4, Summer 2010, 95.

CHAPTER 3
IS THIS JUST A PHASE?

50 **Oliver Sacks's quote is from the following article:**
- Oliver Sacks. "Altered States," *New Yorker*, August 27, 2012, http://www.newyorker.com/magazine/2012/08/27/altered-states-3 (accessed September 3, 2014).

55-60 **For a quick overview of Barry Schwartz's theories on the paradox of choice, see the following TED talk:**
- Barry Schwartz. "The Paradox of Choice," filmed July 2005, TED video, 19:37, www.ted.com/talks/barry_schwartz_on_the_paradox_of_choice/transcript?language=en (accessed March 14, 2013).

Colin Farrell's interview was found in the following magazine:
- Chris Ayres. "Colin Farrell: 'I didn't think I had much longer to live,'" *The Times Magazine*, December 2012.

CHAPTER 4
WHY DO ROAMERS ROAM?

65 **Sambar quote taken from**
- Thomas Friedman. *The World Is Flat* (London: Penguin, 2005, 2006), 28.

68 **European and French statistics are from these two sources:**
- Eurostat Press Office, "Foreign citizens and foreign-born population," *EU citizens living in another Member State accounted for 2.5 percent of the EU population in 2011* (Luxembourg, July 11, 2012).
- European Commission, *European Commission upholds free movement of people*, January 14, 2014, http://europa.eu/rapid/press-release_MEMO-14-9_en.htm (accessed September 9, 2015).
- Lucy Ash. "London, France's sixth biggest city," *BBC News Magazine*, May 30, 2012, http://www.bbc.co.uk/news/magazine-18234930 (accessed December 30, 2012).

Immigrants children leaving the West and "returning" to their ancestral homelands:

- Kirk Semple. "Many U.S. Immigrants' Children Seek American Dream Abroad," *New York Times*, April 15, 2012, www.nytimes.com/2012/04/16/us/more-us-children-of-immigrants-are-leaving-us.html?pagewanted=1&_r=0&ref=us&src=me (accessed December 28, 2012).
- "Why would you leave the West for India?" *BBC News*, October 12, 2012, www.bbc.co.uk/news/world-asia-india-19992062 (accessed December 28, 2012).

69   **For an amusing history of aviation, from the point of view of passengers and crew members see:**
- Omelia, Johanna, and Michael Waldock. *Come Fly with Us: A Global History of the Airline Hostess,* Collectors Press, 2006.

71-72   **Information on the historical cost of long-distance phone calls derived from here:**
- "Journeys: The Telephone," *Connected Earth*, www.connected-earth.com/journeys/Firstgenerationtechnologies/Thetelephone/Internationalnetworks/index.htm (accessed March 15, 2013).

71-72   **North-to-North migration statistics:**
- International Organization for Migration, *World Migration Report 2013 — Key Facts and Figures,* 2013, www.iom.int/files/live/sites/iom/files/What-We-Do/wmr2013/en/WMR2013_FactSheet_EN_final.pdf (accessed June 8, 2015).
- International Organization for Migration, *World Migration Report 2013 — Key Facts and Figures,* 2013, www.iom.int/files/live/sites/iom/files/What-We-Do/wmr2013/en/WMR2013_FactSheet_EN_final.pdf (accessed June 8, 2015), 3.
- Incidentally, the biggest North-to-North migration corridors are Germany to the United States (1.3 million); followed by the United Kingdom to Australia; and Canada, the Republic of Korea and the United Kingdom to the United States, according to the *World Migration Report 2013*.
- "European Commission upholds free movement of people," European Commission, January 14, 2014, http://europa.eu/rapid/press-release_MEMO-14-9_en.htm (accessed September 9, 2015).

European unemployment statistics:
- European Commission Eurostat, *Unemployment statistics*, October 2014, http://ec.europa.eu/eurostat/statistics-explained/index.php/Unemployment_statistics (accessed December 17, 2014).

73-74   **China emigration statistics:**
- "BoP until you drop," *The Economist*, August 4, 2012, www.economist.com/node/21559949 (accessed October 24, 2012).

- Ian Johnson. "Wary of Future, Professionals Leave China in Record Numbers," *New York Times*, October 31, 2012, www.nytimes.com/2012/11/01/world/asia/wary-of-future-many-professionals-leave-china.html?hp&_r=0 (accessed November 5, 2012).

On the economic recovery of various E.U. countries, see:
- Lewis Goodall. "UK v rest of G7: How's our driving?" May 9, 2013, www.bbc.co.uk/news/business-22462175 (accessed July 14, 2013) and www.tradingeconomics.com (accessed July 14, 2013).
- Lorenzo Totaro and Alessandra Migliaccio. "Italy's Economy Fails to Rebound," *Bloomberg*, February 13, 2015, www.bloomberg.com/news/articles/2015-02-13/italy-fails-to-rebound-from-recession-challenging-premier-renzi (accessed April 22, 2015).
- Ed Cumming. "Italians buy up London as recession bites," March 9, 2012, www.telegraph.co.uk/property/propertynews/9131103/Italians-buy-up-London-as-recession-bites.html (accessed July 15, 2013)
- Ami Sedghi. "Europe: where do people live?" *Guardian*, January 26, 2012, www.guardian.co.uk/news/datablog/2012/jan/26/europe-population-who-lives-where (accessed July 15, 2013).
- "Unemployment statistics," Eurostat http://ec.europa.eu/eurostat/statistics-explained/index.php/Unemployment_statistics#Youth_unemployment_trends (accessed April 22, 2015).
- Fiona Ehlers. "Crisis Forces Young Italians to Move Abroad," *Der Speigel Online*, June 8, 2012, http://www.spiegel.de/international/europe/euro-crisis-forces-many-italian-young-people-to-leave-a-848509.html (accessed January 3, 2013).

75   **For more information about international work experience visit Brynne Herbert's blog:**
- Brynne Herbert, MOVE Guides: *The Globalization of Work*, October 20, 2012, http://insights.moveguides.com/the-globalization-of-work/ (accessed January 7, 2013).

76   **On how to land a foreign job:**
- Natasha Stidder, "Working in East Asia: Experience of the region becomes a vital asset," *Financial Times*, June 15, 2011, www.ft.com/cms/s/0/f0cfb9c0-9764-11e0-af13-00144feab49a.html?siteedition=intl#axzz3CJc6cptH (accessed September 4, 2014).

77-78   **On Scientist Svante Pääbo:**
- Elizabeth Kolbert, "Sleeping With The Enemy," *New Yorker*, August 15, 2011, http://www.newyorker.com/magazine/2011/08/15/sleeping-with-the-enemy#ixzz1vCPDr4Xw (accessed September 1, 2014).

On genetics and the potential of a "restless gene":

- David Dobbs, "Restless Genes," *National Geographic*, January 2013, http://ngm.nationalgeographic.com/2013/01/125-restless-genes/dobbs-text (accessed March 6, 2015).
- Dan TA et al. Eisenberg, "Dopamine receptor genetic polymorphisms and body composition in undernourished pastoralists: An exploration of nutrition indexes among nomadic and recently settled Ariaal men of northern Kenya," *BMC Evolutionary Biology* 8 (June 2008), 173.

CHAPTER 5
IT'S THE ECONOMY, STUPID

81   **LGBT wealth:**
- Jennifer Hoyt Cummings, "How to live up to your LGBT marketing," *Reuters*, June 28, 2013, www.reuters.com/article/2013/06/28/us-lgbt-wealthmanagement-idUSBRE95R0JW20130628 (accessed October 31, 2015).
- Fiona Rintoul, "Wealth managers chase the Pink Pound," *Financial Times*, May 19, 2013, www.ft.com/cms/s/0/8c5417ea-a1dd-11e2-8971-00144feabdc0.html (accessed June 26, 2013).

82   **HSBC's Expat Explorer Surveys**
- "Expat Explorer Survey 2015," www.expatexplorer.hsbc.com/#/country/singapore accessed June 26, 2013. I tried to get an interview with HSBC to discuss these demographics but they did not respond to my requests. HSBC's more recent Expat Explorer Surveys no longer publish their research methodology and statistics about the survey respondents' gender, citizenship, incomes, etc.

83-84   **For more information on Savills's World Cities Index and global property prices, see the following sources:**
- "Spotlight: The World in London," July 2012, Savills Research, pgs 4 and 8.
- Yolande Barnes, "12 Cities: Cities on the Move," October 5, 2015, www.savills.co.uk/research_articles/188297/192481-0 and www.savills.co.uk/research_articles/188294/192538-0.
- "World Cities Review," Autumn 2011, Savills Research, 20.
- "Housing Prices in Four Global Cities," February 2011, Savills Research / Residential, 2 and 6.
- Daniel Thomas, "A World Apart", *Financial Times*, June 3, 2011, www.ft.com/intl/cms/s/2/1e07b7ca-8c6c-11e0-883f-00144feab49a.html (accessed October 9, 2014).
- Kirk Williams, "Vancouver's housing 2nd least affordable in world ," *CBC News*, January 21, 2014, www.cbc.ca/news/canada/british-columbia/vancouver-s-housing-2nd-least-affordable-in-world-1.2505524 (accessed May 8, 2015).

- James Surowiecki, "Real Estate Goes Global," *New Yorker*, May 26, 2014, www.newyorker.com/magazine/2014/05/26/real-estate-goes-global.
- Rob Carrick, "Can you afford a home in these cities?" *The Globe and Mail*, July 2, 2014, www.theglobeandmail.com/globe-investor/personal-finance/mortgages/can-you-afford-a-home-in-these-cities/article19435194/ (both accessed October 10, 2014).

85 **Hong Kong and Singapore respond to skyrocketing property prices:**
- Ramy Inocencio, "Hong Kong punctures property bubble," *CNN.com*, November 13, 2012, http://edition.cnn.com/2012/11/13/business/hong-kong-property-tax/ (accessed January 12, 2015).
- Hong Kong Trade Development Council, "Economic and Trade Information on Hong Kong," *HKTDC Research*, April 26, 2013, http://hong-kong-economy-research.hktdc.com/business-news/article/Market-Environment/Economic-and-Trade-Information-on-Hong-Kong/etihk/en/1/1X000000/1X09OVUL.htm (accessed April 30, 2013).
- Shu-Ching Jean Chen, "Good Run Continues for Hong Kong's Property Market," *Forbes*, January 12, 2015, www.forbes.com/sites/shuchingjeanchen/2015/01/12/good-run-continues-for-hong-kongs-real-estate-market/ (accessed September 14, 2015).
- Rachel Chang, "Permanent residents hit by changes," *The Straits Times*, January 12, 2013.

86 **Remittances Data from the following sources, with special thanks to Seyed Reza Yousefi, Consultant Economist at the World Bank, for helping me interpret the raw data:**
- World Bank, "Annual Remittances Data (updated as of April 2015)," *Migration & Remittances Data*, http://econ.worldbank.org/WBSITE/EXTERNAL/EXTDEC/EXTDECPROSPECTS/0,,contentMDK:22759429~pagePK:64165401~piPK:64165026~theSitePK:476883,00.html (accessed April 28, 2015).
- Rachel Glickhouse and Mark Keller, "Explainer: Expatriate Voting Laws in Latin America," Americas Society/Council of the Americas, May 10, 2012, www.as-coa.org/articles/explainer-expatriate-voting-laws-latin-america (accessed October 31, 2015).
- World Bank, "Bilateral Remittance Matrix 2014" and "Bilateral Remittance Matrix 2013," *Migration & Remittances Data*, http://econ.worldbank.org/WBSITE/EXTERNAL/EXTDEC/EXTDECPROSPECTS/0,,contentMDK:22759429~pagePK:64165401~piPK:64165026~theSitePK:476883,00.html (accessed May 1, 2015).

87 **On migrants and their levels of education:**
- "A world of exiles," *The Economist*, January 2, 2003, www.economist.com/node/1511765 (accessed July 3, 2013).
- Alex Glennie and Laura Chappell, "Jamaica: From Diverse Beginning to Diaspora in the Developed World," Migration Policy Institute, June 2010, www.migrationinformation.org/feature/display.cfm?ID=787 (accessed July 3, 2013)
- OECD and United Nations Department of Economic and Social Affairs joint report, "World Migration in Figures," (2013) and www.telegraph.co.uk/news/politics/10258081/Two-million-quit-Britain-in-talent-drain.html and www.theguardian.com/higher-education-network/blog/2013/jun/04/higher-education-participation-data-analysis (accessed September 18, 2014). Over 3.5 million UK citizens live abroad in the OECD and 40 percent of them have a university degree. See page 6 of the OECD report.
- OECD and United Nations Department of Economic and Social Affairs joint report, "World Migration in Figures" (2013).

88-89 **On the remuneration and hiring of expats vs. locals see:**
- Leslie Kwoh, "Asia's Endangered Species: The Expat," *Wall Street Journal Online*, March 28, 2012, http://online.wsj.com/article/SB100014240527023041771045773 05780300265926.html (accessed April 5, 2012).
- Leslie Kwoh, "Asia's Endangered Species: The Expat," *Wall Street Journal Online*, March 28, 2012, http://online.wsj.com/article/SB100014240527023041771045773 05780300265926.html (accessed April 5, 2012).
- "Brazil executives' salaries top London, New York," *Reuters*, December 10, 2010, www.reuters.com/article/2010/12/10/brazil-executives-idUSN1028825320101210 (accessed April 28, 2015).

89 **On countries who do not offer highly skilled migrant visas:**
- Merco Press, *Brazil reviewing immigration policy and is looking for "brains and human capital,"* April 2, 2013, http://en.mercopress.com/2013/04/02/brazil-reviewing-immigration-policy-and-is-looking-for-brains-and-human-capital (accessed October 10, 2013).

89-91 **For information on countries that are attracting their diaspora back home, see:**
- Talent Corp Malaysia, *Returning Expert Program*, www.talentcorp.com.my/malaysians-abroad/returning-expert-program/ (accessed August 4, 2013).
- Gürkan Çelik, "Turkey pulls, The Netherlands Pushes?" *Turkish Review*, June 30, 2011, www.turkishreview.org/tr/newsDetail_getNewsById.action?newsI d=223107 (accessed January 14, 2013).

- Jonah Fisher, "Nigeria's thriving economy lures expats back home," *BBC,* October 20, 2011, www.bbc.co.uk/news/world-africa-15382981 (accessed July 25, 2013).
- "Nigeria GDP Growth Rate," *Trading Economies,* www.tradingeconomics.com/nigeria/gdp-growth (accessed July 25, 2013).
- Peter Cox, "Better Prospects Result in Brain Gain for Africa," *Voice of America News,* February 13, 2013, www.voanews.com/content/africa-brain-gain-thanks-to-growing-african-economies/1602881.html (accessed July 24, 2013).
- Vivienne Walt, "The Repatriate Generation," *Time,* August 15, 2011, www.time.com/time/magazine/article/0,9171,2086837,00.html#i xzz2a8DeOZDD (accessed July 26, 2013).
- Xan Rice, "China's economic invasion of Africa," *The Guardian,* February 6, 2011, www.guardian.co.uk/world/2011/feb/06/chinas-economic-invasion-of-africa (accessed July 25, 2013).
- "Little to fear but fear itself," *The Economist,* September 21, 2013, www.economist.com/news/middle-east-and-africa/21586583-slowing-demand-raw-materials-will-not-derail-african-economies-little-fear (accessed October 11, 2013).
- African Economic Outlook, www.africaneconomicoutlook.org/en/outlook/forecast/ (accessed May 8, 2015).

91-92   On China, international education and its diaspora:

- Patti Waldmeir, "China parents count cost of sending children to overseas universities," *Financial Times,* December 29, 2013, www.ft.com/cms/s/0/98c4a5ac-63c1-11e3-b70d-00144feabdc0.html#axzz3OdBEOsko (accessed January 12, 2015).
- James Manyika and Sree Ramaswamy Susan Lund, "Preparing for a new era of work," *McKinsey,* November 2012, www.mckinsey.com/insights/organization/preparing_for_a_new_era_of_knowledge_work (accessed June 6, 2013).
- "Plight of the sea turtles," *The Economist,* July 4, 2013, www.economist.com/news/china/21580470-students-coming-back-home-helped-build-modern-china-so-why-are-they-now-faring-so-poorly (accessed May 8, 2015).
- ibid.
- Ian Johnson, "Wary of Future, Professionals Leave China in Record Numbers," *New York Times,* October 31, 2012, www.nytimes.com/2012/11/01/world/asia/wary-of-future-many-professionals-leave-china.html?hp&_r=0 (accessed November 5, 2012).

93   **For more details on liberalizing global migration:**

- "Border follies," *The Economist*, November 17, 2012 (also www.economist.com/news/finance-and-economics/21566629-liberalising-migration-could-deliver-huge-boost-global-output-border-follies)
- American Social History Productions, *History Matters*, http://historymatters.gmu.edu/d/7027/.
- Jill Lepore, "The Last Amazon," *The New Yorker*, www.newyorker.com/magazine/2014/09/22/last-amazon (accessed October 6, 2014).
- "What did World War One really do for women?" *BBC*, www.bbc.co.uk/guides/z9bf9j6 (accessed May 12, 2015).

94   **On New Zealand and Chile's immigration policies:**

- Ministry of Business, Innovation and Employment, *Immigration New Zealand's Vision 2015*, (MB 12370 INZ 2015 factsheet_v3).
- Partnership for a New American Economy and Partnership for New York City, *Not Coming to America: Why the US is Falling Behind in the Global Race for Talent* (May 2012).
- "The lure of Chilecon Valley," *The Economist*, October 13, 2012, www.economist.com/node/21564589 (accessed October 14, 2013).
- Start-up Chile, http://startupchile.org/about/faqs/ and http://startupchile.org/about/the-program/ (accessed August 3, 2013). Perhaps this dynamic atmosphere is what garnered such a positive response from Santiago de Chile to my online survey.

CHAPTER 6
NOT COMING TO AMERICA—A CASE STUDY

96   **Eritrea imposes a 2% diaspora tax, but in 2011 the UN's Security Council condemned the practice as a thinly disguised form of extortion, see:**

- United Nations, December 5, 2011, www.un.org/News/Press/docs/2011/sc10471.doc.htm

96   **On American expat taxes see:**

- David Futrelle, "Renouncing Your Citizenship to Stick It to the Tax Man? Not as Easy as it Looks," *Time*, June 22, 2012, http://business.time.com/2012/06/22/renouncing-your-citizenship-to-stick-it-to-the-tax-man-not-as-easy-as-it-looks/ (both accessed November 2, 2015)

96-97   **Facebook statistics and responses to Eduardo Saverin's emigration from the U.S.:**

- Facebook, http://newsroom.fb.com/company-info/ (accessed October 5, 2014).
- Jesse Drucker, "Facebook's Saverin May Save $67 Million on U.S. Tax Bill," *Bloomberg*, May 17, 2012,

www.bloomberg.com/news/2012-05-16/facebook-s-saverin-may-save-67-million-on-u-s-tax-bill.html (accessed May 9, 2013),

- Robert W. Wood, "Why Facebook's Co-Founder Just Defriended America," *Forbes*, May 11, 2012, www.forbes.com/sites/robertwood/2012/05/11/why-facebooks-co-founder-just-defriended-america/ (accessed May 9, 2013).

- Ex-PATRIOT Act text taken from Ingrid Lunden's *Schumer And Casey's Ex-PATRIOT Act: Details Of How They Plan To Get Saverin's $67M And More* http://techcrunch.com/2012/05/17/schumer-and-caseys-ex-patriot-act-details-of-how-they-plan-to-get-saverins-67m-and-more/ (accessed May 6, 2013).

97-101 On FATCA and why more Americans are renouncing their citizenship:

- Giles Broom, "Wealthy Americans Queue to Give Up Their Passports," *Bloomberg*, May 1, 2012, www.bloomberg.com/news/2012-05-01/wealthy-americans-queue-to-give-up-passports-in-swiss-capital.html (accessed May 5, 2013).

- Robert W. Wood, "Americans Renouncing Citizenship Up 221%, All Aboard the FATCA Express," *Forbes*, February 6, 2014, www.forbes.com/sites/robertwood/2014/02/06/americans-renouncing-citizenship-up-221-all-aboard-the-fatca-express/ (accessed October 5, 2014).

- Robert Frank, "Record 3,415 Americans give up citizenship," *CNBC*, February 10, 2014, www.cnbc.com/id/102413492 (accessed May 8, 2015).

- Roma Luciw, "U.S. tax crackdown hits Canadian residents," *The Globe and Mail*, Monday, June 20, 2011, www.theglobeandmail.com/globe-investor/personal-finance/us-tax-crackdown-hits-canadian-residents/article2067393/ (accessed May 6, 2013).

- Report of Foreign Bank and Financial Accounts (FBAR) Section 4.26.16.4.5.1 (07-01-2008), FBAR Willfulness Penalty — Authority, www.irs.gov/irm/part4/irm_04-026-016.html (accessed November 2, 2015)

- Helena Bachmann, "Mister Taxman: Why Some Americans Working Abroad Are Ditching Their Citizenships," *Time*, January 31, 2013, http://world.time.com/2013/01/31/mister-taxman-why-some-americans-working-abroad-are-ditching-their-citizenships/#ixzz2SUnmHAWc (accessed May 8, 2013).

- Al Lewis, "Tax man makes it hard to be an American," *The Wall Street Journal: Marketwatch*, May 18, 2012, http://articles.marketwatch.com/2012-05-18/commentary/31756872_1_bank-accounts-citizenship-tough-irs (accessed May 8, 2013).

- Al Lewis, "Tax-dodgers are proudly un-American," *The Wall Street Journal: Marketwatch*, May 4, 2012, www.marketwatch.com/story/tax-dodgers-are-proudly-un-american-2012-05-04 (accessed May 8, 2013).
- Responses to Helena Bachmann, "Mister Taxman: Why Some Americans Working Abroad Are Ditching Their Citizenships," *Time*, January 31, 2013, http://world.time.com/2013/01/31/mister-taxman-why-some-americans-working-abroad-are-ditching-their-citizenships/#ixzz2SUnmHAWc (accessed May 8, 2013).
- Camilla Turner, "Boris Johnson to pay 'six-figure' American tax bill," *The Telegraph*, January 22, 2015, www.telegraph.co.uk/news/politics/11361816/Boris-Johnson-to-pay-six-figure-American-tax-bill.html (accessed May 1, 2015).
- Ben Wright, "Toxic Citizens?" *The Wall Street Journal*, June 13, 2010, http://online.wsj.com/article/SB1000142405274870040021045752 90451594973266.html (accessed May 6, 2013).
- Helena Bachmann, "Mister Taxman: Why Some Americans Working Abroad Are Ditching Their Citizenships," *Time*, January 31, 2013, http://world.time.com/2013/01/31/mister-taxman-why-some-americans-working-abroad-are-ditching-their-citizenships/#ixzz2SUnmHAWc (accessed May 8, 2013).
- Isabelle Eichenberger, "Swiss expats caught in middle of US tax conflict," *Swiss Broadcasting Corporation*, February 16, 2012, www.swissinfo.ch/eng/specials/expat_woes/Swiss_expats_caught_in_middle_of_US_tax_conflict.html?cid=32137500 (accessed April 30, 2013).

102-103 On Eduardo Saverin's tax bill and how much he may owe the IRS

- Sanat Vallikappen and Jesse Drucker Sheridan Prasso, "Facebook's Saverin to Pay Hundreds of Millions in Tax," *Bloomberg*, May 18, 2012, www.bloomberg.com/news/2012-05-17/facebook-co-founder-turns-30-000-savings-to-3-billion.html (accessed May 10, 2012).
- Estimated by Thomas H. McNutt of the American Chamber of Commerce in Singapore.
- Brian Solomon, "Eduardo Saverin's Net Worth Publicly Revealed: More Than $2 Billion In Facebook Alone," *Forbes*, May 18, 2012, www.forbes.com/sites/briansolomon/2012/05/18/eduardo-saverins-net-worth-publicly-revealed-more-than-2-billion-in-facebook-alone/ (accessed May 10, 2013).
- Andrew M. and Scott A. Bowman Katzenstein, "Facebook's Saverin Left U.S. as a Taxpayer, Not a Traitor," *Bloomberg*, May 25, 2012, www.bloomberg.com/news/2012-05-24/facebook-s-saverin-left-u-s-as-a-taxpayer-not-a-traitor.html (accessed May 6, 2013).

- Jesse Drucker, "Facebook's Saverin May Save $67 Million on U.S. Tax Bill," *Bloomberg*, May 17, 2012, www.bloomberg.com/news/2012-05-16/facebook-s-saverin-may-save-67-million-on-u-s-tax-bill.html (accessed May 9, 2013).

Americans abroad know they have an annual date with their labyrinthine tax office, but other roamers shouldn't sit on their laurels.

- Living and working anywhere within the E.U. is so easy today that Europeans can forget that tax obligations vary from country to country. Roamers who have been domiciled in the U.K. for seventeen years, for example, automatically become subject to U.K. inheritance taxes. Only if they move out of the U.K. for three years or more are they excluded. For example, if Dieter from Austria moves to the U.K. and lives there for eighteen years, then moves to Germany and dies two years later, his estate will still be subject to U.K. inheritance taxes. If Dieter dies more than three years later, Her Majesty's Revenues and Taxes will no longer have any claims on his estate.

104   **On the number of immigrants to the U.S. vs. other countries**

- "Migration and Remittances: Top Countries," The World Bank, siteresources.worldbank.org/INTPROSPECTS/Resources/33493 4-1199807908806/Top10.pdf (accessed May 17, 2012).

- Adam Ozimek, "Is the U.S. the most immigrant friendly country in the world?" *Forbes*, November 18, 2012, http://www.forbes.com/sites/modeledbehavior/2012/11/18/is-the-u-s-the-most-immigrant-friendly-country-in-the-world/ (accessed May 17, 2013).

- Anna Fifield, "US hits skilled visas quota in just days," *Financial Times*, April 5, 2013, www.ft.com/cms/s/0/1a7231a6-9e37-11e2-bea1-00144feabdc0.html#axzz3YtjOJfDH (accessed May 1, 2015).

105   **On confounding immigrants with roamers:**

- James Surowiecki, "The Track-Star Economy," *The New Yorker*, August 27, 2012.

106   **Kunal Bahl, Snapdeal and entrepreneurial American immigrants:**

- Greg Bensinger and Spercer E. Ante, "eBay Forms Partnership With India's Snapdeal," *The Wall Street Journal*, June 3, 2013, online.wsj.com/article/SB1000142412788732442390457852369071 6834954.html (accessed November 2, 2015).

- "On hiring with Kunal Bahl, Snapdeal, 'We are looking for raw passion and killer motivation,'" *Your Story*, February 15, 2012, yourstory.in/2012/02/on-hiring-with-kunal-bahl-snapdeal-we-are-looking-for-rawpassion-and-killer-motivation/ (accessed November 2, 2015).

- "Strict US immigration policies contribute to high unemployment," *RT*, August 4, 2012, rt.com/usa/us-immigration-economy-visa-education-863/.

107-109 On American immigration and STEM industries:

- Conor Friedersdorf, "Why the Ex-Patriot Act Is a Creepy Law," *The Atlantic*, May 18, 2012, www.theatlantic.com/politics/archive/2012/05/why-the-ex-patriot-act-is-a-creepy-law/257368/ (accessed May 6, 2013).
- U.S. Department of Homeland Security, Office of Immigration Statistics, *Yearbook of Immigration Statistics:2011* (Washington, D.C.: United States. Department of Homeland Security, 2012), 5 and 8. Legal permanent residents are also known as "green card" recipients.
- Partnership for a New American Economy and Partnership for New York City, *Not Coming to America: Why the US is Falling Behind in the Global Race for Talent* (May 2012), 8.
- Partnership for a New American Economy and Partnership for New York City, *Not Coming to America: Why the US is Falling Behind in the Global Race for Talent* (May 2012), 18.

Singapore's immigration strategy and birth rates:

- Department of Singapore Statistics, *Key Annual Indicators*, 2012, www.singstat.gov.sg/stats/keyind.html (accessed December 27, 2012, based on Mid-Year Estimates).
- Statistics from The World Bank, *Data: Fertility rate, total (births per woman)* , http://data.worldbank.org/indicator/SP.DYN.TFRT.IN (accessed July 17, 2013).

CHAPTER 7
ALL POLITICS IS LOCAL

111-112 For a thoughtful piece on the future role of national governments see:

- Parag Khanna, "The End of the Nation-State?" *The New York Times*, October 13, 2013: SR5.
- Ibid.

On the 2006 Lebanon War and Canadians of Convenience see:

- *The Evacuation of Canadians from Lebanon in July 2006: Implications for the Government of Canada.* The Standing Senate Committee on Foreign Affairs and International Trade Report published May 2007. The Honourable Senator Consiglio Di Nino, Chair The Honourable Senator Peter A. Stollery, Deputy Chair. www.senate-senat.ca/foraffetrang.asp

112-113 On dual citizenship and the number of citizens living abroad:

- United Nations High Commissioner for Refugees, www.unhcr.org/pages/49c3646c26.html (accessed September 15, 2015).
- Jason Schachter, United Nations Economic Commission for Europe Statistical Division, "Dual citizenship trends and their implication for the collection of migration statistics," (paper

presented at UNECE/Eurostat Work Session on Migration
Statistics, Chisinau, Republic of Moldova, September 15, 2014),
Slides 10-
11,www.unece.org/fileadmin/DAM/stats/documents/ece/ces/ge
.10/2014/mtg1/presentations/10._UNECE_Dual_citizenship.pdf
(accessed November 21, 2015).

Number of American citizens with dual nationality:

- "The problem of dual citizenship," by The Times Editorial Board,
  Los Angeles Times 26 December, 2014,
  www.latimes.com/opinion/editorials/la-ed-dual-citizenship-
  20141228-story.html (accessed November 20, 2015)
- Maria LaMagna, "When one passport isn't enough," July 4, 2012,
  CNN, http://edition.cnn.com/2012/07/04/us/dual-
  nationals/index.html (accessed November 21, 2015).

Number of Dutch citizens with dual nationality:

- Statistics Netherlands, press release August 6, 2015, "Statistics
  Netherlands: 1.3 million people in the Netherlands hold dual
  citizenship," www.cbs.nl/en-
  GB/menu/themas/bevolking/publicaties/artikelen/archief/2015
  /aantal-nederlanders-met-dubbele-nationaliteit-gestegen-naar-13-
  miljoen.htm (accessed November 21, 2015).

Number of Australian citizens with dual nationality:

- Michael Bradley, "You may be surprised by how you could lose
  your citizenship," Jun 29, 2015, *ABC News*,
  www.abc.net.au/news/2015-06-25/bradley-how-you-could-lose-
  your-citizenship/6572382 (accessed November 21, 2015).
- Parliament of Australia, "Dual Citizenship in Australia "(Current
  Issues Brief 5 2000-01, Social Policy Group, 28 November 2000),
  www.aph.gov.au/About_Parliament/Parliamentary_Departments
  /Parliamentary_Library/Publications_Archive/CIB/cib0001/01C
  IB05 (accessed November 21, 2015).

Number of Canadian citizens with dual nationality:

- Audrey and François Crépeau Macklin, *Multiple Citizenship, Identity
  and Entitlement in Canada*, IRPP Study No. 6, Institute Research on
  Public Policy, June 6, 2010. p. 7. (4 million Canadians with dual
  nationality vs. Jason Schachter UNEC ESD report, which states
  only 1 million Canadians have dual nationality).
- Christopher DeWolf, "In Hong Kong, Just Who Is an Expat,
  Anyway?" December 29, 2014,
  http://blogs.wsj.com/expat/2014/12/29/in-hong-kong-just-who-
  is-an-expat-anyway/ (accessed March 21, 2015).

Number of Indian citizens living overseas:

- The Ministry of Overseas Indians put the number at ten million in
  2012, but other figures put the number at closer to twenty million.
  http://moia.gov.in/services.aspx?ID1=300&id=m8&idp=59&mai
  nid=23 (viewed April 28, 2013) and
  http://nriinternet.com/Did_you_Know/NRIs_Population_WOR
  LDWIDE/.

114   **On rogue traders:**

- "Biography," nickleeson.com, www.nickleeson.com/biography/full_biography_02.html (accessed December 19, 2014).
- My conclusions are informed by an article by Simon Goodley, "Investment Bankers accused of 'creating own monsters,'" *The Guardian, UBS Crisis Special*, October 2011.

117   **On foreigners and cultural clashes while abroad:**

- "Swiss man admits vandalism, faces caning in Singapore," *AFP: Asia One News*, June 25, 2010, http://news.asiaone.com/News/AsiaOne+News/Singapore/Story/A1Story20100625-223926.html (accessed December 19, 2014).
- Barbara Surk, *The Huffington Post*, April 4, 2010, www.huffingtonpost.com/2010/04/04/dubai-kissing-couple-jail_n_524736.html (accessed December 19, 2014).
- Dhananjayan Sriskandarajah and Catherine Drew, "Viewpoint: Expats chasing dreams, Brits Abroad" *BBC News*, Monday, December 11, 2006, http://news.bbc.co.uk/2/hi/uk_news/6163219.stm (accessed November 2, 2015).

118   **Immigration and Emigration figures are derived from here:**

- World Bank, "Migration and Remittances: Top Countries," *The Migration and Remittances Factbook 2011*, http://siteresources.worldbank.org/INTPROSPECTS/Resources/334934-1199807908806/Top10.pdf (accessed May 5, 2015). By 2010, Russia had imported 12.3 milion and exported 11.1 million people. Britain had seven million immigrants in the country and 4.7 million Brits were living abroad. India imported 5.4 million people and exported 11.4 million. Germany wasn't far from reaching the dual top 10- it had imported 10.8 million immigrants by 2010, and had exported 3.5 million of its own citizens.
- According to the U.K.'s 2010 census, most immigrants to the United Kingdom come from the following ten countries: India, Poland, Pakistan, Ireland, Germany, South Africa, Bangladesh, the United States, Jamaica, and Kenya. These figures, however, are frustratingly inaccurate. For example, the U.K.'s 2010 census does not distinguish between Brits who were born in Germany while their parents worked on German military bases during the Cold War and "echt Germans" who were born in Germany, speak German, have a German passport and have since become U.K. citizens. As Helen Pidd in *The Guardian* writes, "The full census data on passports held and language spoken has not yet been released. That will give us a far better picture on how many real Germans have made this rainy island their home. Until then, there is no scientific way of finding out how many Bavarians and Berliners really lurk on these shores." Helen Pidd, "Britain's German-born population prefers life under the radar," *The*

Guardian, 14 December 14 2014,
www.theguardian.com/uk/2012/dec/14/german-born-
population-uk-census (accessed May 5, 2015). Eurostat statistics
use a different measure for calculating the number of foreigners in
any given E.U. country. In their list foreign-born nationals living in
the UK, which specifies the country of citizenship on January 1,
2013, the most migrants are citizens of India, Ireland, Pakistan, the
United States and Lithuania. Eurostat, "Main countries of
citizenship and birth of the foreign foreign-born population,
January 1, 2013 (1)," European Commission Eurostat,
http://ec.europa.eu/eurostat/statistic (accessed May 5, 2015).

119   **David Foster Wallace on voting:**
  • David Foster Wallace, "Up Simba," *Consider the Lobster* (London:
    Hachette Digital, 2006), Kindle edition.

122-124 **On the wealth and power of cities, and their popularity with
         foreigners:**
  • "Expats vote Singapore best place to live and work" *HSBC Expat
    Explorer survey*, September 15, 2015, www.hsbc.com/news-and-
    insight/2015/expats-vote-singapore-best-place-to-live-and-work
    (accessed November 1, 2015)
  • Mike Hales and Andres Mendoza Pena, *2012 Global Cities Index and
    Emerging Cities Outlook*, AT Kearny Inc., 2012, 3.
  • PriceWaterhouseCoopers, "Global city GDP rankings 2008-2025,"
    UK Media Centre PwC - UK Economic Outlook November 2009,
    www.ukmediacentre.pwc.com/Media-Library/Global-city-GDP-
    rankings-2008-2025-61a.aspx, p. 23 (accessed April 12, 2012).
  • Canada, Switzerland, France, Hong Kong, the U.A.E., and
    Germany make up the rest of the top 10, with China sliding in at
    number 11. Hydrogen Group, "Global professionals on the
    move—2013," (2013), 9-10.
  • iOMe Challenge, "Strategic Research Institute at St. Norbert
    College, USA," *iOMe Millennials on Social Security*, October 2011,
    http://bit.ly/nG5kWo (accessed April 10, 2012).
  • Richard Florida, *The Rise of the Creative Class* (New York: Basic
    Books, 2004), 96.
  • A special thanks must go out to Santiago de Chile, who are over-
    represented in this survey with 19 responses. It may be smaller
    than other big cities, but they have a big heart.

126-128 **On voting from abroad:**
  • Sikander Shaheen, "Voting for expats not possible ," *The Nation*,
    April 25, 2013, www.nation.com.pk/pakistan-news-newspaper-
    daily-english-online/elections-2013/25-Apr-2013/voting-for-
    expats-not-possible (accessed May 20, 2013).
  • Suzi Dixon, "Lords calls to extend expat voting rights," January
    25, 2013, www.telegraph.co.uk/expat/expatnews/9808027/Lords-
    calls-to-extend-expat-voting-rights.html (accessed April 25, 2013).

- www.letcanadiansvote.com/ (accessed April 19, 2014).
- Sabir Shah, "Around 120 countries allow expatriates to vote, 62 do not," *The International News*, March 29, 2013, www.thenews.com.pk/Todays-News-2-168092-Around-120-countries-allow-expatriates-to-vote,-62-do-not (accessed May 20, 2013).
- David Adams, "Venezuelan expatriates saddened by narrow election defeat," *Reuters*, April 15, 2013, www.reuters.com/article/2013/04/15/us-venezuela-election-expats-idUSBRE93E06520130415 (accessed April 26, 2013).
- Philipp Köker, "Zeman wins at home but Schwarzenberg abroad: Differences in voting results in the Czech presidential election," www.presidentialactivism.com, January 30, 2013, http://presidentialactivism.wordpress.com/2013/01/30/zeman-wins-at-home-but-schwarzenberg-abroad-differences-in-voting-results-in-the-czech-presidential-election/ (accessed April 26, 2013).
- Brooke Anderson, "Expat voting an electoral reform success story," January 26, 2013, www.dailystar.com.lb/News/Local-News/2013/Jan-26/203801-expat-voting-an-electoral-reform-success-story.ashx#axzz2RXUtJiIS (accessed April 26, 2013).
- Patrick Winn, "Are expats America's laziest voters?" *Global Post*, October 9, 2012, www.globalpost.com/dispatch/news/regions/asia-pacific/thailand/121008/expats-america-voters-US-election-2012-expatriate-vote (accessed July 1, 2013).
- "Returning officers: More expatriates are electing political representatives at home," *The Economist*, July 2, 2012, www.economist.com/node/21556222 (accessed April 30, 2013).
- NZPA, "Overseas votes could decide next week's election," *National Business Review*, October 30, 2008, http://m.nbr.co.nz/article/overseas-votes-could-decide-next-weeks-election-37142#bmb=1 (accessed April 28, 2013).
- Rachel Glickhouse and Mark Keller, "Expatriate Voting Laws in Latin America," May 10, 2012, Americas Society/Council of the Americas, www.as-coa.org/articles/explainer-expatriate-voting-laws-latin-america (accessed June 8, 2013).
- Ibid.
- "Returning officers: More expatriates are electing political representatives at home," *The Economist*, July 2, 2012, www.economist.com/node/21556222 (accessed April 30, 2013).
- Of course this is a self-selecting group—a person who is willing to fill out a survey for a perfect stranger (and for which they receive no compensation) is also more likely to make the effort to vote.

129-130 On France's first capitalist revolution
- Lauren Collins, "L'Etranger," *The New Yorker*, February 25, 2013, 63.

On politicians who lose credibility by spending too much time abroad:

- David Runciman, "Fire and Ashes: Success and Failure in Politics by Michael Ignatieff—review," *The Guardian*, November 27, 2013, www.theguardian.com/books/2013/nov/27/michael-ignatieff-fire-ashes-review (accessed September 25, 2014).
- Richard Tomlinson and Sandrine Rastello, "Strauss-Kahn Bailouts Give IMF Chief Popularity Over Sarkozy," *Bloomberg*, January 26, 2011, www.bloomberg.com/news/2011-01-26/strauss-kahn-bailing-out-euro-gives-imf-s-chief-popularity-sarkozy-misses.html (accessed September 30, 2014).

131-133 Information on overseas constituencies is from the following sources:

- Alexandre Léchenet, "La gauche l'emporte chez les Français de l'étranger," *Le Monde*, June 18, 2012, www.lemonde.fr/politique/article/2012/06/18/la-gauche-l-emporte-chez-les-francais-de-l-etranger_1720178_823448.html#6WfSACyMGOV8gbDW.99 (accessed December 19, 2014) and private research.
- International Institute for Democracy and Electoral Assistance, *Voter turnout data for France*, www.idea.int/vt/countryview.cfm?id=53 (accessed May 30, 2013).
- Lizzy Davies, "French expats prepare to vote in parliamentary elections," *The Guardian*, June 1, 2012, www.guardian.co.uk/world/2012/jun/01/french-expats-vote-parliamentary-elections (accessed April 27, 2013).
- Department of Foreign Affairs, Trade and Development Canada, "Circular Note No. XDC-1264 of September 8, 2011," *Foreign Elections in Canada and Foreign Electoral Constituencies*, www.international.gc.ca/protocol-protocole/policies-politiques/circular-note_note-circulaire_xdc-1264.aspx?lang=eng.
- Foreign Affairs and International Trade Canada, *Statement by Minister Baird on Tunisian Elections*, September 22, 2011, www.international.gc.ca/media/aff/news-communiques/2011/272.aspx?lang=eng (accessed April 26, 2013).
- Australian Bureau of Statistics, "2006 Census of Population and Housing: Media Releases and Fact Sheets," June 27, 2007, http://abs.gov.au/AUSSTATS/abs@.nsf/7d12b0f6763c78caca257061001cc588/5a47791aa683b719ca257306000d536c!OpenDocument (accessed September 18, 2015).
- James Panichi, "The diaspora fights back," *Inside Story*, December 4, 2008, http://inside.org.au/the-diaspora-fights-back/ (accessed May 31, 2013).
- Ibid.
- At the time of writing, France, Italy, Tunisia, Croatia, Colombia, the Dominican Republic, Ecuador, Macedonia, Morocco, and Portugal have overseas electoral districts.

- Brian Knowlton, "Evaluating the Expat Factor," *New York Times*, August 27, 2012, www.nytimes.com/2012/08/27/us/politics/votes-from-expatriates-could-play-crucial-role-in-election.html (accessed June 8, 2013).

133-134 On governments supporting their citizens overseas with public-private ventures:
- Alastair Gee, "Technological Advances," *Monocle*, no. 69, December 13/January 14.
- See more at: http://advance.org/who-we-are/#sthash.zC8GnjJP.dpuf (accessed May 30, 2013).

134-136 On foreign citizens voting in the country where they live:
- Sylvia Zappi, "Législatives: les Français de l'étranger abstentionnistes expliquent leur non-vote," *Le Monde*, June 8, 2012, www.lemonde.fr/politique/article/2012/06/08/legislatives-les-francais-de-l-etranger-abstentionnistes-expliquent-leur-non-vote_1715155_823448.html (accessed May 30, 2013).
- "Give disenfranchised expats the vote," January 29, 2014, *The Local*, www.thelocal.de/20140129/eu-give-disenfranchised-expats-the-vote (accessed November 1, 2015).
- Peter Spiro, "Noncitizen Voting Makes Sense. Why Don't Liberals Agree?" *Bloomberg View*, June 19, 2013, www.bloombergview.com/articles/2013-06-19/noncitizen-voting-makes-sense-why-don-t-liberals-agree- (accessed May 6, 2015).
- Simon Thompson, "Voting Rights: Earned or Entitled?" *Harvard Political Review*, December 3, 2010, http://harvardpolitics.com/united-states/voting-rights-earned-or-entitled/ (accessed May 6, 2015).
- "SWEDEN.; Abolition of the Passport System," *The London Times*, republished in *The New York Times*, November 6, 1860, www.nytimes.com/1860/11/06/news/sweden-abolition-of-the-passport-system.html (accessed November 1, 2015).

CHAPTER 8
MI CASA, SU CASA: ROAMERS ON HOME

144-145 For a perceptive article about living abroad and one's relationship to home, see:
- Gianpiero Petriglieri, "Moving Around Without Losing Your Roots," *The Harvard Review Blog Network*, October 3, 2012, http://blogs.hbr.org/cs/2012/10/moving_around_without_losing_your_roots.html (accessed December 2, 2012).

146 Several rival global cities indexes exist, but this is the one used throughout *Roaming*:
- "2014 Global Cities Index," AT Kearney, www.atkearney.com/research-studies/global-cities-index/full-report (accessed September 8, 2014).

147-151 Writers on what home means to them:

- Yotam Ottolenghi and Sami Tamimi, *Jerusalem* (Berkeley: Ten Speed Press, 2012), 14.
- Pico Iyer, "Where Is Home?" June 2013, www.ted.com/talks/pico_iyer_where_is_home.html?v2=0#81071 7 (accessed July 20, 2013).
- David Sedaris, "A Long Way Home," *The New Yorker*, April 2013, 28-31.

152-153 On foreigners in China:

- Zhu Zhe and Xu Wei, "Green Card Access Eased," *China Daily*, September 16, 2015, http://usa.chinadaily.com.cn/epaper/2015-09/16/content_21893963.htm (accessed October 22, 2015).
- Mark Kitto, "You'll Never Be Chinese: Why I'm leaving the country I loved," *Prospect Magazine*, August 8, 2012, www.prospectmagazine.co.uk/politics/mark-kitto-youll-never-be-chinese-leaving-china (accessed September 24, 2014).

153-154 Germany and foreign Ph.D.'s:

- Craig Whitlock and Shannon Smiley, "Non-European Ph.D.s In Germany Find Use Of 'Doktor' Verboten," *The Washington Post*, March 14, 2008, http://articles.washingtonpost.com/2008-03-14/world/36842340_1_doctoral-degrees-nazi-era-law-boston-university (accessed June 12, 2013).
- David Sedaris, 31.

155-159 For insightful and sensitive views on identity, see the following sources:

- Amin Maalouf, *In the Name of Identity: Violence and the Need to Belong*, trans. Barbara Bray (New York: Penguin, 2003), 2-3.
- Charlotte Alfred, "Protesters Say Ferguson Feels Like Gaza, Palestinians Tweet Back Advice," *The Huffington Post*, August 14, 2014, http://www.huffingtonpost.com/2014/08/14/ferguson-gaza_n_5679923.html (accessed October 14, 2014).
- Amin Maalouf, *Origins: A Memoir*, trans. Catherine Temerson (New York: Farrar, Straus and Giroux, 2009).

CHAPTER 9
WE'LL ALWAYS HAVE PARIS: ROAMERS ON LOVE, DIVORCE, AND OTHER JUICY STUFF

162 On long-term relationships, see

- Esther Perel, "The secret to desire in a long-term relationship," February 2013, www.ted.com/talks/esther_perel_the_secret_to_desire_in_a_long_term_relationship/transcript?language=en (accessed March 8, 2015).

163 National Statistics on couples vs. singles:

Few governments compile data on non-cohabiting partners so it's hard to gauge accurately genuine singles and those who have a partner. A few studies, though offer clues. See:

- Mary Madden and Lee Rainie, "Romance in America," *Pew Research*, February 13, 2006, www.pewinternet.org/2006/02/13/romance-in-america/ (accessed October 17, 2014).
- Office for National Statistics, www.ons.gov.uk/ons/index.html.
- Matt Chorley, "Revealed: How married couples are now a minority…," *Mail Online*, March 28, 2014, www.dailymail.co.uk/news/article-2591541/Revealed-How-married-couples-minority-half-Brits-choose-live-just-stay-single.html (accessed October 17, 2014).

163   On those who are single by choice:
Studies that support this:

- Bella DePaulo, "How Many People Choose to Be Single?" *Psychology Today*, September 23, 2013, www.psychologytoday.com/blog/living-single/201309/how-many-people-choose-be-single (accessed October 16, 2014).
- Janelle Nanos, "Single by Choice," *Boston*, January 2012, www.bostonmagazine.com/2012/01/single-by-choice-why-more-of-us-than-ever-before-are-happy-to-never-get-married/ (accessed November 2, 2015).

Marriage to a foreigner as a leading factor for Americans living abroad:

- Amanda Klekowski von Koppenfels, "Political Transnationalism in a New Light?" in Migration and Organized Civil Society: Rethinking National Policy, 79-95 (Abingdon: Routledge, 2013).

165   On Long Distance Relationships, see:

- Gregory Guldner, "Long Distance Relationships," The Former Center for the Study of Long Distance Relationships, www.longdistancerelationships.net (accessed December 6, 2013).

170   You can read Christine's own inspirational story on Glamomamas. Christine has also written a chapter called "The First 6 Months" about adjusting to a new country. It can be found in the appendix to *Roaming* in the ebook and Kindle versions:

- http://glamomamas.com/takes-village/ first published in *Harper's Bazaar Singapore*—November 2010 (viewed December 15, 2013).

172   For those interested in Third Culture Kids or a deeper look at raising children abroad, see:

- David C. Pollock and Ruth E. Van Reken, *Third Culture Kids*. Boston: Nicholas Brealy, 2009.
- Robin Pascoe, *Raising Global Nomads: Parenting Abroad in an On-Demand World*. Vancouver: Expatriate Press Limited, 2006.

173   International School data taken from the following sources:

- American Cooperative School of Tunis, www.acst.net/about.cfm?subpage=697515 (accessed March 10, 2015).

- Canadian International School of Hong Kong, www.cdnis.edu.hk/facts/facts-sheet.html (accessed January 20, 2013).
- The International School of Helsinki, www.ish.edu.hel.fi/page.cfm?p=368 (accessed March 10, 2015).

179   On living longer and baby boomers:
- Compiled by Earth Policy Institute from United Nations Population Division, World Population Prospects: The 2010 Revision, electronic database, at http://esa.un.org/unpd/wpp/index.htm, updated May 3, 2011 (accessed August 29, 2014).
- Del Webb Baby Boomer Survey 2013, *HEY KIDS: MOVE OUT & MOVE ON*, (Press Release).

185   Percentage of Americans who hold a passport:
- U.S. Department of State—Bureau of Consular Affairs, http://travel.state.gov/content/passports/english/passports/statistics.html (accessed March 10, 2015).

On larger personal networks, but weaker close ties:
- Richard Florida, *The Rise of the Creative Class* (New York: Basic Books, 2004), 7.

CHAPTER 10
THE BOTTOM LINE: ROAMERS ON WORK, NON-WORK, AND THE TRAILING SPOUSE

188   On the extensive working hours of professionals:
- Paul Hodkinson, "Chart of the Day: which professions demand the longest hours?" *eFinancial News*, August 22, 2013, www.efinancialnews.com/story/2013-08-22/working-hours-comparison-industries-banks (accessed October 27, 2014).

189-190 On the link between multilingualism and soft skills:
- Fraser Lauchlan, Marinella Parisi, and Roberta Fadda, "Bilingualism in Sardinia and Scotland: Exploring the cognitive benefits of speaking a 'minority' language," *International Journal of Bilingualism*, April 16, 2012.
- R.L.G., "Johnson: Do different languages confer different personalities?" *The Economist Blog: Prospero*, November 5, 2013, www.economist.com/blogs/prospero/2013/11/multilingualism?fsrc=scn/fb/wl/bl/differentpersonalitieslanguage (accessed November 7, 2013).

On job satisfaction:
- "Job Satisfaction: 2014 Edition," The Conference Board, June 2014, www.conference-board.org/publications/publicationdetail.cfm?publicationid=2785 (accessed July 14, 2015).
- Jena McGregor, "Only 13 percent of people worldwide actually like going to work," *The Washington Post*, October 10, 2013,

www.washingtonpost.com/blogs/on-leadership/wp/2013/10/10/only-13-percent-of-people-worldwide-actually-like-going-to-work/ (accessed July 14, 2015).

195-196 On the trailing spouse:
- "Mindful Migrations: 2015 Global Mobility Trends Survey Report," Brookfield Global Relocation Services, (U.S.A., 2015), 13.

199-200 On gay multicultural couples moving abroad:
- Julia Preston. "With No Shortcut to a Green Card, Gay Couples Leave U.S." *New York Times*, February 17, 2013, www.nytimes.com/2013/02/18/us/with-no-shortcut-to-a-green-card-gay-couples-leave-us.html?pagewanted=all&_r=0 (accessed April 19, 2013).

CHAPTER 11
WHERE DOES IT ALL END? ROAMERS ON GROWING OLD AND UNSETTLING DOWN

202 Quote about the Dalai Lama taken from:
- Evan Osnos. "The Next Incarnation," *New Yorker*, October 4, 2010, 63.

203 On the downsides to expat life:
- Marcus Mabry and Jan Benzel, "The Dark Side of the Expat Life," *New York Times*, March 21, 2013, http://rendezvous.blogs.nytimes.com/2013/03/21/the-dark-side-of-the-expat-life/?_php=true&_type=blogs&_r=0 (accessed April 15, 2013).

205 Millennials expect to stay in a job for 3 years:
- Jeanne Meister, "Job Hopping Is the 'New Normal' for Millennials," *Forbes*, August 14, 2012, www.forbes.com/sites/jeannemeister/2012/08/14/job-hopping-is-the-new-normal-for-millennials-three-ways-to-prevent-a-human-resource-nightmare/ (accessed August 2, 2013).

213 On growing older:
- Catherine Mayer. *Amortality: The Pleasures and Perils of Living Agelessly*, (London: Ebury Digital, 2011), Kindle edition.
- Ryan Jaslow, "Sexually transmitted disease rates rise among elderly: Why?" *CBS News*, February 6, 2012, www.cbsnews.com/news/sexually-transmitted-disease-rates-rise-among-elderly-why/ (accessed November 3, 2014).

Why we get happier after the age of 46:
- "The U-bend of life," *The Economist*, December 16, 2010, www.economist.com/node/17722567 (accessed November 2, 2015).